What Hollywood is saying about
BEN and TOM

"These guys probably ripped off everything in this book just like they do in all their screenplays. That would explain why it's actually kind of good."

—**Ed Helms**

"Tom and Ben are two of the writers currently working in Hollywood. I can add they make a 'profit' on each of their writing jobs, as I believe they have very little overhead. Therefore, they are clearly qualified to write this book. Having not read it, I can tell you that it is uproariously funny, perhaps the best book on writing ever."

—**Zak Penn, film screenwriter and director**

"Tom and Ben's valuable insight into writing for a Volkswagen bug and creating the 'Lawrence of Arabia of Ping Pong films' make this book far more informative to the young dramatist than the vastly overrated Aristotle's *Poetics*."

—**Jonathan Glickman, film producer,
president of MGM, Motion Picture Group**

"Ben and Tom are a great fit for me. I love working with talented writers and then telling people everything was my idea. This is a great book that I pitched to them a while back . . . I'm thrilled that they finally got around to writing it."

—**Danny DeVito**

"Some screenwriters have a knack for capturing the heart and soul of characters, the nuance of themes, the richness of the human experience. And some are like Tom and Ben."

—**Shawn Levy, film director and producer**

WRITING MOVIES

FOR FUN AND PROFIT!

How We Made a Billion Dollars at the Box Office
and You Can, Too!

ROBERT BEN GARANT
& THOMAS LENNON

Foreword by John Hamburg

A Touchstone Book
Published by Simon & Schuster

New York   London   Toronto   Sydney   New Delhi

Touchstone
A Division of Simon & Schuster, Inc.
1230 Avenue of the Americas
New York, NY 10020

First Touchstone trade paperback edition July 2012

TOUCHSTONE and colophon are registered trademarks of Simon & Schuster, Inc.

For information about special discounts for bulk purchases,
please contact Simon & Schuster Special Sales at
1-866-506-1949 or business@simonandschuster.com.

The Simon & Schuster Speakers Bureau can bring authors to your live event.
For more information or to book an event contact the Simon & Schuster Speakers
Bureau at 1-866-248-3049 or visit our website at www.simonspeakers.com.

Manufactured in the United States of America

3   5   7   9   10   8   6   4   2

The Library of Congress has cataloged the hardcover edition as follows:

Garant, Robert Ben.
Writing movies for fun and profit! : how we made a billion dollars at the box office
and you can, too! / by Robert Ben Garant & Thomas Lennon.
p.   cm.
1. Motion picture authorship.   I. Lennon, Thomas.   II. Title.
PN1996.G34   2011
808.2'3—dc22   2011011985

ISBN 978-1-4391-8675-6
ISBN 978-1-4391-8676-3 (pbk)
ISBN 978-1-4391-8677-0 (ebook)

*This book is dedicated to entertainment lawyers everywhere—
especially Karl Austen*

A portion of the authors' proceeds from this book are being
contributed to the USO of Metropolitan Washington,
a private, nonprofit organization dedicated to serving
active duty military members and their families
in the greater Washington, D.C., region.

CONTENTS

Introduction by the sellout authors:

> If you're gonna sell out, make sure you make big money. That's the best part of selling out—the money! This book will tell you how we made over a billion dollars for the studios and bushels of dollars for ourselves, <u>and earned the love and respect of film critics everywhere</u>.*

Foreword by John Hamburg   ix
Introduction   xi

PART ONE: SELLING YOUR MOVIE

1. Getting Started in Hollywood   3
2. Why Isn't Anyone Buying My Brilliant Script?   11
3. How to Pitch Your Movie   18
4. Joining the Writers Guild of America, West   24
5. I SOLD IT! Now What Happens?   29
6. Idiot Check   38
7. Coverage! or How a Kid Getting College Credit Can Make or
   Break Your Movie!   51
8. Have I Made It Yet?   55
9. They Love My Script! . . . and I Got Fired?   59
10. Why Does Almost Every Studio Movie *SUCK* Donkey Balls?   62
11. The Art of Nodding or How to Take Notes   71
12. Directors   82
13. Producers   89
14. *Herbie: Fully Loaded*   92
15. Redlighting or How to Get Your Movie Un-Greenlit!   101
16. Turnaround   108

*That last part is not true.

17. How to Pimp Your Movie   110
18. Naysayers   114
19. The Silver Lining   116
20. Our Lunch with Jackie Chan   120
21. Credit$ 124
22. Living in Los Angeles   130

PART TWO: WRITING A SCREENPLAY

23. If Your Screenplay Doesn't Have This Structure, It Won't Sell,
    or Robert McKee Can Suck It   147
24. In a Few Pages, We'll Teach You How to Formulate
    Characters in a Script   154
25. How to Write a Screenplay   166
26. Writing Action and Description   170
27. Advice for Writing with a Partner   175
28. Rewrites: You Want It When? And I'm Getting Paid What?!?!?!!? 180
29. Martin Lawrence Has a Few Thoughts or How to Take Notes
    from a Movie Star   188
30. Arbitration or Who Wrote This Crap?   193
31. Sequels!   198
32. Getting the Book Rights   201
33. I'm Drinking Too Much. Is That a Problem?   204
34. Final Thoughts   208

Appendix: Sample Outlines   211
Glossary   295
Acknowledgments   313
Index   315

All that—plus FREE SAMPLES!

FOREWORD BY JOHN HAMBURG

Writer of *Little Fockers, I Love You, Man,*
Meet the Fockers, Zoolander, and *Meet the Parents*

I've known Tom Lennon and Ben Garant since the time they were young, hungry sketch comedians fresh out of New York University, trying to make a go of it in the big city. And from those humble beginnings, it's been an honor and pleasure to watch two of the funniest, most talented comedic minds I have ever come across completely sell out and get rich by churning out an endless supply of mindless Hollywood screenplays.

Now, having just purchased this tome, you're probably asking yourself, "Why the hell did I just shell out twenty bucks for a how-to book by the writers of *Herbie: Fully Loaded*?" That's a great question which I do not have the answer to. You clearly made an impulsive decision, and now you have to live with it. What I do know is that, when it comes to writing big, commercial, hit movies, Tom and Ben truly know what they are talking about. They treat the job like professionals—more like terminators really—and their talent, insane work ethic, and practical approach to movie-making has made them two of the most successful scribes in the industry.

Whereas most of us try our hardest to dress down for our meetings with studio executives, when Tom and Ben go to pitch, as legend goes, they wear matching suits—expensive black suits—so that the execs who may potentially shell out millions of dollars for these guys to write their next potential franchise know that they mean business (having directed Tom as a gay man with whom Paul Rudd goes on a "man date" in *I Love You, Man* I also know that black is incredibly slimming on him).

So, in spite of what I wrote a couple of paragraphs back, you have actually made a very wise decision to purchase this book. Aside from the trademark Lennon/Garant wit we've seen in movies like Vin Diesel's *The*

Pacifier and the Queen Latifah/Jimmy Fallon vehicle *Taxi*, this is the most practical, no-nonsense, and useful book I've ever read on what it really takes to make it as a writer in the movie business.

John Hamburg
New York City
November, 2010

INTRODUCTION

Quit now, or you might just get rich!

So you want to write movies for ~~fun and~~ profit?

By now you've noticed that the words "fun and" have been crossed out from the title of this book—and for good reason: this is not some fruity Robert McKee screenwriting guide that's going to help you "crack" your story—this book is not for "fun." It is the guide to <u>writing hit movies that make you and the studio piles of money</u>. Period. Yes, we know there was a period at the end of the sentence, but we added the word "period" too, to show you how very serious we are, exclamation point.

Now, if you want to write "art-house" films, please put this book down immediately and go gaze longingly out the window. We have no practical information for you on how to write Atom Egoyan films or the kind of films that they show at the Angelika Film Center in Robert

McKee–loving Greenwich Village. We do have an appreciation for art-house films, especially the ones where you see Helen Mirren's boobs.

This book is not about screenwriting *"theory."* As Grandpa used to say: *Screenwriting theory and a MetroCard will get you a ride on the subway.* This book is full of the practical information that nobody else can tell you about surviving and conquering the Hollywood studio system. This is information <u>you need to know</u>, and <u>you will find it only here</u>. And in case you don't believe us, with our screenwriting we've made:

$1,467,015,501

and counting at the box office.

Yes, three commas mean <u>billion</u>, people. And people often get confused. A billion is ONE THOUSAND MILLION, not one hundred million. Grandpa used to say: "One hundred million dollars and a Metro-Card, and you can buy your own train. Like those two dudes in *Wild Wild West*."

In this book, you will learn everything you need to know about how to sell and write your own GIANT, FOUR-QUADRANT BLOCK-BUSTER! *(Hell, yes, we put "selling" before "writing." Any crusty old film school professor can tell you how to write a script—but if they knew how to <u>sell</u> one, they wouldn't be working at some crappy film school!)*

You'll learn how to pitch, why to write a spec, when to shut up and nod, and what to do with the giant mountains of cash you're going to earn writing movies in fabulous Hollywood, California!

"How do I get an agent?" "What's a producer do?" "How do I format my script correctly to turn it in to 20th Century Fox?" "Should I use Windex or soap and water to clean the see-through glass hood on my new Lamborghini?"

You'll learn all this and more in this easy-to-read guidebook to making millions and millions of dollars the old-fashioned way—writing movies for some giant Hollywood studio! (We even include a few compli-

mentary samples of movie treatments and outlines—yours free with the purchase of this book!)

So what are you waiting for! Turn the page and dive in—a wonderful world of ~~fun and~~ profit awaits!

R. B. Garant & Thomas Lennon
(Dictated, but not read)

PART ONE
SELLING YOUR MOVIE

If you don't sell it, it's not a screenplay.
It's a stack of paper for the recycling bin.

GETTING STARTED IN HOLLYWOOD

DAVID MICHEL LINCOLN

As the title of this chapter implies: YES—you need to be in Hollywood, California, if you're going to make even TINY piles of money writing movies. Once you are rich and established, THEN, and only then—can you move into a fabulous brownstone next to Ethan Hawke in New York's independent-movie-loving West Village. But until you're a huge success, you need to be in Los Angeles. Period. Exclamation point.

"Why?" you ask. "I'm a writer, I can write anywhere." Well, guess what:

THAT'S BuL7$*!t

If you're serious about screenwriting, you must be in Los Angeles, California. It is the world headquarters of the movie industry. (Outside of India, which is the REAL world headquarters of the movie industry. They make so many movies it's ridiculous.)

You need to have access to the studios all the time, and they need to have access to you. You <u>have</u> to live in L.A. so that you can go to the studios and meet face-to-face. At any time. Movies take YEARS to get made—it could take eight to ten YEARS to get a movie going. Stars will get attached, fall out . . . your star will pick up a "tranny" on Santa Monica Boulevard, go to rehab, punch a cop, impregnate a nanny . . . or the worst fate imaginable: their level of fame will cool off the tiniest bit.

> You NEED TO BE AROUND the people who are making the decisions.
> You need to be on their radar.
> <u>You need to be in L.A.</u>

You need to be there, doing punch-ups and round tables and sometimes REWRITING ALL OF ACTS I AND III after a horrible table read. (This happens more often than you might imagine.) There's also almost always a writer or team of writers on call for movies that are in production. You need to prove to the studios that you can be a hero to them by: Coming up with new scenes, dialogue, gags, structure. Being available. And figuring out a way to make their ideas work.

There is, quite simply, ONE THING every studio executive wants.

"TO MAKE SUCCESSFUL FILMS?" you ask.

No. TO NOT GET FIRED, dummy. Successful films are a bonus, but the turnover for executives at the studios is fast, and "not getting fired" is the immediate goal around town. Many executives won't last the length of a whole movie's production at a studio. THEY WANT TO STAY AT THEIR JOBS, and you need to help them.

BE THE PERSON WHO HELPS THEM NOT GET FIRED.

That means you <u>need</u> to be around.

HERE'S WHAT YOU WILL NEED TO GET STARTED IN HOLLYWOOD

1. The Right Tools

The industry standard for all scripts is a computer program called Final Draft (www.finaldraft.com). You must write in this program; there is no other accepted format. It's also a really great program and phenomenally easy to use. It's also a little bit expensive, so save your receipt and use the program to GET RICH QUICK. If you already have Final Draft (which, if you're holding this book, is quite likely), learn how to properly format your script (See chapter 6, "Idiot Check."). The vast majority of scripts are formatted WRONG.

2. An Agent or Manager

Yes, you need an agent. And to get one these days, you must be creative. Simply sending out your script is perhaps the LEAST likely way to get one. Sending out your script unsolicited is about as appealing to agents as a cold call from a discount butt sandwich company. A method that will have a much higher success rate would be to write a short script, funny, scary, or touching, and SHOOT IT. Get it up on YouTube or FunnyorDie (or the hundred other sites like those). BE CREATIVE. Do a reading, put up your play, enter a screenwriting competition. Try ANYTHING. You will have to. But the absolute fastest way is to HAVE SOMETHING PRODUCED. Something concrete they can point to and say, "There's talent." Even if it's thirty seconds long and only on the internet, a finished product gives you a huge advantage over a script on paper. If you don't know any actors, take a class at the Upright Citizens Brigade in Los Angeles; you will meet tons of actors. (They have a theater and school in New York, too, but you already know YOU ARE NOT SUPPOSED TO BE IN NEW YORK, DUMMY.)

Remember, the movie software that comes FREE on any Mac computer has better editing programs than ever existed for most of the history of the movie industry. If Orson Welles were alive today, he would be thrilled and amazed at the moviemaking power of a flip camera and the simplest laptop computer.*

So—

Why do you need an agent or manager?

*If Orson Welles were alive today, his penchant for chili cheese fries would have made him approximately the size of the Griffith Park Observatory (pictured here, for scale).

For SEVERAL reasons.

Most studios will not take unsolicited material. They won't even look at your script unless an agent or manager hands it to them. And it has to be a rep ("representative"—that means agent or manager) whom the studio has done business with in the past. (Your buddy Rick can't just print up cards that say "Agent Rick" on them and expect to be able to get your script into a studio.) The studios do this to weed out the riffraff.

You need someone to negotiate your deals for you. To negotiate well, your reps need a LOT of information (what deals have been negotiated similar to yours and for how much money, how much cash does the studio have at the time, etc.). They need information, negotiating skills, the charm of a diplomat, nerves of steel, and the balls of a great white shark.* The negotiations can get REALLY nasty. (Especially as you get more expensive!) Your reps and the studio will really play hardball as your quote gets higher and higher. You don't want to be the one negotiating for yourself; you want to be the "good guy." Let your reps be the pricks.

Some writers not only have an agent and a manager, they also have an ENTERTAINMENT LAWYER. (We have all three. And our lawyer is the scariest one on our team. He's a nice guy and all . . . he's just ready to chew your heart out and spit in back in your face at the drop of a hat.)

An entertainment lawyer? Really?

YES! His job is JUST to negotiate deals. He's usually the one guy on your negotiating team who doesn't have a buddy-buddy relationship with the studio. Because he's NOT the one who's out there every day, schmoozing and getting jobs for his clients. He's a lawyer—his job is to be hated/feared. AFTER your reps have gotten you in the door and you've gotten the job, the LAWYER swoops in to help negotiate the deal. He usually gets us 25 percent more cash than we would have gotten without him.

Back to managers and agents:

---

*Memo to assistant: Google whether great white sharks have balls or not.

So they get your script in the door, they negotiate your deal—and . . .

Good reps have relationships with people at the studios. They're usually pretty gregarious people. They go to a lot of parties and are friends with people in every area of the business—"talent" and studio execs and producers. They know which exec, at which studio, is buying what kind of scripts at any given time. If you have a spec, they have a good sense of which studio or producer might want it. And they are always sniffing around to find you work and to set you up with people who might hire you.

Trust us. You need a manager and/or an agent. An entertainment lawyer too.

Do you need an agent AND a manager? Not always. We like having both, because between all of them, they cast a VERY WIDE NET to find us work. And when we're making big business decisions, we like getting advice from different points of view. They don't always agree with each other on what our next move should be—and that's a good thing. It makes us think about our next moves very carefully.

But not everyone has both. (Oh, and those people do not come free. They all take a percentage of what you earn.)

What's the difference between a manager and an agent, anyway?

For one thing, agents tend to be more specialized: we have a features agent, a TV agent, an acting agent, and a literary agent—four guys, each handling one aspect of our career, all at the same talent agency. They each have tons of clients, but they can handle it, because they are focused on one aspect of your career. Managers tend to focus on your *entire* career—every aspect of what you do.

Managers tend to have fewer clients, and they focus on the big picture, or where your career is going. This may be overstating the difference between managers and agents—but agents tend to be focused on your next job; managers tend to ask you questions like "Where do you see yourself in five years?"

Here's how one of our managers explains the difference:

WHAT IS THE DIFFERENCE BETWEEN
A MANAGER AND AN AGENT?
Peter Principato
founder, Principato Young Entertainment
(and Tom's manager)

A recent age-old question. These days, I think there are more managers than there is actual talent to represent. That is because it is honestly easier to become a manager than it is to become an agent. An agent is, by definition, a licensed employment agency, while anyone can hang a shingle on the door and say they are a manager. Even though the job requirements are similar and the agent/manager paradigm continues to change, there are different types of agents and different types of managers.

Agents are glitzy; Managers are down-to-earth

First of all, the simplest way I can explain the difference between agents and managers is to look back at high school, as show business is just a bigger blown-out version of high school to begin with. You have your cliques, still made up of high school stereotypes: the popular crowd, the nerds, the slow kids, and the indescribables, with the studios and networks playing the role of athletic departments and school clubs and the power shift changing with each and every project that people put out. That said, agents are like the specific subject teachers (math, social studies, english, science, etc.), and managers are like the guidance counselors. Managers help make the right choices, guide a career, look toward the future, really get to know a client's hopes and dreams, and try to lay a path to make them come true. This doesn't mean that there are not agents who do the same, but for the most part the agents have expertise in a very specific area. You have your film talent agents, film literary agents, TV literary agents, TV talent agents, personal appearance agents, book agents, etc. Best-case scenario? Managers try to have an expertise in ALL these areas and understand how to navigate the big picture, to make sure a client, who may have many talents and abilities, is utilizing all of these assets and not just concentrating on one specific area.

Agents are heat seekers; Managers are caretakers

Also, agents tend to have much larger client lists to fulfill the needs of opportunities being offered and to control a market share of the business, while managers tend to have fewer clients to focus on. Now that doesn't mean that managers will not have a good amount of clients. Agents tend to like to represent people with existing credits and a body of work so that they can plug them into opportunities more easily, while managers tend to take chances early on in a client's career, helping build a body of work to attract an agent. These days agents and managers work hand in hand with each other and balance out the relationship, giving the clients more eyes and manpower to create and find opportunities to build a career on.

Agents love money; Managers love art and commerce

Gone are the days—although some people still handle their business this way—when the agents controlled all the info and flow of that info, and managers work out of their homes with one or two clients and take care of all the personal needs of a client; we have evolved and the business invented the personal assistant, and while more and more agencies grow in power, influence, agendas, and prestige, the bigger they get, the more critical the need for the modern-day manager has become. It is a new day. A day when the agent and the manager work hand in hand while watching their backs! Having been both, it is a fine line indeed, but one thing is clear: the need for both has become most urgent. Until, of course, a client decides they don't want either and just sticks with an attorney to make deals. OY!

I think, to sum it up most clearly:

Agents wear suits; Managers wear jeans

3. Discipline

The single most important ingredient in your success and the thing that will separate you from amateur screenwriters (pronounced: everyone in the world) will be your work habits. Here is a general rule of thumb: AL-

WAYS BE WRITING. To work for the studios, you need to write compulsively. You should feel COMPELLED to write every day. Always. It's that simple. If you don't feel the desire to write every day—skip it. And let everyone else in the world get rich writing screenplays.

Why do you need to write compulsively? Because so much of your work will be thrown away.

To survive in the studio system, you cannot fall in love with everything you write. Be prepared to throw LOTS of it away and start over from scratch. As a studio writer, you are more contractor than artiste. Look at it as though they have hired you to "write" *them* a new kitchen or bathroom. Don't let it break your heart when you have to throw out a week's worth of writing. It happens all the time, for reasons you can't predict—the star of the film may have just made a CROQUET film and subsequently will not GOLF or even hold a MALLET in your film because it will seem as if they've "done that before." So you will have to rewrite an entire sequence. You will be rewriting all the time. Learn to love it. Or at least not hate it. And most important, LEARN from your rewriting. Keep making the script better.

To be a working writer, you should be able to write anywhere and all the time. Practice that art. Write everywhere you go, even if it's just scenes or sketches. Find a time of day, every day, when you can just write without distractions. It may vary from day-to-day, so try out different times and see what works for you. And for chrissake: TURN OFF YOUR E-MAIL AND WEB-BROWSING APPLICATIONS. Seriously. These will steal a solid twenty minutes per hour or more of your writing time.

If you've put in a solid four to five hours without distractions: then, and only then: reward yourself by turning off "safe search" and Googling: HELEN MIRREN > TOPLESS > IMAGES.

WHY ISN'T ANYONE BUYING
MY BRILLIANT SCRIPT?

DAVID MICHEL LINCOLN

There are many self-proclaimed "screenwriting gurus"—though how you get to be a "guru" of something you've never actually *done* is beyond us. Screenplays are like blueprints. A guy who's drawn up a lot of blueprints that have never actually been made into buildings is not an "architecture guru," he's an "unemployed douchebag." A guy who talks about screenwriting but who's never sold a screenplay is not a "screenwriting guru," he's a "lecture circuit bullshit artist." From now on, that's what we'll call them.

. . . Where were we? Oh, yeah:

There are many *lecture circuit bullshit artists* who say that to write a good screenplay, the most important thing is to come up with "a story that *needs* to be told." They use that phrase over and over: Is yours "a story that *needs* to be told"?

Here's a little homework for you. Go see what movies are playing in your local theaters right now. We'll wait.

. . .

Okay, now—can you honestly say any of those movies playing has a story that "NEEDED to be told"? *Really?* Was *Transformers 2: Revenge of the Fallen* "a story that *needed* to be told"?

Even with the *great* movies? *The Matrix. Casablanca. Terminator. The Pacifier.** Are those stories that *"needed* to be told"? A documentary about a guy wrongfully accused of murder, and the guy is still on death row right now—sure. That story *"needs* to be told."

Studio Movies need to be one thing:

ENTERTAINING.

Some producers will say that the movie being entertaining is the ONLY important thing. Screw character development, screw story. We don't go quite that far. But after we turn our script in, they usually hand it over to another writer, who proceeds to take out the story and character development SO THAT THE MOVIE IS SHORT AND ENTER-TAINING.

A movie where Luke Skywalker and his dad go through therapy and work out their issues would probably make a good story. But unless they blow up a couple Death Stars along the way and get Princess Leia wet AND in a bikini (two different scenes) then—story-schmory. Even movies about serious topics need to be entertaining *first.* (Remember, we're not talking indies here. We're talking about STUDIO MOVIES.) *Norma Ray, Silkwood*—entertaining as hell. They're studio movies. They aren't slow, and they keep you on the edge of your seat.

If you're running around Hollywood and you can't understand why your GREAT STORY isn't selling . . . then check: Is your movie as entertaining as *Die Hard*?

If not—

* Do we really put *The Pacifier* up there with *Casablanca*? Yes. Yes, we do. But don't trust us. GO BUY IT ON DVD RIGHT NOW; MAKE THAT DECISION FOR YOURSELF.

GO BACK TO THE DRAWING BOARD

There's another consideration if your movie isn't selling: Is your movie a lot like OTHER MOVIES that play in the theater? We don't mean a rip-off of some specific movie, like a *Terminator* rip-off (those go straight to DVD, because no movie stars will do them). We mean:

**Is it like the <u>kinds</u> of movies that play in
multiplex theaters and make money?**

Is it an epic tale about people from different religions in a five-way never-requited love pentagon set in a leper colony during the Spanish Inquisition? That's gonna be a tough sell, buddy. Not a great date movie. Best of luck to you.

Is it a love story about a Hugh Grant–type guy who walks dogs for a living? SOLD! Is it about a bank heist that gets stopped by an off-duty cop who plays by his own rules? SOLD! Is it a comedy about an underdog in love with a girl out of his league?! OH MY GOD! WE LOVE IT!

Rule 1: No one wants you to reinvent the wheel.

Let's put it this way: Do you like movies that challenge and confuse you? We do. Sometimes. *Eraserhead* is great. But not every night. Can you take your in-laws and their kids to see *Eraserhead*? Can you pop *Eraserhead* into your Blu-ray when your family is over for Christmas to shut everybody up for two hours? Can you give a DVD of *Eraserhead* to your folks for their birthday?

Don't get us wrong, we love *Eraserhead*. But 95 percent of Americans, if you forced them to watch *Eraserhead*, would want to punch that movie in the face and would punch YOU in the face for making them watch it. If you want to make movies like that, make an indie. Make a movie with people who don't care about box-office receipts.

**Rule 2: Most people do not go to the movies to be challenged.
They go to the movies to be entertained.**

Of the writers we know who HAVEN'T been able to break into the business—a lot of them think they can break into the movie business by writing a script that breaks all the rules. QUITE THE OPPOSITE. <u>Follow all the rules, to the letter</u>.

The OTHER reason that your brilliant screenplay you've been taking all over town isn't selling—<u>is just that</u>:

DON'T HANG YOUR DREAMS ON

YOUR <u>ONE</u> BRILLIANT SCREENPLAY.

We know a few writers who've failed because, when their one screenplay didn't sell, they kept tweaking it, and honing it, and rewriting it, based on whatever feedback they got from the last studio. A studio that passed on it.

This is a big mistake.

One of the biggest.

If everyone passed on your script—consider it dead. Bury it. Dig it up again years from now when you're as big as Tarantino, and they'll greenlight your old unsold scripts.

But you will never become a great screenwriter or write a great screenplay by rewriting the same script over and over again. This brings us back to a theme we're going to hit a lot:

ALWAYS BE WRITING

Always be writing. *Always be writing.*

<u>Always be writing</u>.

Always be working on a new script. There are more reasons to always be writing a new script than there are In-N-Out Burgers in the greater metropolitan Los Angeles area. (See Chapter 22, "Living in Los Angeles.")

1. If your first script doesn't sell, you NEED to have another one so that maybe *it* will sell, instead.
2. If your first script **does** sell, then you **NEED** to have another one so that maybe it will sell *too*. After a studio reads your script, whether they buy it or not, the next thing they're going to say to you is—"So what's next?"
3. If you're looking for representation, they may not like the first thing you wrote; you should have more than one script.
4. If you're looking for representation and they LOVE your first script, they need to know you're not a one-hit wonder. An agent once told us, "I don't represent scripts. I represent writers." Have a bunch of scripts.

5. <u>THIS ONE IS THE BIG ONE</u>: You get better at something only by doing it over and over. Do it constantly. Do it maniacally.

If you want to be a painter, a boxer, or race professional racing midgets, the only way to get better at it is by doing it every day, for many hours a day, with great discipline, for years and years.

People make the mistake of thinking that their first script is going to be great. <u>It won't be</u>. They think that they are born with a style and that style will be PERFECTED *before* they've ever even written "FADE IN." It <u>won't</u> be. Your style will develop. It will grow. You will get better. Your style will change.

Don't believe us?

Try this little experiment!

(It will take you a year, maybe two—<u>but you HAVE to do it</u>.)

STEP ONE: Write a screenplay. Then read it. Then rewrite it.
Keep rewriting it until it is the GREATEST SCREENPLAY IN HISTORY.

REPEAT with screenplay 2. Keep rewriting it until it is the
GREATEST SCREENPLAY IN HISTORY.

REPEAT with screenplay 3.

Now—

Go back and reread SCREENPLAY 1. Go, do it. We'll wait.

• • •

• • •

Did you go back and read your first screenplay? It *sucks*, right?

See—you've learned a TON by writing a bunch of screenplays!

> **Rule 3: You don't become a good writer by thinking about it.**
> **You don't get better by talking about it. You get better by <u>writing</u>.**

If your brilliant screenplay isn't selling—learn from your mistakes, and WRITE ANOTHER ONE.

Now—stop reading this book, and GO WRITE ON YOUR SPEC. Then come back and read the next chapter. It's terrific!

HOW TO PITCH YOUR MOVIE

Knowing how to <u>pitch</u> your movie is the only thing standing between you and piles of money up to your armpits. Money that can be traded for jet skis, piñatas, and hot fudge sundaes served off the bare bottoms of Brazil's most attractive models. So PAY ATTENTION. These few simple steps will show you how to pitch properly. Take notes, <u>this is important</u>! (Just kidding about the notes, we already wrote it all down for you—just rip these pages out of the book and <u>stick to them</u>. Yes, even if you're in a bookstore and haven't purchased this book, YOU SHOULD STILL RIP THESE PAGES OUT AND KEEP THEM HANDY!)

For the perfect pitch, your movie needs two things:

1. A new idea that is easy to describe in terms of OTHER SUCCESSFUL FILMS.

    Like we've said, be original, but don't reinvent the wheel. Invoking the name of a film that has MADE A TON OF MONEY in your pitch is <u>never</u> a bad thing in Hollywood. For example: "It's *Die Hard* meets *Home Alone*— set at a Chuck E. Cheese. PG. But instead of Bruce Willis to the rescue, it's an eight-year-old. And Hans Gruber is an animatronic raccoon gone haywire." (This idea will probably sell, and it's yours free with the purchase of this book.)

2. The main character must be the kind of flawed-but-amazing character a <u>MOVIE STAR wants to play</u>.

Remember: only a movie star or studio head can get your movie greenlit. There are six or seven studio heads in the entire world and fifteen to twenty movie stars. So shoot for a movie star, and your odds of getting your pitch made into a film will be three times as good. If a movie star wants to make your movie, the studio head will hop on board immediately. All you can do once a star is attached is to pray that he doesn't <u>accidentally pick up a transvestite prostitute in front of a news crew on his way home</u>. Or star in *Gigli*. It happens, even to the best of us.

A flawed-but-amazing character should be something like: "GREG (36) is the only dad in the all-moms CARPOOL. Despite his amazingly good looks, he's shy around women. <u>He's too caught up in his work to notice that he's missing his son DANNY (7), growing up before his eyes.</u>" Like it or not, the example that studio heads throw at us ALL THE TIME is *Liar Liar.* Jim Carrey is a TOTALLY LIKABLE, PERFECT FATHER with ONE FLAW: he lies.

(FEEL FREE TO USE THIS CHARACTER, "GREG," COMPLIMENTS OF THE AUTHORS, WITH YOUR PURCHASE OF THIS BOOK.)

And now the Art of the Pitch. In a few rules:

1. **Dress well.**
   DO NOT show up at a pitch in a Cabo Wabo T-shirt and flip-flops. The way you look at a pitch should inspire confidence. It should say to the buyer: "I don't write as a hobby, <u>I write as a profession.</u>"

Left: Sammy Hagar in a Cabo Wabo T-shirt: <u>No</u>.
Right: William Faulkner: <u>Yes</u>.

2. **Be able to describe your movie in one sentence.**

For example: "It's an animated version of *The Commitments* with Santa's reindeer, showing how the sleigh-pulling team got together for the first time." (You can't have that one. Universal owns that one.)

3. **Keep your pitch short.**

NO JOKE. Keep it short. Do not waste their time. Keep your pitch to under fifteen minutes. If possible, to around twelve or thirteen minutes. Most humans, especially those in the movie industry, have very short attention spans. Don't abuse them. Keep it short, and let them ask questions afterward.

4. **Act out as much as you can.**

Don't be afraid to actually <u>play</u> the characters.

Take an improvisation or acting class to hone your skills for pitching. Make your pitch *a performance*. It's more fun for you and them—and it's also the clearest way to tell the story. It's the way we're most accustomed to *hearing* stories told—we're used to hearing them performed. Don't be shy. This is your one chance. Play every character and moment to the hilt—<u>but do not violate number 3</u>.

5. **Practice your pitch.**

<u>Out loud</u>. Say the pitch out loud over and over again, until you're so relaxed telling it that you could tell it on a Tilt-A-Whirl. <u>Practice the pitch</u>. Saying it out loud will also call attention to problems, glitches, and awkward parts of the pitch, which you can correct. If you have friends who will listen to it—TEST IT OUT ON THEM. The more you rehearse the pitch, the better it will be. It will also help you time the pitch.

6. **Be gracious.**

Seven times out of ten, your pitch WILL NOT SELL, and for reasons beyond your control. Don't be surprised to hear things like "Adam Sandler already has a competing lion tamer movie in the works, so we can't buy a lion tamer idea right now." Even if they don't buy your pitch, remember: YOU ARE A WRITER. THEY NEED WRITERS. So be gracious, charming, and generally wonderful to be around—and you may well still get hired!!! To fix another writer's script, or work on the "SOMALI PIRATES idea they're all excited about at Paramount."

RULE 4: If you don't sell a pitch, that's okay.

More often than not, they want you to work on an idea THEY came up with anyway. If you leave the room with them thinking: "We won't do his '*Die Hard* in a Chuck E. Cheese' idea, but that guy's obviously a good writer." You've won! You're in the door. They'll call you in on another project. If you're easy to work with, YOU WILL GET HIRED AGAIN. And again. Be gracious, polite, and the least amount of a dick you can possibly be. Hollywood is a small town, and the assistant you're complaining to today will be running the studio next year.

WRITER SAFETY TIP: DON'T PITCH DRUNK!

ROBYN VON SWANK

Okay, truth be told: we never actually pitched "drunk," per se. But we did pitch Disney with hangovers so bad that we had a moderate case of "the spins." And we were pretty confused in general, and we struggled to remember even the general idea of the slobs-versus-snobs comedy we had been working on. (The general idea was: In the Future, Earth has run out of beer. Hops will not grow in our hostile environment. A team of ragtag losers who failed the space program is assembled to make an intergalactic BEER RUN to another planet.)

But . . . we were so hung over that not only was it hard to pitch, it was also almost IMPOSSIBLE to eat the chicken Caesar salads in front of us in the wonderful Disney executive dining room called "The Rotunda." That's pretty hungover, indeed. The night before, the very funny David Cross of *Mr. Show* had bought us a round of tequilas after a bunch of beers at a terrific bar called the Three of Clubs,* and the rest is a movie

*Three of Clubs is apparently actually called: Three Clubs, 1123 N. Vine Street, Los Angeles, CA 90038, www.threeclubs.com.

that never happened called *Beer Runners*. (Still a moderately good idea, and NOT yours free with purchase of this book.)

Remember: pitching is a performance; you need your rest! Pitching with a hangover can happen easily, especially if you are a New York writer who's been flown out to Los Angeles for "meetings." Be careful. L.A. is a fun town (in very small doses) and you'll keep thinking: "It's so early here!* Sure, I'll have one more." Next thing you know, you're holding on to the table for dear life and staring down a chicken Caesar salad as though it's your mortal enemy. Sad. And when you're so hungover that you almost have the shit-n-spins—you probably don't SMELL that great either! And people in this town already think writers stink, so don't give 'em any more ammunition, Mr. Faulkner!!! Be sensible. Head back to the hotel room and watch either a hit film on pay-per-view or some of the wonderful, award-winning pornography that our cousins in the San Fernando Valley have assembled!

---

*Los Angeles is in the Pacific time zone, three hours earlier than New York City.

JOINING THE WRITERS GUILD OF AMERICA, WEST

Yes, there is a Writers Guild of America, East, but as we mentioned—unless you are Woody Allen, you are supposed to be in Los Angeles. You should visit New York in the fall and see it the way it's supposed to be seen: from the Taipan Suite in the Mandarin Oriental hotel.

So forget about the Writers Guild, East. They're like our first cousin that we accidentally made out with that one time before we realized why she seemed so familiar.

The Writers Guild of America, West, is the union you'll need to be in, if you're not already. They provide, well . . . protection. Like Tony Soprano protection? You ask. No. Not like that. The Guild will NOT help you get rid of a dead goomar. We asked one time.

But they do protect you from the studios, who—let's face it, would do away with the creative unions if they could. They'd save a fortune if the Writers Guild wasn't looking out for us. The Guild has contracts with all the studios, and they protect you with contract minimums, a health and pension fund, and collecting residuals. All kinds of great stuff. And a website where you can look things up easily. And a script library at their offices in Los Angeles. For all of this, you pay a small protection fee: 1.5 percent of your earnings as a writer. A small price to pay, considering you don't have to be the one who checks to make sure you got paid at the 1.2 percent rate for the network prime-time TV showing of your movie. I don't even know who you would call to ask about that. So . . .

"How do I get into this wonderful guild?" you ask.

It was a while ago, so we kind of forgot how we got in. (Might have been selling our pitch of *Let's Go to Prison*, a decent rental right up until the last ten minutes or so.)

So to answer that question simply, we asked the former president of the Writers Guild, West, and our homey, Patric Verrone.

Hey, Patric, what's the easiest way to get into the WGA?

Hey, guys, great question. In my opinion, the easiest way to get into the Writers Guild is to write the same exact thing that every one of the over ten thousand writers who already belong to the Guild wrote: something totally original and unique that none of the over ten thousand writers who already belong to the Guild wrote. Not to be facetious, but if you ask one thousand writers how they broke in, you'll get a thousand different answers. Go ahead, ask. I'll wait here. And while I'm waiting, I'll let you know that there are a few other requirements for Writers Guild membership (for both the Writers Guild, East, in New York and the West in Los Angeles). First, your original and unique piece of writing needs to be of an audiovisual nature (film, TV, radio, new media). Second, because the guilds are labor unions under federal law, membership standards are based on actual labor. In other words, you have to do writing that's considered "work." (Unfortunately, it can't just be done for fun, as the title of this book might suggest.) Thus, you have to be paid for your writing (it doesn't have to be produced; just bought or optioned). Most important, you have to perform the work under a Writers Guild contract for a producer who has signed the WGA Minimum Basic Agreement. Naturally, every writer wants to work under a WGA contract because it means that you get paid a minimum salary; receive residuals when your writing is reused; have your name credited on the finished product; and get health insurance, a pension, and other benefits. But not every producer is willing to meet the standards of a WGA contract (especially in reality TV and animated films), so it's up to every writer to insist on that contract and its terms. If you do, you'll be eligible for membership and you'll get to tell your totally original and unique story about the easiest way to get into the Writers Guild.

—Patric Verrone, former president, WGAW

See, there you go. It's that easy. If you consider that easy. (Which it's not, really.) Technically, you need to build up "points" to join, but the number of points you need can be met with just ONE screenplay sold to a studio. So follow all the other advice in this book, and get yourself into the Guild. Your teeth will thank you for the wonderful dental coverage.

And once you're in the Guild . . . the perks just keep on coming. We're talking about partying your ass off with Patron Gold, luxury boxes, and stone-cold foxes. Because that's how we roll in the WGAW.*

*This part is pretty much not true. That's not really how we "roll." But there are occasional mixers, with some really nerdy guys and ladies. And occasional movie screenings. And there's a PRETTY GOOD place to lock your bike in the WGA underground parking garage on Fairfax. DO NOT PARK YOUR BIKE AT THE RAILING OUT FRONT. THE SECURITY GUY WILL YELL AT YOU.

★ ★ ★ **FREE MOVIE IDEA** ★ ★ ★
Yours Free with the Purchase of This Book*

"WHACKED"

Approximate Budget: $18 Million
Box-Office Gross: $97 Million Worldwide
Awards Potential: Supporting Actor Golden Globe for Michael Caine

Jonah Hill stars as a lovable loser who goes from ZERO to HERO in this hilarious "ball-busting" croquet sports/comedy.

Jonah stars as LUKAS, a twentysomething nerd studying at a community college in New Jersey. To make ends meet, he works at a tacky miniature golf place, where rich kids make fun of him. BUT he's really good at miniature golf. When Lukas's brilliant/wealthy/stoner roommate (Chris Mintz-Plasse) DROPS OUT of college and heads to Alaska to "find himself," Lukas finds himself holding his now "off the grid" roommate's ACCEPTANCE LETTER to the Rhodes Scholar program at Oxford University. Lukas decides to accept the scholarship and go to Oxford, England, POSING AS HIS ROOMMATE. Why? Because he has a crush on his classmate (Sienna Miller), who just got accepted to Oxford.

Lukas is a fish out of water right away, which we see in hilarious scenes like one where he LEARNS TO TIE A BOW TIE and how to eat kippers and blood sausage for breakfast. He'll say funny things like "Watch the hands, Dumbledore," to his aging ROWING INSTRUCTOR when they're out punting on the river.

All the OXFORD SNOBS pick on him and knock him down again and again until page 32, where Lukas gets invited by SIMON (Cillian Murphy) to a weekend in the country for a grand croquet tournament (for the SPECIFIC reason of humiliating him).

Now it's *Rocky*, with croquet—Jonah Hill in the Rocky role and Michael Caine as "Ol' Squiggs" training him.

*A note on the "Free Movie Ideas" in this book: <u>We're not kidding about these</u>. All of these ideas are yours free, with book purchase. Feel free to pitch and sell each and every one, no kidding! Hell, try to sell the sequels to them, too! And if you do, why not check out: CSO Yachts at www.csoyachts.com. They've got some of Europe's most dazzling and flat-out expensive yachts for sale! Bon voyage!

Ol' Squiggs and Lukas hit it off. Squiggs is the aging groundskeeper, and he too is from a humble background. "See a lot of me'self in you, kid . . . now let's start whackin' some balls."

Act II: They train.

Act III: Lukas KICKS ASS in the tournament, winning Sienna Miller away from Cillian Murphy.

Note: Sound track features all British ska hits from Madness and The Specials.

I SOLD IT! NOW WHAT HAPPENS?

First off—CONGRATULATIONS.

You just sold a f*%#in' movie! You are now a Professional Screenwriter. You're gonna run into a lot of people in Hollywood who say they're screenwriters. A great majority of those people are Full Of Shit. They've never sold anything but lattes. You, however, are a Professional Screenwriter. Take a minute to enjoy that.

Then: breathe in the fact that now—**the pressure is on**. It is <u>very</u> <u>easy</u> to sit around a bong and talk a big game. Actually WRITING SCREENPLAYS for a living, however, takes talent, brains, perseverance, hard work, tact, cunning, and shoe leather.

Okay—so you sold a movie, a pitch, or a spec. Now what?

Well, expect some congratulatory phone calls from your reps and from the studio execs who bought your movie. The studio will say, "We're all really excited." But before you get those calls, there will be . . .

THE NEGOTIATION

A studio liked your pitch or spec. Here's what happened after you left their office.

The executive who you pitched to went to their BOSS. Unless you pitched to the BOSS, the president of the studio. That's rare. Will Smith pitches his movies to the president. Almost everybody else pitches to someone below them.

So the exec you pitched to went down the hall and pitched your movie to their Boss. (That's a comforting thought, huh? Your fate is in the hands of some dude who heard you describe your movie <u>once</u>.) The Boss liked it and said "WE'LL TAKE IT!" Sometimes the Boss says NO.

Sometimes the Boss says, "I like it, but not enough to buy it. I'd like the writer to come in and pitch it to me themselves." (Maybe so they can ask you a few questions or see if you're okay with their notes.)

These days, the economy being what it is **(Thanks a lot, [<u>insert name of current president here</u>!],** sometimes even if the Boss *wants* to buy it, they have to run it by a few people. They might run it by the MARKETING department, to see if they think they can sell your movie. Sometimes they even have to run the movie past CORPORATE.

So they liked your movie. They want your movie. So they called your reps. They asked for YOUR QUOTE. What's a QUOTE? **Your QUOTE is the industry term for how much money a major studio paid you for the LAST comparable movie you wrote.** You have a QUOTE for an original script, a QUOTE for a sequel you've written, a QUOTE for a week of rewrites, etc. If someone who was NOT a major studio paid you to write a movie, you do not have a quote. If some indie company paid you a billion bucks to write a movie, that is NOT a QUOTE.* Studios acknowledge only payments made to you by themselves or other major studios.

Which brings us to the big question everyone asks:

How much money am I gonna make?

*That is a ridiculous scenario.

That depends on a lot of things:

Is this is the first movie you've ever sold?

If it is, you DO NOT HAVE A QUOTE. If you don't have a quote, the WRITERS GUILD has standard minimum payments for writing a screenplay. As of the printing of this book, the minimum payment for an original screenplay is **$109,783.**

They <u>have</u> to pay you AT LEAST that much.

You get paid in installments, as you do the work:

$43,875 for commencement (to start writing)

$43,875 for turning in the first draft

Then they give you notes, and you get paid.

$22,033 to turn in the FINAL DRAFT.

Guild minimum for a spec script is **$80,427.**

But be warned—sometimes it takes MONTHS to get paid. We think the record for us was once eleven months, from getting commenced to getting the check.

The good news is—you'll get more than Guild minimum when:

MORE than one studio wants to buy your movie. Then you get to hear two of the most wonderful words you can hear as a writer:

Bidding war!

Woo-hoo! Two studios (or, super woo-hoo, *more* than two studios) have to outbid each other for your movie. And that's superfun. Then who knows—the sky is the limit.

OR—if you DO have a quote:

Your SECOND movie deal will always be bigger than the first. Even if your FIRST MOVIE didn't get made, it's usually a 10 percent bump-up. The studio's (and your reps) figure: you sold one movie, you know how to write—so you're going to get a raise.

If your last movie actually *did* get made:

We gotta ask—DID IT FLOP? IF YOUR FIRST MOVIE FLOPPED . . . sorry, you might not ever work again. It doesn't matter if it wasn't your fault: if the director screwed it up and the movie didn't resemble your script at all. It doesn't matter. You might be done. Hope you finished college and learned a skill. Tough racket, huh?

If your last movie made its money back:

You'll get more than a 10 percent bump. Maybe 30 percent. Maybe more. Depending on how your last movie did.

If your last movie made a fortune:

Hear that BEEP BEEP BEEP? That's the MONEY TRUCK backing up to your house! Screenplays written by proven moneymaking screenwriters regularly sell for over a million bucks. Usually in the $1 million to $3 million range. There are about twenty guys who get paid that, and higher.

WARNING: Seven figures may seem like a lot of money. Because it is. But you'll take home only about a fourth of that. No joke—for every buck you get paid, you'll actually SEE about 25 cents.

But . . . one-fourth of seven figures is still pretty damn good. It ain't Stiller money, but it beats working at Carl's Jr. Here's who-all gets a chunk:

AGENT: Usually 10%.

MANAGER: Usually 10%.

LAWYER: Could be 5%. Could be more. Could be less. Some charge by the hour.

BUSINESS MANAGER: Could be 5%. Could be more. Could be less. Some charge by the hour.

WRITERS GUILD DUES: 1.5%.

FEDERAL INCOME TAX: We're in a very high bracket (and hopefully you will be too).

CALIFORNIA STATE INCOME TAX: Ugh. Forget it, this state is a MESS. It's BROKE. And who has to pay? Us—the rich people. Life is so unfair.

Other Things That Your Reps Will Negotiate For

BACK END: A percentage of the profits. You won't get that. We don't care who you are—if you're reading this book, odds are about one in a gajillion that you're going to get a percentage of the profits. If you DO get that—call us, and tell us how you pulled it off. (Don't call us. E-mail our agent at CAA, Scott Greenberg.)

A PRODUCER or DIRECTOR DEAL: If you want to produce, that's a whole other book. People often ask us, "What *IS* a producer, anyway?" Producers might do anything—from being involved in every single creative decision in a movie to doing NOTHING at all, just collecting a fee. But they were involved in some early aspect of the development of the movie. Maybe it was their idea and they hired the writer. Maybe they found the script and took it to the studio.

And if you want to direct . . . that's *also* way too much to fit into this book. We'd recommend watching *Living in Oblivion, Hearts of Darkness,* and *Lost in La Mancha.* If you STILL want to direct after those . . . more power to ya.

RETAINING SEPARATED RIGHTS TO YOUR MATERIAL: So that they have to come to you AND PAY YOU if they make the movie into a TV show or lunch boxes. You will get these only if the Writers Guild determines that you get a WRITTEN BY credit on an original screenplay. This kinda shit gets *really* complicated and has its own chapter (See Chapter 21, "Credit$.") As a member of the Writers Guild, you'll get paid when they do sequels, books, and video games, anyway—but not NEARLY as much as you would if you had SEPARATED RIGHTS. And you won't get creative control.

CREDIT BONUS: Extra money if you receive full or partial credit on the final film. (See chapter 21.)

LAST-WRITER BONUS: Extra money if you are the last writer—meaning either that you were the ONLY writer who worked on the script or, after they hired twenty other writers to do changes, they rehired YOU at the end of the process to fix what all those other douchebags did to your script. This happens ALL THE TIME.

BOX-OFFICE BONUS: Extra money if your movie hits certain prenegotiated amounts at the box office—$100 million, $150 million, etc. WOO-HOO! Buy a boat!

PASSIVE PAYMENTS ON REMAKES, SEQUELS, AND THE LIKE: The Writers Guild's rules say that if they make a sequel of your movie, you AUTOMATICALLY get paid 50 percent of your writing fee (the one you got paid for the first movie) for the sequel—WHETHER YOU WORK ON IT OR NOT!

So if you got paid a million bucks to write *Super Banana*—you're gonna get a $500,000 check when they make *Super Banana II: Back in the Saddle,* and you don't even have to lift a finger. Neat, huh? And your reps can prenegotiate for MORE than 50 percent. Obviously you get paid MORE if you *do* write it. You always get paid more for sequels. Sequels mean the first one did really well . . . or at least well enough to make a sequel.

You also get paid if they remake your movie or make your movie into a TV show, but the amount varies. The Guild has standard minimums, and they're not bad.

We'll be honest—a lot of this stuff is stuff YOU ARE NOT GOING TO GET FOR A LONG, LONG TIME. Until your movies have made about a billion bucks at the box office. The main thing you'll negotiate for is money.

Okay . . . whew. Your reps and the studio have to agree on all that stuff—it sometimes takes weeks.

Then, after the deal is closed:

You'll get a contract in the mail, or you'll go to your rep's office and sign it. Your reps will call and say, "We're all feeling really good about the deal." The studio'll call and say, "We're all really excited."

We always send our reps a little gift—our agent, our manager, our lawyer, and any producers involved.

Tom usually sends red wine. Ben usually sends sake.

Okay, you signed the deal. Now what?

You don't start writing right away. Usually you have ONE MORE MEETING with the studio. You shake hands, they give you a Diet Coke or bottled water, they say how happy they are to be in business with you, and then—they'll usually GIVE YOU A FEW NOTES.

<u>DON'T PANIC</u>: they very rarely pull a bait and switch ("I know you sold us an intergalactic heist comedy, we want you to write a period drama about Mao Tse-tung"). We're sure that's possible . . . but we've never heard of that happening.

Those sorts of cockamamie notes usually come later, after you've given the studio the first draft. (See Chapter 10, "Why Does Almost Every Studio Movie SUCK Donkey Balls?")

When you go in for this meeting, don't forget: ACT REALLY GRATEFUL AND EXCITED. Hopefully, you'll actually *be* really grateful and excited. We say this only, because we heard a story of a guy who decided he was hot shit now that he was a professional screenwriter. He went in and argued with the executive who JUST BOUGHT HIS MOVIE about some minor point—and the studio yanked the deal right out from under him. Nothing was signed yet. (Oops. Sor-ry.)

Now you start writing. Unless you sold a spec. Then you start REWRITING, based on the studio's notes. And unless you're Quentin Tarantino, you're gettin' NOTES, pal.

How long do you have to WRITE THE SCRIPT?

There are standard time periods you have to write a script; they're the same for every project:

To write the first draft: **ten weeks**.
When you turn it in, the studio has **six weeks** to read it
and get back to you with their notes.
After they give you notes: you have **six weeks** to do those revisions.

They'll start calling you about week seven and asking you "How's it coming?" and "When do you think you'll be turning it in?" Spyglass Films starts this on about day two. But keep in mind, if they're bugging you for the script—THEY'RE STILL ENGAGED IN THE PROCESS. Don't worry when people are bugging you for the finished script. Worry when people <u>AREN'T</u> bugging you for the script. You or your project may have cooled off. Don't worry. You have ten weeks. But turning it in a little early is ALWAYS a good thing. Eight weeks is good. They'll know you didn't rush, but they're still getting it early.

Most movie deals *used* to be composed of a FIRST DRAFT and ONE SET OF REVISIONS. That means they CAN'T fire you after your first draft. They have to at least give you notes and let you TRY to "fix" the script, AKA do their notes. (See Chapter 10, "Why Does Almost Every Studio Movie SUCK Donkey Balls?")

But now, with the economy in the toilet **(Thanks a lot, [insert name of current president here!]**, most studios (especially Paramount) are only doing ONE-STEP DEALS. You get paid, you write a draft, you turn it in—that's it. The studios are saving a fortune that way.

Some deals also have an OPTIONAL POLISH. That means they give you another set of notes (after you've done your SECOND draft) and you have **TWO TO FOUR WEEKS** to do them. But just because it's a "polish," that DOES NOT mean it will be less work. Sometimes doing their notes will mean completely throwing out 50 percent, 75 percent, even 100 percent of the script and rebuilding it from the ashes. Their note may be: "We need to change the characters and the setting and the story"—and they'll still call it a POLISH and give you **TWO** weeks.

That's why you HAVE to be very good, very fast, and very disciplined. Sometimes it's crunch time.

Oh, and the six weeks they contractually have to get their notes back to you? They breach that ALL THE TIME. You're supposed to get paid a penalty when they do that. You won't get that penalty. Ever.

We saved the best news for last:

The best thing about selling your first script:

NOW YOU'RE IN THE DOOR!

Hollywood is a town that's TERRIFIED of sticking its neck out for any unproven commodity.

NO ONE wants to be the FIRST ONE to hire a new young writer. Getting your first job in Hollywood is a MILLION times harder than getting your SECOND. (Unless your first movie tanks—but worry about that later.) After you've written a script for a studio, you're "in the club." Your agents and reps will be sending you scripts to rewrite and setting up meetings to hear the studios' ideas all the time. Your phone will ring constantly. Until you f@&k up.

Tonight, go celebrate. Go out for sushi, smoke a bowl, and pop a good movie into the Blu-ray.

Now that you're a writer—you can write it all off.*

---

*Subject to U.S. and state tax laws.

IDIOT CHECK

You are now only ten short steps away from turning in your script!

1. Make sure your script is the right length.
2. Make sure your script is formatted correctly.
3. Make sure your title page is correct, has the right date, and is also formatted correctly.
4. Spell-check your script.
5. Fact-check your script.
6. Clear your revision marks, and make a clean PDF of your script.
7. Clearly mark your OFFICIAL draft and save it someplace where YOU can find it. AND BACK IT UP.
8. Register your script with the WGA.
9. Double-check—have you been paid yet?
10. Make sure you're turning it in to the right person or people—AND TURN IT IN.

1. Make sure your script is the right length.

If it's a comedy, it should be about 100, 110 pages. A little longer if it's a drama. We'll repeat that. It's important:

The correct length of a script is: around 100, 110 pages for a comedy, a little more for a drama.

39

Is it really so specific? **YES**. **YES, IT IS**. *We've handed in scripts to studio people and seen them WEIGH the script with their hand to see if it's the right length.*

To the studio, script length equals how much the movie will cost. (Most movies we write are about a million bucks per page.) And most scripts are usually about a MINUTE of screen time per page.

Turning in a script that's the right length shows that you know what you're doing. If your script is WAY too long, you might as well have turned in a dead fish wrapped around a turd. It's as good as dead.

Your buddy may tell you that if a script is REALLY good, it can be longer. Yes, a lot of screenplays are longer. But—most *published* screenplays you can buy online are not the FIRST DRAFT of that script. They're the SHOOTING DRAFT. And scripts get longer as you get notes.

We turn in our first drafts at around 100, 110 pages. And we've had lots of movies made. And they've made $1.5 BILLION at the box office. Your buddy, who wrote the 270-page script—how much money has his movies made? If your buddy is James Cameron, we defer. But bear in mind, *Avatar* and *Titanic* were three hours—but his first scripts, the ones that got him started, like *The Terminator*? Probably shorter. *Terminator* runs only 107 minutes.

If your script is too long—cut it down.

- Cut unnecessary scenes. If your script is 130 pages, we promise you, there are some unnecessary scenes. And any scene that doesn't move the plot forward is unnecessary.
- Trim any lengthy descriptive action paragraphs. They are boring and hard to read.
- Trim any long speeches. Go watch one of your favorite movies. You'll notice—there *AREN'T many long speeches*. The longest speech in *Star Wars* is Leia's "Help me, Obi-Wan Kenobi" speech. It's only about 1½ minutes. And it's ALL THE PLOT YOU NEED for all three *Star Wars* films. In *Casablanca,* Rick's longest speech is his "You're getting on that plane" speech. It's about 1½ minutes. If your screenplay has any speeches longer than 1½ minutes, make sure they are better than Humphrey Bogart's "You're getting on that plane" speech. If you have TWO speeches that long—cut one entirely.

Then, when there's nothing left to cut and your script is *still* 115 pages . . . CUT ANOTHER FIVE PAGES. We do a thing we call **WORD TETRIS:** go through your script, and take out WORDS that make one line of action or dialogue into two lines.

Change:

"Bob takes his hand from his pocket for Tom to
    shake. Tom shakes it."

To:

"Bob offers his hand to Tom, who shakes it."

If you go through an entire script doing this, you can cut FIVE PAGES from your script without cutting a single thing!

2. Make sure your script is formatted correctly.

There is a standard format for screenplays (as well as a standard format for SITCOMS, ONE-HOUR DRAMAS, etc.). Here's what a standard script looks like. **Note where the TRANSITIONS, SCENE HEADINGS, CHARACTERS, ACTION, DIALOGUE, and PARENTHETICALS go.**

Transitions go here, like this:

FADE IN:

Then you write your SCENE HEADING, describing where the next scene is taking place. Like:

EXT. [*EXTERIOR*] A SEEDY BROTHEL — CAIRO — NIGHT

INT. [*INTERIOR*] SEEDY BROTHEL — CONTINUOUS

You write the action here. Keep your action to the point. No one wants to read long paragraphs of slow, superdetailed description. Save that for your romance novel:

RICK (mid-40s) enters.

                    RICK
          Rick's dialogue goes here.

Rick looks out the window, bored with this scene.

                    RICK (CONT'D)
                    (to himself)
          I thought this was a brothel. When
          is something interesting going to
          happen?

                                        CUT TO:

EXT. [*ESTABLISHING SHOT*] THE PENTAGON — DAY

INT. THE PENTAGON — CONTINUOUS

Several HIGH-LEVEL GENERALS stand around a map.

                    GENERAL SMITH
                    (furious)
          Get me Rick Manderson — pronto!

The General's attaché, TIFFANY (20), blond and VERY stacked, picks up the phone and dials.

CUT TO:

INT. SEEDY BROTHEL — CONTINUOUS

Rick answers the phone.

                    RICK
     Moshi moshi?

               TIFFANY (O.S. [*off screen*])
     Please hold for General Smith.

INTERCUT:

INT. THE PENTAGON — CONTINUOUS

                    GENERAL SMITH
                    (into phone)
     Where the hell are you, Rick?

                    RICK
     Where the hell do you think I am?
     I'm in a seedy brothel in Cairo.
     The same one where you and I . . .

He trails off. OFF HIS LOOK, we . . .

DISSOLVE TO:

FLASHBACK:

EXT. CESSNA — HIGH ABOVE THE ATLANTIC—1967

INT. CESSNA — CONTINUOUS

"Come Fly with Me" plays. A strapping, shirtless YOUNG RICK (18 years old) flies the plane, sitting in a YOUNG GENERAL SMITH'S lap.

```
                              DISSOLVE BACK TO:

INT. SEEDY BROTHEL — PRESENT DAY

Rick wipes a tear from his eye.

                                        Etc., etc.
```

Some studios have formats they REQUIRE you to use. Their requirements are varied and <u>very</u> technically specific. Some studios want you to double-space the line before the SCENE HEADING. Some have specific MARGINS and headings for you to use.

For example, 20TH CENTURY FOX requires this layout:

Under the Document menu, choose Page Layout.

In the *Margins* tab you will see your top and bottom margin options. These must be set at:

```
Top      1.12" (For the Mac)      1.13" (For a PC)
Bottom   1.00"
Header and Footer Margins should both be .50".
```

In the *Options* tab you will see your line spacing options. This must be set at <u>normal</u>.

Under the Format menu, choose Elements . . .

In the *Font* tab, make sure all fonts are set to Courier 12.

In the *Paragraph* tab, you need to check each of the elements by going down the list on the left and checking the margins (or "indents") on the right.

Element	Left	Right
General	1.25"	7.25"
Scene Heading	1.25"	7.25"
Action	1.25"	7.25"
Character	3.25"	6.25" *(Flexible)*
Parenthetical	2.75"	5.75" *(Flexible)*

Element	Left	Right
Dialogue	2.25"	6.25"
Transition	4.25"	7.25" *(Flexible)*
Shot	1.25"	7.25"

Please note that the latest versions of Final Draft . . . have slightly different defaults than earlier versions. For the most part they have shifted the margins by ¼" on the left and adjusted the right so that the actual measurement is the same.

The following newer Final Draft defaults are also acceptable under Fox format.

Note that you are allowed to change the dialogue element to the more generous 4" measurement if you wish.

Element	Left	Right
General	1.50"	7.50"
Scene Heading	1.50"	7.50"
Action	1.50"	7.50"
Character	3.50"	7.25" *(Flexible)*
Parenthetical	3.00"	5.50" *(Flexible)*
Dialogue	2.50"	6.00" *(6.5" right indent accepted)*
Transition	5.50"	7.12" *(Flexible)*
Shot	1.50"	7.50"

Under the Document menu, choose More & Continueds.

For the Dialogue breaks options please check mark the following:

Bottom of page for the (MORE) label.

Top of next page for the (CONTINUED) label *(upper caps preferred).*

For the Scene breaks options please check mark the following:

Bottom of the page for the (CONTINUED) label.

Top of next page for the CONTINUED: label

CONTINUED (#)—*(This function will do a page count for a scene.)*

Title Page

The preferred font is Courier. Use 24 point size for the title and 12 point for the rest of the page.

WARNER BROS. has a few rules of its own:

WARNER BROS. STANDARD SCRIPT FORMAT

Stage direction and shot headings (also known as slug lines) have a margin of 1.7" on the left and 1.1" on the right. Remember **TWO BLANK LINES PRECEDE EACH SHOT HEADING.**

Dialogue has a left margin of 2.7" and a right margin of 2.4".

Character names over dialogue have a left margin of 4.1".

Parenthetical direction within dialogue has a left margin of 3.4" and a right margin of 3.1"

Scene/shot numbers: When a script is numbered in preproduction, the left number is placed 1.0" from the left edge of the page and the right scene number is placed 7.4" from the left edge of the page.

Top page margin is .5" (3 single lines) before the page number. A single blank line separates the page number from the body of the script, which begins with either a CONTINUED: or a new shot heading/slug line.

Bottom page margin is at least .5" (3 single lines) following the (CONTINUED) or the end of a scene.

Total page length is a maximum of 60 lines, including page number and CONTINUEDs (but not including the 3 line margin at the top and bottom of the page).

Paper size is 8.5" wide and 11" long.

<u>*Font*</u> is 12-point Courier New.

Etc., etc.

It's complicated, right? That's why you should . . .

GET A SAMPLE SCRIPT FROM THE STUDIO. Ask your reps to get it for you. AND (advice of the obvious): <u>MAKE YOUR SCRIPT LOOK LIKE THE ONE YOU GOT FROM THAT STUDIO</u>.

Again, the best formatting software, as we've said, is:

Final Draft! www.finaldraft.com

See Chapter 1, "Getting Started in Hollywood." You should have bought Final Draft by now. We can't stress it enough. This software is a NECESSITY. If you are serious about writing a screenplay—BUY IT. Online is the easiest way to buy it. Do it. Now. We'll wait for you.

• • •

See! Final Draft practically formats your script for you. You can set it to whatever format you're writing—SCREENPLAY, WARNER BROS. SCREENPLAY, SITCOM—you name it. It has spell check, it can add footers and headers, it can mark your REVISIONS in different colors to keep track of which set of REVISIONS you're on. It will even REGISTER your script with the WGA for you.

3. Make sure your title page is correct, has the right date, and is formatted correctly.

EVERY script needs a TITLE PAGE. It comes before page 1 of the script.

It should look like this:

THE NAME OF YOUR MOVIE
(goes here. We usually write it in a slightly larger font.)

by

(You put your name here)

&

(If you have a partner, put their name here)

(If your script is based on some other property — a book,
comic book, or something — you write that here)

Based on some book, by some dude.

Revisions by

(The names of the douchebags who rewrite your script will
go here, in the order that they were hired.)

Current Revisions by

(The name of the douchebag who's <u>currently</u> rewriting
your script will go here.)

(The date you turned in the draft goes here.
Change this date, with each subsequent draft.
KEEP THIS ACCURATE AND UP-TO-DATE,
or finding which draft you're working on will be very confusing.)

Some people put their
Name *and*
Address *and*
Phone Number *(Or those of your REPS. We never do*
that. Usually the STUDIO will put their name and a COPYRIGHT
LAW statement here, when it reprints your script.)

Again, FINAL DRAFT will do this for you. That's—

Final Draft! www.finaldraft.com

4. Spell-check your script.

This may seem obvious, but DO IT. Then DO IT AGAIN. Typos, even small ones, make your script and YOU look unprofessional. We proofread our script several times—then we *always* PAY someone to proof it again. We pay him about $100. It's worth it.

Oh, and "it's" is <u>always</u> a contraction of "it is." You'd be surprised how often this comes up.

5. Fact-check your script.

Make SURE all of your references are CORRECT. If one mistake glares out to someone who's reading it ("The Battle of Waterloo wasn't in 1820! Who are these morons?!?"), that might be the ONE THING that makes the person PUT YOUR SCRIPT DOWN before finishing it, the straw that broke the camel's screenplay. Mistakes make you look dumb. Check all your dates, name spellings, geography, state capitals, famous quotes, song lyrics, "timely references" in a period piece—anything that's from the REAL WORLD better be 100 percent right. Do it. Fact-check. Get on Google, get on Wikipedia, or go to the public library.*

6. Clear your revision marks, and make a clean PDF of your script.

In Final Draft: go to EDIT and hit SELECT ALL. Then hit CLEAR REVISIONS in the TOOLBAR. Sometimes you have to do it twice. Check that all of the revisions are cleared. Then go to FILE. Scroll down to SAVE AS and SAVE AS a PDF.

Always turn in your scripts as PDFs. "Why?" you ask. Well, we've had a producer, a director, and even an actor "tweak" our scripts without telling us. It's unprofessional, but it happens. A PDF, unlike a Final Draft file, is a locked document. Meaning: a Final Draft file can be tweaked,

---

*Obviously this is a joke. DO NOT GO TO THE LIBRARY. The library is for creepy internet predators and homeless people.

changed, or . . . rewritten by the new writers who get hired AFTER you. If you turn in PDFs, at some point they will have to come to you for a Final Draft version of the script. Sometimes this is the only way you will know you've been replaced!

If you're turning in a SECOND DRAFT or POLISH, turn in:

- One PDF version WITH revision marks, marked "MARKED REVISION" (title it something like **YOURMOVIE: second draft 1/23/11/MARKEDREV**).
- <u>And</u> one PDF clean version (**YOURMOVIE: second draft 1/23/11/ CLEAN**).

7. Clearly mark your OFFICIAL draft and save it someplace in your computer where YOU can find it. AND BACK IT UP.

Put all of your previous drafts (the ones that you AREN'T GOING TO TURN IN to the studio) into a folder. Do not DELETE them—SAVE THEM. You will need them later. (See Chapter 30, "Arbitration or Who Wrote This Crap?") Then save your OFFICIAL draft, the one you're giving to the studio, somewhere where it will be easy to find. You're going to need it in six weeks, when the studio has notes.

<u>Then back it up—in multiple places</u>.

8. Register your script with the WGA.

Go to the Writers Guild of America's script registry website; www.wgaw registry.org.

You can register your script online or by mail. It costs $10 if you're a Guild member, $20 if you're not. If you're turning in a script to a studio— trust us, you're in the Guild. But, whether you're in the Guild or not—

ALWAYS REGISTER YOUR SCRIPTS.

ALWAYS. It will protect your script from being stolen by a studio (which doesn't happen often, but does happen). More important, it will protect you from OTHER WRITERS. (See Chapter 30, "Arbitration or Who Wrote This Crap?")

9. Double-check—have you been paid yet?

Check with your agent or manager: Have you gotten your commencement check yet? DON'T TURN YOUR SCRIPT IN UNTIL YOU HAVE GOTTEN PAID.

Sometimes, your agent calling the studio and telling them "The script is done" is the only thing that'll get some executive to pick up the phone and get you <u>paid</u>.

10. Make sure you're turning it in to the right person or people— AND TURN IT IN.

You'll turn in your script by e-mailing the PDF. When your career is just starting, you'll e-mail it to your reps, and they'll turn it in to the studio for you. Then they'll bill for delivery. Woo-hoo! More money!

Sometimes your reps will have a note or two. Listen; they're part of your team. But in the end, remember: it's YOUR script. (Until you turn it in, that is. Then it's the studio's script.)

As your relationships with the studios grow, you'll eventually e-mail your scripts directly to your executive, your producers, your director, sometimes also to the movie stars attached (if they're involved in the creative process). We e-mail stuff right to the studio, then CC our reps. Always CC your reps. So they have a copy, <u>and so that they can BILL. You ain't doing this for your health</u>. The air in L.A. is terrible. <u>You're doing it for the money</u>.

And whatever you do: **MAKE SURE YOU'RE GIVING THE SCRIPT TO <u>EVERYONE</u>** WHO'S SUPPOSED TO GET A COPY and no one else. If you forget to CC someone who's supposed to get a copy—<u>they will take it personally. They will be mad</u>. NEVER DO THAT.

Also, don't accidentally e-mail it to someone who's NOT supposed to get it. The studio will FREAK OUT. And they may sue you.

That's it. Turn that bad boy in. Then sit back and wait for the accolades and Academy Awards to come pouring in!*

---

*This has never happened to us. But we'll take a check over accolades and Academy Awards any day. Yachts are more fun than trophies.

7

COVERAGE!
OR
HOW A KID GETTING COLLEGE CREDIT
CAN MAKE OR BREAK YOUR MOVIE!

So you finished the draft of your screenplay, and you turned it in to the studio! Congratulations, the script is in! Go celebrate at any restaurant in Los Angeles that's not Pink's Hot Dogs. Pink's Hot Dogs is a disgusting cesspit, and we have no idea why Martha Stewart keeps glorifying it. That jailbird must be getting some graft.

ROBYN VON SWANK

Now you play a waiting game while the head honchos of the studio read your script.

But here's the catch:

THE HEAD HONCHOS OF THE STUDIO
DON'T READ YOUR SCRIPT.

Nope, not at all. Very unlikely, on the first draft anyway. Junior executives usually know that they'll get only one "read" by their boss (studio talk for the boss will only read ONE draft—the best one—so it better be good). And the junior execs sure aren't going to turn in your FIRST draft, which probably has Act III problems.*

So before ANYBODY IN POWER reads your script, the Story Department will read it. And they will provide the higher-ups with what's called "coverage."

Huh? That sounds like the people at the top are just reading the CliffsNotes version of your script. Well, guess what—they are!

All that time you spent figuring out the perfect placement of the ellipses, every time you added the most sublime comma, and the hours you agonized over whether to use a dash or a colon to bring the wonderful gumbo of your masterpiece to its sizzling perfection . . .

Yes, nobody read that stuff—those little things that make up your so-called screenplay, the thing you wrote that they paid you (hopefully) a ton of money for. Not yet, anyway.

"Why don't they read it?!" you ask. *"I worked really hard on it,"* you whine.

Well, stop whining. Studio executives can't be expected to just "read" every script they've purchased. Do you read every script you purchase? . . . Bad example. But it's true. The studio executive probably has A LOT of scripts in development. And movies that are prepping, or shooting, take precedence. And there's only so many hours in the day, and at some point, they have to go relieve their nanny, who has a life too.

---

* *All* scripts have Act III problems, according to them.

The person who is REALLY going to read your script is a person whose job is ONLY THAT. A reader. Usually a young person whom you will never meet or even know where in the building he or she is working. Most of the "readers" in the studios are good "readers" who've proven to the higher-ups that they're good at providing summaries of scripts, which is an art, just like writing screenplays. In fact, sometimes executives will handpick WHO among the readers will do coverage on which scripts, because they know better than anyone: positive coverage on a script can speed up the process of actually getting the thing made, by making it more likely that their boss will actually read the screenplay (that thing that you wrote).

Good coverage can be a real boost to your script. Think about it; if you're going to read something and someone has already told you, "It's great!" you're more likely to think it's great too. If somebody's said it has Act III problems, has no marketing angle, and the lead role is uncastable—you're screwed.

This is another reason that the responsibility falls on you to make your script a DELIGHT TO READ. Work on the readability of your script. Make it breezy. *And for chrissake—trim some stuff.* Nobody wants to read a 130-page script. Not even on an iPad in Cabo.

So before you turn your script in, your job is to think: What would you say about your script if you hadn't written it?

These are the things your script's "reader" will "grade" you on:

What's the rating of the movie?
G or PG is best, for a HUGE box office. R can succeed big, but you've eliminated about HALF of the moviegoing audience with this rating. If you make an R-rated movie, just about every single person in America who goes to see R-rated movies has to go see yours. Like in the case of *The Hangover,* which is a great example of how a relatable premise can translate into bags of American currency.

What's the target audience for the movie?
It had better be A LOT of people. And a lot of people who actually go to the movies. Writing a movie that appeals to the Amish is pointless. Or to people over fifty. Sorry, old-timers.

How expensive is the movie?
If the audience for it is big enough, it's okay to be expensive, but don't go nuts.

How can the movie be cast?
If there's a juicy role for some movie star who can open a movie—great. In fact, this is not optional. There HAS to be a juicy role for some movie star who can open a movie.

Can the movie be MARKETED?
The marketing department will tell you in two seconds if it can or can't. Movies that can be marketed: *Toy Story! Transformers! The Hangover!* For movies that CAN'T be marketed: check out *Storytelling* by Todd Solondz. Or pretty much any movie by Todd Solondz. Jeez, cheer up, Todd.

And last, the vaguest question but still fairly important:

Is it any good?

That's a tough one, and you may not be able to answer it, because you wrote it. Don't worry, the kids doing the coverage will tell you if it's good or not. But do a mental checklist of the categories they're looking at, and you'll be ahead of the game. Correct answers to those questions mean that your movie is more likely to MAKE MONEY. And that's what studios want to make—MONEY. They may say they make movies—but if there were a way for them to make MONEY <u>without</u> making movies, they would!

HAVE I MADE IT YET?

The easy way to tell what the studio's opinion of you is . . .

Where do they let you park?

The studios tell you EXACTLY how important you are to them by the parking pass they give you when you pull onto the lot. A complete break-down, follows, divided into categories of importance and unimportance.

DISNEY
Important = Alameda Gate. Outdoor executive spots opposite Team Disney. Way to go! Don't bump the car next to you, it's expensive.
Not Important = Buena Vista gate, or, GOD FORBID, the underground structure off Alameda. Which is literally worse than parking in any of Dante's Nine Circles of Hell. Well, after circle two, the one for lust. So, worse than the bottom seven circles of Dante's Hell.

FOX
Important = Pico Gate. "Gold Door" spots right outside the front door. Likely you are parked next to James Cameron. These parking spaces are the jewel in the crown of all studio parking. If you get one of these spots, take a picture of your car there. It may never happen again.
Not Important = Galaxy Gate Parking Structure. Like riding out a typhoon

in downtown Calcutta. Every man for himself. You could get murdered down here, and nobody would find you for weeks; hell, nobody would even bother to look. Just another screenwriter. Leave 'em as a treat for the rats. Yes, it's that bad, and worse. Probably some sort of monster lives in the bottom level, and the THOUSANDS OF CARS JAMMED IN THERE are the only thing keeping it in. There are a few parking attendants down there, handpicked from insane asylums—weeping, flailing, and shrugging their shoulders, as if they're in no way affiliated with the parking aspect of the parking structure.

WARNER BROS.

Important = Gate 4, VALET. Yes, there's a valet at the Warner's offices. And a couple of VIP executive visitor spots. They are clearly labeled "VIP," and they sum it up: you are a very important person. For now, at least.

Not Important = Either of the two structures that are NOT EVEN ON THE LOT. There's one across the street on Olive and another down on Forest Lawn. Technically a "walk-on" not a "drive-on." If you're parking in either one of these . . . yikes. What did you do? They must have HATED the draft you turned in, and now you have a LONG WALK to think about how you disappointed them and everybody else. But mostly yourself. *Proud of yourself now? Basset Hound Switcheroo* could have been a FRANCHISE, dammit. And you FUMBLED ON THE ONE-YARD LINE. Next summer was all about *Basset Hound Switcheroo*! MARKETING ALREADY HAD SOME MOCK-UP POSTERS MADE, WITH A FUNNY BASSET HOUND SAYING *"UNLEASHED!"* Well, way to go, jerk.

PARAMOUNT

Important = Melrose gate, VALET. Yes, Paramount has a very good valet section. Ask the guy in the car next to you if he happens to have some Grey Poupon. He won't laugh, because almost nobody remembers those commercials anymore.

Not Important = The open parking lot that's JUST TO THE LEFT of the Valet. You'll find a spot, sure. And it's out in the open, under the big fake panorama of sky, no real shame in that . . . BUT YOU'RE ALSO CLOSE ENOUGH TO THE VALET TO KNOW THAT YOU WEREN'T ALLOWED TO PARK THERE. Yep. And there're so many open spots in the Valet area? Well, you fell just short of making that list. Chew on that as you walk the extra 300 feet to your meeting.

UNIVERSAL

Important = Gate 4, the outdoor lot just below Building 100. Sunshine, the gentle sounds of traffic whizzing by on Lankershim, a nice view of a billboard for an upcoming Universal Picture. Ah. C'est la parking.

Not important = The horrifying Building 100 Parking Structure. Not fit for humans to park in. Designed off plans of Spanish castles, specifically intended to CONFUSE and DELAY the invading Moors. If you have to park here—YOU WILL BE LATE FOR YOUR MEETING. We don't care how early you are. You will circle, and circle like a ghost ship . . . up and up and . . . HOLY CRAP, THERE'S STILL NO SPOTS. Isn't this like, level 4 already??? WHO ARE ALL THESE PEOPLE, AND WHAT THE HELL ARE THEY DOING AT UNIVERSAL??? WHY DIDN'T I JUST PARK AT CITYWALK AND WALK DOWN THE HILL??? OR AT THAT METRO STATION PARKING LOT ACROSS THE STREET??? We haven't fact-checked these numbers, but there have probably been millions of suicides in this parking lot. From despair. Think about that. Millions of suicides that may or may not have happened. Really makes you think, doesn't it?

DREAMWORKS

Important = INSIDE the big brown gate off Amblin Drive, inside the DreamWorks compound, which looks like a gorgeous hotel in New Mexico, only more beautiful than the one you were picturing in your head. How good are these parking spots? Well, this is where Steven Spielberg parks. So there. That good. Some people might argue that this fact makes them the best parking spots in the world. And they may be.

Not Important = The little lot OUTSIDE the DreamWorks gate. You will then have to walk back across the street, and they will open the huge, CAR-SIZED gate for you—but you are now carless. It will be a little reminder that you haven't quite made it yet.

(As a side note: DreamWorks has the tightest security of any studio. It's intense. When you arrive, don't be surprised if you are scrutinized by the guards at the gate for a while. Even if you are supposed to be there. It is, in fact, much faster to enter the United States with a valid passport than it is to enter DreamWorks with a pass FROM DREAMWORKS.)

57

MGM

Important and Unimportant = There is simply no way to tell how important you are at MGM. Their new offices are in a high-rise building in Century City. The parking structure behind it is new, modern, and . . . fairly convenient. It's also a very short walk to the Century City Mall, right across the street. ARRGH. So frustrating to not have some sort of parking hierarchy in place over there! It's distressing and may lead to confusion. We beg you, MGM, make up some cockamamie pecking order, like different-color dashboard passes at least. So we know how you feel. Possibly "laminates" like at a rock concert, with varying levels of access, or some sort of star or letter grade system.

SONY/COLUMBIA PICTURES

Important = Valet Parking through the Madison Gate. Parking fit for a sultan. Or even better: fit for Will Smith. And the valets here know their stuff. They're playing in "the show." They'll make you feel like the reincarnation of Irving Thalberg, stepping back into his dream factory.

Not Important = Overland Avenue Gate, Parking Structure, or, as it should be called, the Culver City Tower of Terror. Six awful levels, straight up, winding around like an operatic nightmare concocted by Guillermo Del Toro. A labyrinth of your worst parking-related nightmares. Parking here will make you lose your faith in God. How could a God who loves us as his children, look down and let this kind of parking happen? Was that a spot? No, some idiot parked their motorcycle there. There's one . . . nope, Smart car. Why, God, why?

Well, you probably got this terrible parking space because your script has Act III problems. How do we know? BECAUSE ACCORDING TO THEM, ALL SCRIPTS HAVE ACT III PROBLEMS.

If you choose to complain about your terrible parking space, turn to page 59.

THEY LOVE MY SCRIPT! . . . AND I GOT FIRED?

You did it! You turned in your first script! The next sure sign that you've "made it" as a professional screenwriter is—your ass will be FIRED. Welcome to the luau, pal. The technical term for this event is "fresh eyes," as in "Everybody sooooo respects how far you've gotten us with this Martin Lawrence/Canadian curling movie . . . but we've decided that we need some FRESH EYES."

"Fresh eyes" are a new writer or team of writers, usually someone who's worked with the star, studio, or director before. To say that you will be fired a few times is an understatement; if you're working for the studios, there's a 99 percent chance that you will be fired off of EVERY SINGLE SCRIPT YOU EVER WORK ON. Wear it like a badge of honor, and remember: if you got fired off of your script, it means they HIRED someone else, investing more money in it—bringing it closer to production. Getting fired means the movie is moving forward! (Kaching!)

That's the deal. That's how it goes. Don't take it personally. Remember: they're nervous. Executive turnover is FAST, and they need to hedge their bets. If they think there's a slight chance another writer will get them five yards further down the field, they'll take it. Sometimes they just have to appease the star. Even if they truly LOVE your script, they may be forced, contractually or otherwise, to let the star's favorite writer do a pass. (See Chapter 10, "Why Does Almost Every Studio Movie *SUCK* Donkey Balls?")

Here's the important part: HOW YOU REACT.

Again, this is your chance to be awesome. DO IT—BE AWESOME. Don't pout, don't kick up dust, don't complain, and don't do anything that could be described as "douchey." No matter how mad it makes you, be gracious. Because there's a 99 percent chance you'll get fired, and a 55 percent chance you'll get REHIRED! (Better odds than blackjack!) It happens all the time. You will, if you play your cards right, get fired from and rehired to your own scripts all the time. When you make it to the very top, you'll find that you're usually replaced by or are replacing the same writers too!

Here's a flow chart of how the fire/hire system should work, if you remember to be wonderful:

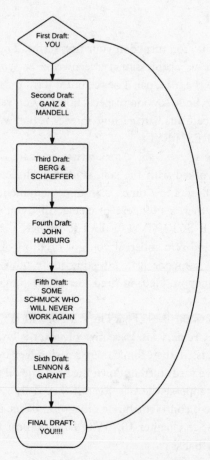

There's also a seedier underbelly to this already seedy underbelly, and that's this: whoever replaces you might be a bit unscrupulous in making changes to your script. Watch out for this, especially with writers who haven't had a lot of films produced. They'll change character names, locations, and props. If you get rehired to fix one of your old scripts—CHANGE THEM BACK. Why? you ask. *Why would they change something that works for no good reason?*

FOR CREDIT! (See Chapter 30, "Arbitration or Who Wrote This Crap?" and read about how screen credit turns into royalties that can be traded for hydrogen-powered motorcycles and Victoria's Secret underpants.)

Remember: getting fired takes practice. You'll be angry the first few times. After that it gets easier! (See Chapter 33, "I'm Drinking Too Much. Is That a Problem?")

WHY DOES ALMOST EVERY STUDIO MOVIE *SUCK* DONKEY BALLS?

Short answer: **development.**

. . . But let's back up for a second.

A lot of movies get screwed up even though they have a perfectly good script. Maybe the movie gets miscast. Maybe it's a bad director or not enough money to pull off the movie, not enough *time* to pull it off. Or no chemistry between the leads, or maybe the leads flat-out hate each other. Sometimes on-set egos, power struggles, or laziness get in the way. Sometimes the cast doesn't trust the script, sometimes they don't trust the director. And, scariest of all—

Sometimes, even if everyone involved in the movie is *great* and passionate and talented . . . *sometimes the movie just doesn't come together.* <u>Sometimes things work on paper that just don't get translated to the screen.</u> Let's face it—

<u>Most movies suck.</u>

Ninety-five percent of them. This is not a new phenomenon. Since the beginning of movies, the majority of movies in any given year have

ALWAYS sucked. The year *Casablanca* came out, Warner Bros., also came out with dozens of other movies YOU'VE NEVER HEARD OF. Because they sucked.

And you, as the writer, can't worry about that: you're just the writer. ("*'JUST* the writer'?!? B-b-but . . . it's *my* movie!") First off—no, it's not *your* movie. It's *the studio's* movie. You sold it to them, remember?

Second: you can't worry about things that are beyond your control. You'll go nuts.

Will people blame YOU, the writer, if your *genius* script turned into a turd of a movie? <u>Yes</u>. Some people will. A lot of people. Walk it off.

There will also be people who *don't* blame you. A lot of folks in the industry will say, "I don't understand why that movie sucked, I heard the script was great."

Either way, after the script is done, there's nothing you can do about the subsequent creative decisions, good or bad.

When you accept this fact, you'll sleep better.

What *should* you worry about? Worry about *your* part of the process: the WRITING.

Let's talk about how movies get screwed up DURING the writing process. There's a word for that in Hollywood. And that word is:

Development.

Now, despite popular belief, not everyone in the movie business is an idiot. There are lots of smart, talented people working in the studios. Problem is, like in any industry—<u>there are a lot more idiots than smart people</u>. And all those idiots do a lot of damage. They do damage at every step of the creative process—but most movies get destroyed during development.

What is development?

So you brought the studio a movie, and they liked it so much they bought it. Then, ten weeks later (eight would be better) you gave them the script you told them you'd write.

So now you're done, right? . . . Ha! Ha ha ha ha! Ha ha! Hahaha-hhahahahhahha.

Ha! HA! HA! HA! HA!

Ha! Ha! Ha!

Ha ha ha ha ha ha ha ha ha ha ha! Ha! Ha ha ha ha!
Ha ha! Hahahahhahahahhahha hee hee hee.

Ha! HA! HA! HA! HA!

Ha ha ha ha ha ha ha ha ha ha ha! Ha! Ha ha ha ha!

Ha ha ha ha ha ha ha!!!!!

Ha ha ha ha ha ha ha ha ha ha ha! Ha! Ha ha ha ha! Ha ha! Hahahahha-hahahhahha. Ha ha ha ha ha ha ha ha ha ha ha! Ha! Ha ha ha ha! Ha ha! Hahahahhahahahhahha.

Ha! Ha! Ha!

Hehehehehehhhe. Pfftf—HA! Hahahahaha! Ha ha ha ha ha ha ha ha ha ha ha! Ha! Ha ha ha ha! Ha ha! Hahahahhahahahhahha.

Ha! HA! HA! HA! HA!

Ha ha ha ha ha ha ha!!!!!

Ha ha ha ha ha ha ha ha ha ha ha! Ha! Ha ha ha ha ha ha ha ha ha ha ha!
Ha! Ha ha ha ha! Ha ha! Hahahhahahahaha.

Okay. So . . .

What is the development process?

"Development" happens when you turn in your script to the studio,
and the executive (or executives) who read it don't like it enough to make
it into a movie or to pass it along to their boss. So they're going to try to
figure out how to make it "better." Sometimes that means *fixing* what's in
your script; sometimes that means *changing* what's in your script.

They are going to *develop* the idea—into a different, *better* idea.
This is also called

"DEVELOPMENT HELL"

The reason a lot of studio movies suck donkey balls is simple: Before
your movie gets made it has to get to the president of the studio. The
president of the studio is usually a very smart woman. But between you
and the president of the studio there are between four and twenty executives who have to *approve* your script. <u>And some of those executives are
going to be idiots.</u>

Don't get us wrong. Sometimes you do get good notes. GOOD EX-
ECUTIVES can actually HELP your script. The simple truth is, smart
people give good notes, dumb people give bad notes. Always listen with
an open mind.

Casablanca, maybe the best movie ever. Jack Warner developed the
SHIT out of that script. *While they were shooting.* It had AT LEAST four
teams of writers, probably MANY more. And it worked out GREAT.
*Screenwriting is ALWAYS going to be collaborative. ALWAYS. Again, we are
not writing novels.*

**The problem is, there are A LOT more DUMB executives than
smart ones.** Especially when you're just starting out as a writer, and
you're dealing with JUNIOR EXECS (many of whom are not going to

last in the business). That's when you get notes that do not help a script. They are a waste of time, changing scripts without making them better— lateral moves that can go on for YEARS. Or worse. And all it takes is one bad executive to ruin a movie.

Why Bad Notes Happen to Good Scripts

- Sometimes an executive simply doesn't *get* your script. (See Chapter 14, "*Herbie: Fully Loaded.*")
- Sometimes they get it but they don't like it (even though their boss, WHO BOUGHT IT, does).
- Sometimes they're just dumb as paint.
- Sometimes they want to get some idea of theirs into the movie, even if it doesn't work, so they can take credit for it, to gain headway in their career at the studio. ("You know that GREAT scene where Godzilla steps on a building—*that was mine.*")
- Sometimes they have a movie <u>they</u> wanna do, *some other movie not your own*, and they haven't been able to get it made yet—so they try to make YOUR movie into THEIR movie. (They've wanted to make a romance about a football player and a nerdy girl for years, so they're gonna try to shoehorn THAT plotline into the pirate movie you're writing.)
- Sometimes they don't like the executive who bought your movie. Politics are rampant.
- Sometimes they don't like you. This doesn't happen often. If you're a writer, most executives won't even remember you.
- Sometimes they think *they* should be president, and they think the way to do that is to develop your movie in some new direction—to prove THEY'RE smarter than the person who *bought* your movie.
- Sometimes they get obsessed with some tiny little point and they're going to let that unravel an entire script. We had an executive once who was a clean freak; she couldn't stand the thought of people eating outside or in a garage. It TOTALLY destroyed a script. Sometimes it's even semantic. "The protagonist isn't likable enough" is a big one. *When you hear that note, without any specific, practical example of LINES or ACTIONS that make your hero unlikable: <u>you are screwed</u>*. It means the executive is probably kinda dumb. **Those words—"Your protagonist isn't likable enough"— usually mean that you're dealing with an executive who has nothing to say, but he's gonna say it anyway.**

- And sometimes an executive will just start TALKING, spitballing in the room—and you'll realize: this guy didn't even read my script! Or they don't remember it! Or they're giving me the notes from some OTHER script he read that weekend.

Scary, huh? It's happened to us, and <u>IT WILL HAPPEN TO YOU</u>.

The good news:

We've been in the movie business for about twelve years. That's one-eighth as long as there's been a movie business. And we can say something with all honesty:

Most smart executives rise to the top, and most of the not-so-smart executives get fired.

. . . eventually.

Either they got fired or they quit to "spend time with their family" or to "try their hand at the creative/production side" or they go to work at NPR. (That means they got fired.)

Sometimes they drift around from studio to studio, not rising too high above entry-level positions before they get fired. Sometimes they go to work with a production company. And that's good news for you. If they're at a production company—YOU CAN AVOID WORKING WITH THEM.

Studios, you can't avoid. They're the ones that make the movies. And there are only a dozen of them: Warner Bros., Paramount, Sony, Columbia, 20th Century Fox, Buena Vista (Disney), Universal, Lionsgate, Fox Searchlight, the Weinstein Company, Summit Entertainment, Focus Features, and Overture Films.

But despite the fact that the idiots usually get canned, there will always be plenty of BAD executives around, and make no mistake, they will make sure that your movie sucks donkey balls.

So—how do you stop these nimrods from ruining your movie?

- If you'd like to learn a few tips, turn to Chapter 11, "The Art of Nodding or How To Take Notes."
- If you'd like to follow Professor Kirby into SPACESHIP 44–7, turn to page 293, "The Treasure of the Space Incas, Continued."

WAITING FOR THE STUDIO TO GET BACK TO YOU WITH NOTES?

Then why not spend the afternoon checking out a famous Hollywood landmark:

DAVID MICHEL LINCOLN

THE CRAZY ROLLER-SKATING DUDE ON ROBERTSON?!

Yes, Angelenos know and love (or fear) this guy. Some folks call him "Crazy Robertson," others know him as the dude in skintight black leggings who disco roller-skates up and down Robertson Boulevard pretty much every single day. He's a real treat for the eyes—*if you consider a fifty-year-old man with a beard and leggings so tight that you can clearly see the outline of his genitals a treat!* (Count us in!!!)

To top it all off, HE'S A PRETTY GOOD ROLLER SKATER. Not amazing by any standards, no, and certainly not as good as even the very worst disco roller skaters you'd see in Central Park, New York City. But what he lacks in technical prowess, he makes up for in *joie de vivre*! And in *c'est la guerre* . . . and *cherchez la femme*—by which we mean: yes, <u>he's crazy as hell</u>. Or at least he SEEMS pretty crazy.

To see him: park at any of the PUBLIC PARKING options on Robertson Boulevard between Beverly and 3rd Street. (Careful if you park in front of the Ivy; Lindsay Lohan sometimes crashes cars there.*)

Then KEEP YOUR EYES PEELED, HE'S HARD TO SPOT! (Just kidding, he's a six-foot-tall dude with a beard on roller skates whose balls you can pretty much see.)

Enjoy!

Why not make an afternoon of seeing "Crazy Robertson" and get a quick bite at any of the top-notch restaurants nearby:

The Ivy. Where they have lunch in *Get Shorty* and Danny DeVito orders stuff that's not on the menu.

Chaya Brasserie. Incredibly hip; the hostess usually looks like a professional model, only slightly hotter.

Newsroom Cafe. So "L.A." that it's almost annoying. Try the Blue Corn Waffle or the whatever Sambazon Acai is or even the Hemp Granola, you fruitcake!

*True.

THE ART OF NODDING
OR
HOW TO TAKE NOTES

Great news! They read your script, and now the studio (or producer) has some notes! Fun! Wait . . . not fun. Notes means there are things they didn't like in your script, which, as we all know, is f#@king perfect. But—they're the ones paying you, so yes, you have to do the notes. Remember, it's not your script. It's theirs. They bought it from you. For lots of money.

> N.B.:*
> *Notes you do for a studio = You get paid to do*
> *Notes you do for a producer = A "producer's draft"*

And for a producer's draft you DON'T GET PAID, ever. And the producer can give you a ton of notes, and you have to do them all for free! Another reason that having an outside producer on your script can be next to useless. There is an art to nodding and smiling while they tear your script to pieces.

Taking notes is easy, but it takes a bit of practice and a Jedi level of control over your ego.

---

*Abbreviation of the Latin words *Nota Bene.***
   ** *Latin words for "Note Well."*

Here are the steps to doing it right and getting hired again and again (and subsequently getting as rich as a low-level sultan!)

Rule 1. ACTUALLY TAKE NOTES. Meaning: <u>WRITE DOWN WHAT THEY SAY</u>. Don't just sit there listening like a turd, write down everything that they say, and do it for two reasons: One, <u>KEEPING YOUR HANDS BUSY LIKE THIS WILL HELP PREVENT YOU FROM MAKING THE "RAGE FACES" THAT YOU WILL BE INCLINED TO MAKE WHEN YOU HEAR THEIR CRAPPY IDEAS</u>. And two, you will remember and incorporate far more of their notes if you've written them down. Most studio heads will be VERY HAPPY if in your next draft you include a literal line or phrase that they said during the notes meeting. For example: If the studio head says, "I feel like our main character is a guy who never appreciated the things in his life that are right under his nose," your next draft should include dialogue like this:

```
                RICK
    Until that genie made me switch
    lives with that ol' basset hound,
    I never appreciated the things in
    my life that were right under my
    nose.*
```

<u>Yes, it can be that literal</u>. It will show that you understood, and you will be hired again, and the studio will love it. No joke.

Rule 2. Listen. And show them you're listening by nodding. Subtle but steady nodding is a nice subconscious way that people feel like you are agreeing with them, and that you respect what they're saying. Practice nodding and looking relaxed when you're REALLY ANNOYED, and you'll become a good note taker. After you leave the room, they'll say, "I like that guy. We should let him take a look at our *Basset Hound/Switcheroo* picture."

Rule 3. WHEN THEY'RE RIGHT—AGREE, AND IMPROVE UPON THE IDEA. Subdue your ego. Be the first person to support someone else's good idea. Hell, let the studio president feel like your idea is HER idea. Who cares, if it moves the script forward? Remember, your job is to help them keep THEIR job.

*This line of dialogue is yours free with the purchase of this book.

"MAD."   "THINKING."

Rule 4. WHEN THEY'RE WRONG—LET YOUR DISAGREEMENT BE QUIET AND THOUGHTFUL. Don't be argumentative; it's way too easy to get fired. Be thoughtful. Practice turning your "mad" face into a "I'm thinking about it" face.

Tell them that you'll think about it—and do think about it. See if there's a way to make some version of their crappy idea work. You will always sound VERY CONFIDENT if you say this simple phrase:

"I'm not sure if it's going to work, but I'm definitely going to try it."

Disagreeing and being argumentative "in the room" is pointless. Of course you should have opinions, and of course you should push your point of view, but be like a reed—strong but flexible—or somebody will snap, and as the writer, you're usually the easiest person in the room to fire.

Then: After the notes meeting, alone with your MacBook Pro—focus on the good notes. You're the writer. You're in the driver's seat. Do the good notes, and gloss over or skip the bad ones entirely. And if there is some way to do some version of their bad notes that's actually good—figure it out and do it. For example: if they think farts are hilarious and suggest that your ex-cop hero fart <u>all the time</u> and you give the hero a dog who farts a couple of times, the studio will love that you put "their idea" into the script. Yet you didn't turn your movie into a "farting ex-cop" movie.

If you can do that—make their bad ideas into actually *good ideas*—all of Hollywood will be yours. Remember, no matter what you do, either way <u>you are probably going to get fired</u>. Increase the odds of being rehired as much as you can.

Important script notes from one of the world's most powerful producers:

75

Translation

goal
Har dos Shady
effed guol
birthday

(We think???)

TRUE HOLLYWOOD HORROR STORIES!

Part One

ROBYN VON SWANK

It was three years ago . . . three years ago THIS VERY DAY! Two young screenwriters headed off for a notes meeting on their script for *The Incredible Shrinking Man*. (Note: As of this publishing, the authors of this book have been working on this unproduced script for seven years.)

The screenwriters were excited, as this meeting was with the HEAD OF THE STUDIO! This was the guy who could wave a magic wand and greenlight the film! The meeting began like all meetings: with small talk and gossip—as you'll learn, the first seven to twelve minutes of all Hollywood meetings start with gossip and hefty servings of *Schadenfreude*, where we all laugh and thank the universe that we had NOTHING TO DO WITH THAT ANIMATED MOVIE *Delgo*.*

(Note: Never, ever joke about the disastrous failures made by people IN THE ROOM. It can happen by accident, so best to IMDB the people you're meeting with in advance and don't accidentally tell Martin Brest what you thought of *Gigli*. And if you're not sure, SHUT UP.)

The screenwriters pulled out their notepads. The studio head came on strong, with LOTS of ideas to improve the script. He talked a *Blue Streak*† about what he thought about the film . . . how it really was a *film noir*. He talked, and talked. For almost thirty minutes.

---

* *Delgo* had the worst opening ever for any film on more than 2,000 screens. It is available on DVD.

† *Blue Streak* with Martin Lawrence grossed $117,758,500. It is available on DVD.

Then, when the screenwriters least suspected it, he suggested:

"The main character should have to interact with animals!"

SFX: RECORD NEEDLE SCRATCH.

This was a note that really confused the two screenwriters, as a great deal of Act II of the script, and ALL of Act III of the script they had written involved the diminutive titular character INTERACTING WITH A RABBIT, A PANTHER, AND A RAVEN. All three of which, last time we checked, <u>were</u> animals. The studio head had either:

A. JUST HAD A STROKE THAT WIPED OUT THE PART OF HIS BRAIN THAT REMEMBERED WHAT HAPPENED IN THE SCRIPT HE WAS GIVING NOTES ON.

or

B. NOT READ THE SCRIPT.

Yes, it's true. The answer is B. The studio president gave notes on a SCRIPT HE HAD NOT READ. *(Quel dommage!*)*

Once he mentioned the "interact with animals" thing, the screenwriters noticed that every note he had given up until that point was VAGUE. Just sort of general "here's what would make a good *Shrinking Man* remake"–type stuff. Wow, was it possible? Had he been able to fill thirty minutes with generalizations so that no one noticed that he hadn't read the script he was giving notes on? <u>Thirty solid minutes</u>. That is a real skill. Man, when this guy was in grade school, his book reports must have KICKED ASS. Even on *The Sound and the Fury*, which is REALLY BORING, and he probably just skimmed. To be able to talk for thirty minutes about something you know ABSOLUTELY NOTHING ABOUT—

---

* *Quel* and *Dommage!* are French words.

master that skill, and the world is yours! (And probably a pretty nice hybrid Lexus too!)

They say that to this day you can still hear that studio head, roaming the halls at night, dress shoes clicking as he goes . . . giving notes to nobody . . . without even having read the coverage! MOO-HA HA HA HA!

"TURBULENCE"

Approximate Budget: $100 million (see cast)
Box-Office Gross: $210 million worldwide (see cast)
Home Video/DVD Gross: $50+ million
Awards Potential: Best Song nomination for Randy Newman's original song:
"Nothing to Declare (Except my Love for You)"

ADAM SANDLER <u>OR KEVIN JAMES</u> stars as BENNY, a downtrod-den baggage handler at Chicago's O'Hare International Airport. Benny's life has been a series of missed opportunities due to his major lack of self-confidence. He's a lonely guy. As a hobby he collects LUGGAGE TAGS from places he's never been, exotic airports around the world as he unloads other people's bags. "Oooh, look! Mount Pleasant Airport, Sandwich Islands. You don't see that one very much!" is the kind of sad dialogue that Benny will say to his cool, jaded coworker RON (Jason Schwartzman). Ron will constantly remind Benny that his life is a series of missed opportunities because of his lack of self-confidence. Benny's popular brother GLENN (Will Ferrell cameo) is the star RELIEF PITCHER for the Chicago Cubs. The brothers can't stand each other (Benny wanted to be a pitcher too, but it didn't work out).

But . . . Benny is a HUGE Cubs fan, so this leads to a funny scene in Act I where Benny and Ron have to alternately ROOT FOR, THEN HECKLE Glenn while he's on the mound. Benny, torn, will scream out, *"We want a pitcher, not a belly itcher, please God throw some heat!"* This will get a laugh at the test screening of this film.

Benny's life will be turned UPSIDE DOWN when he and Ron stumble upon a $60 million van Gogh painting in some luggage that's been lost. After much (funny) debate about what to do, Benny sets off to return the suitcase to its rightful owner, PENELOPE, a *surprisingly hot art historian*, played by CAMERON DIAZ.

Turns out the painting is STOLEN from the Japanese Yakuza, who stole it from the Art Institute of Chicago. Penelope was trying to RE-TURN it, when her suitcase got lost, blah blah blah. Mistaken identity, blah blah blah. They get chased by the Yakuza, the FBI, hide out "on the lam"—disguising themselves (yes, fun outfit and hair color changes for her) and sharing a bed in a TERRIBLE MOTEL, which leads to some PG-13 sparks between them when we find out she sleeps in the nude: "Me too," says Benny as he DROPS HIS TOWEL TO THE FLOOR, REVEALING A SLIGHTLY SMALLER TOWEL UNDERNEATH. (Trailer moment.)

All the while, BENNY IS COMING OUT OF HIS SHELL, TURNING FROM LOWLY BAGGAGE HANDLER INTO COOL/SPY–TYPE GUY. They get caught by the Yakuza (funny scene where they're both tied up and getting threatened by the Yakuza guys through their interpreter, played by MASI OKA). Our guys escape and plot a complicated REVERSE HEIST to get the painting back into the Art Institute of Chicago that at one point incorporates Benny throwing a baseball in a PERFECT SLIDER, 66 FEET, TO DISARM AN ALARM INSIDE THE MUSEUM. Benny's sports/living-in-the-shadows thing is vindicated. He and Penelope return the painting, and all is well. They kiss and are about to say good-bye on the steps of the museum at dawn, when Penelope tells Benny that she really is . . .

. . . a BOUNTY HUNTER. Only not for people, for art. That's what she does. Top secret stuff, find and return art: lots of danger, big bucks, and lots of travel to exotic locales. And Benny has proven himself a perfect partner.

They head off into the sunrise as she briefs him on their next mission, which involves a reclusive billionaire who lives in the Sandwich Islands . . . yes, he's finally gonna get to see Mount Pleasant Airport!!! And: CUE THE RANDY NEWMAN SONG!!!

DIRECTORS

Meet the person who's going to make and/or ruin your movie!

"Director," as any union member of a film crew will tell you (while sucking down some craft-service cantaloupe), "is the only entry-level position left in the movie business." Meaning: to get any other job on a crew, you have put in a ton of union hours. You can't START as the property master or sound mixer. Or even as the assistant director. You have to work your way up. The only job you can get on a movie set with no experience whatsoever is: director. Everything else requires union training.

So is it like joining the army and being made a four-star general on the same day? Yes, it is. And it happens all the time. Sometimes the director on the film is the LEAST experienced person on the set. It's not uncommon for a young COMMERCIAL DIRECTOR, MUSIC VIDEO DIRECTOR, or HILARIOUS INTERNET SHORT FILM DIRECTOR to get called up to "the show" and get to direct a feature film with no training or preparation. In this scenario, a person is going from the MOST FUN JOB IN THE WORLD to the HARDEST JOB IN THE WORLD, with no transition. In scuba diving, this event is called "the bends," and it can kill your brain. Just like directing movies can.

NOTE: AT THIS POINT, IF YOU ARE THINKING ABOUT BECOMING A FILM DIRECTOR, PUT THIS STUPID BOOK DOWN AND GO DIRECT A MOVIE, FOR CHRISSAKE. OR A SHORT FOR FUNNYORDIE.COM. STOP READING THIS NONSENSE AND GO DO IT. GOOD DIRECTORS MAKE A

TON OF MONEY. SO MUCH MONEY THAT IT MAKES EVEN THE MOST SUCCESSFUL SCREENWRITER IN HOLLYWOOD LOOK LIKE SOME HORRIBLE...POOR PERSON. Icky little screenwriters, driving around in their Lexi and Mercedeses—poor things.

(Note to editor: Is Lexi the plural of Lexus? Please let us know for the subsequent printings of this book and subsequent Lexus purchases.)

The (screenwriter) authors of this book* once parked one of their shitty cars next to (director) Michael Bay's GLASS-BACK FERRARI. Yes, the back cover is made of glass, so that you can look in and see the exquisite hand-crafting of the engine—which is in the back, for some reason. If you put glass over the engine in some screenwriter's car, all you'd see is an old pair of tighty-whitey underwear that's being used to hold the radiator cap in place.

Good directors are getting 10 million dollars a picture. Plus profit participation.

The old joke where people say: "...but what I really want to do is direct," is said so often BECAUSE IT'S 100 PERCENT TRUE.

EVERYBODY REALLY DOES WANT TO DIRECT.
Because they don't know what's in store for them.

A regular person, who wasn't crazy, you'd have to pay them a million dollars to get them to direct a movie. Somebody who really knows what directing a movie means you have to pay them $10 million.

Being the director of a studio film, while it sounds like a lot of fun, in reality is a job you might not wish upon your worst enemy. At least: *if you're doing it right, it's not that fun.*

Directing a studio film is like being the captain of an aircraft carrier

*The authors of this book are also members in good standing of the Directors Guild of America. Look for their forthcoming book from Simon & Schuster entitled *Directing Movies for Passion and BJs.*

that's pulling out to sea and ALREADY HAS SOME LEAKS IN THE HULL. And there's a fire belowdecks. And a crazy person (movie star) is your COPILOT. And your admiral is a female lead who's NUTS and wants to know her motivation for EVERYTHING, and you can't film her butt, ever. Or the left side of her face. And the script sucks (because it's been rewritten twenty-five times by different writers). *Wait, what? ALL OF THIS, Already? We should turn back to port! STOP THIS AIR-CRAFT CARRIER!!! I WANT TO GET OFF!!!*

Too late. You can't turn back. You're directing a studio movie. Most studio movies cost around $200,000 a day to produce. Sometimes more. Sometimes WAY more. A movie like *Transformers 2: Revenge of the Fallen* costs almost a million bucks a day. We only pay the president of the United States $400,000 per year. Per YEAR. Really makes you think about which racket you wanna get into, huh?

If you want to practice directing studio movies, here's what to do:

Step 1. Watch the documentary *Burden of Dreams* about the making of the 1982 Werner Herzog film *Fitzcarraldo,* in the Amazon.

Then: If you STILL want to direct a movie . . . (Really? Wow. Okay.) Move on to Step 2.

Step 2. Fill your shoes with mustard greens, go stand in the rain on fourteenth and Broadway, and wait for a dolphin to walk by and mistake you for Kim Jong-il.

What did that teach you, Daniel-san? That directing a studio film, more than anything else, is about:

PATIENCE

If you don't like the idea of making a soufflé while two people who have never made a soufflé look over your shoulder and tell you how to make a soufflé, DON'T TRY TO DIRECT A STUDIO FILM.

Patience. As Guns N' Roses said in their beautiful anthem "Patience":

You and I've got what it takes to make it
We won't fake it, Oh never break it.

On second thought, those lyrics are not the least bit helpful. But they do rhyme in a way that only people doing A LOT of drugs in 1988 can rhyme words.

When directing, patience is everything. Because a studio film has more moving parts than, say, a tiny wind-up medieval hand grenade in a Guillermo Del Toro film. Directing a film isn't a full-time job, it's TEN full-time jobs. When you're not on set, you're scouting locations. When you're not scouting locations, you're casting. When you're not casting, you're meeting with the wardrobe designer, storyboard artist, CGI team . . . and on and on. Not to mention the studio executives, who will be sitting on your shoulders like little winged angels/devils from an old-time cartoon. And when they're hungry, you will look like a steak to them.

And while you're making three hundred decisions a day: there are people around you who are QUESTIONING THE THREE HUN-DRED DECISIONS YOU'RE MAKING EVERY DAY. Especially if you're a first-time director. Or if your last movie wasn't a huge hit.

Then, at lunch, twenty lunatics need a decision about something, immediately—and THAT'S WHEN YOU WATCH THE DAILIES OF YESTERDAY'S FOOTAGE. *And you know what? It would have been a lot better if the female lead had let you get that shot of her butt. Dang.* Now you'll have to do some reshoots. But you won't be at the same location to match, so you'll have to build a set to match the place you were. Which means a meeting with the production designer and approving a small MODEL of a set that looks kind of like the place you were. And a butt double. That means you have to set a meeting with the casting director too, to find a butt double. And if the butt doesn't match, you'll need somebody to air-brush the butt double's butt. Then in post you'll have to color-time the airbrushed butt double's butt.

Then, after the very first test screening—you cut the whole scene from the film anyway. Ah, well . . . no harm done. Just MILLIONS of dollars down the toilet, *and your brain has been destroyed and won't ever come back.*

Directing a film is like spinning plates—that you're trying to make a Tibetan sand painting on top of. And while you're doing it: you're always "losing light," according to the director of photography. And the Teamsters are griping about how you're still "wet behind the ears." And the cantaloupe from craft service is TERRIBLE.

Directing studio films is a huge pain. Some might say it's more trouble than it's worth. Unless you get good at it: then you get $10 million a picture, plus points, and you get to live forever in the pantheon of great film directors.

It's easy, as the screenwriters, to say, "Hey, idiotic director, stop ruining our brilliant movies!" But we must also take into account that making a truly great studio film, given the parameters and the number of people involved, is . . . <u>almost impossible</u>. And the director is the eye of the poop hurricane.

It certainly helps if you get a director who respects writing and respects the screenplay. And who knows how hard it is to write a screenplay. Often things you spend MONTHS on in the script will get changed in three seconds on location scout. Cross your fingers that you get a director who respects your writing. But—BEWARE THE DIRECTOR WHO REMINDS YOU THAT HE'S "A WRITER TOO." Ugh. If any director actually SAYS THAT OUT LOUD to you—"I'm a writer too."—you'd better WATCH OUT. That's code for "<u>I'm going to change your script. A LOT</u>." You just bought an e-ticket on a ride called SUCKTOWN CANYON (which is some kind of flume ride through things that suck). WRITER-SLASH-DIRECTORS, when they're just directing, not writing, will make your life a living hell.

There are two kinds of film directors:

1. Facilitators
People the studio trust. The studio knows that it can give them $100 million in cash, a bunch of movie stars, a CGI team, and a huge crew, and they'll come back with the footage required to cut together into a hit film.

Facilitator: from the Spanish *facil,* or "easy." Literally meaning: people *who* make hard things seem easy. Let's call them: Easytators.*

And the other kind of director:

2. Guillermo Del Toro

Okay, we could have said FACILITATORS and VISIONARIES. But saying Guillermo Del Toro is more fun. And holy crap: have you seen this Guillermo Del Toro guy's movies? He's, like, some kind of genius or visionary or sumpin'.

NOTE: AT THIS POINT, IF YOU HAVEN'T SEEN ANY GUILLERMO DEL TORO MOVIES—SPARK UP A JOINT, AND THROW ONE IN THE BLU-RAY PLAYER. BUT YOU MIGHT WANT TO PUT DOWN SOME PLASTIC ON THE COUCH, FOR WHEN YOUR HEAD EXPLODES FROM AWESOMENESS.

You'll never know what kind of director you're going to get until it's too late. And in the end, it doesn't matter—you don't get a vote anyway. So treat your director the way you would your studio executive: HELP THEM KEEP THEIR JOB. Be supportive. Do the rewrites they ask you for. Yes, even for free. The more you can stay involved, the better the chances that they won't ruin your movie. Give them options on any material you write for them (also for free): *If you've written all of the options, then they might not feel that they need "fresh eyes."*

The best way to help a director not ruin your film: be someone they want to keep around. *Fix their problems. Help them out however you can.* Remember: like a rattlesnake, a director is probably more scared of you than you are of him. So puff your chest out, ACT like you're confident, and you'll seem like you are. And in doing this, you'll make everyone feel a lot better.

Film is a "director's medium," as any director's agent will tell you. No matter what anybody says, the director is THE MOST IMPORTANT PERSON ON THE SET. <u>Except for the first assistant director, who is REALLY the most important person on the set</u>. (You can make a movie without a great director. But not without a great first A.D., not a chance.) So work hard, as a writer, to stay on the director's good side: by being helpful.

---

*Note to publisher: Easytators, or "Easy Taters," is a good idea for some kind of deep-fried potato tie-in with the release of this book, at Cracker Barrel, Applebee's, etc.

Even better, eliminate the middleman:

Direct your movies yourself.

Then the fat, lazy screenwriter and moronic, illiterate director are both YOU! Now you can truly hate yourself! (Along with drinking, self-hatred is a big part of directing AND screenwriting!)

If you want to truly be happy in the motion picture business and see your vision reflected in every aspect of a film, there's only one path for you:

BECOME AN EDITOR.

Yep. Editor. <u>Be an editor</u>. The hours are good, the chairs you sit in are "ergonomic," the work itself is satisfying, and you decide whether the footage you've been handed is *Citizen Kane* or *Dunston Checks In*. Plus, your lunch is usually picked up by the postproduction budget! CHA-CHING! Yes, there is such a thing as a free lunch. As long as you're the editor.

PRODUCERS
And What They Will Tell You They're Useful For

Keep in mind: when a film wins the Academy Award for Best Picture, the person who accepts the award is . . .

<u>THE PRODUCER</u>.

Not the director, sure as hell not the writer, and not anybody from the studio. Those folks are lucky if they get thanked. The producer is the face of the movie, and they get to keep the trophy to prove it.

The short version of the producer's job description is: **everything.** The producer is literally responsible for every aspect of the entire film, from getting the rights to the story to hiring writers and steering the screenplay process, the casting, hiring the director, postproduction, and on and on. And of course: firing people.

AND YELLING AT PEOPLE. And they yell at people A LOT. And when yelling isn't enough, they throw phones at people, because everyone the producer is dealing with (if you ask them) is a rotten, spoiled baby who's lucky to be working at all.

And . . . *They're kind of right.* We are lucky to be working in showbiz at all.

Most movie producers are crazy—because being a movie producer is a job that no sane person would want. As far as we can tell, no sane person has had the job yet. Not and succeeded at it, anyway.

Being a movie producer requires a big, bold personality. And, as we mentioned, TONS OF YELLING. It is NOT a job for the meek, the humble, the introspective, or anybody you'd describe as "a really great guy." Since the days of Thalberg and Selznick, the position of producer is one for oversexed, megalomaniac ÜBER-HUMANS who for some reason feel the desire to play wedding planner to a group of dim-witted rodeo clowns, who are also, for the most part, oversexed and megalomaniacal.

Great producers, like Thalberg, die young. Those are the lucky ones. The ones who survive have to deal with the rest of us showbiz types— hiring us, firing us, screaming at us until their stomach lining supernovas or their liver LEAPS out of their body and runs away to go "find itself" at a spa in the Arizona desert.

When high-level executives get FIRED from movie studios, their severance packages often come with a deal to become a "producer on the lot."

IF YOU THINK ABOUT IT, THIS MEANS THAT TO THE STUDIO PEOPLE, <u>BEING MADE TO BE A PRODUCER IS PUN-ISHMENT</u>.

Being a movie producer means having a keen eye for a great novel that will make a thrilling film. It also means making sure that the Jonas Brothers and Demi Lovato are ON THE GODDAMN RED CARPET AT THE PREMIERE, MENTIONING THE GODDAMN NAME OF THE GODDAMN FILM WHILE THE TITLE IS CLEARLY VISIBLE BEHIND THEM ON THE GODDAMN MARQUEE!!! AND GETTING THE OPENING DATE RIGHT!

Yes, LOTS AND LOTS OF YELLING is required. And occasionally throwing a phone, paperweight, or fax machine at an intern.

Note: Throwing electronics at your assistant or an intern is NEVER ACCEPTABLE in Hollywood. Unless your last movie made a shitload of money. Then all bets are off. Then—go nuts. Throw a Bentley at your assistant or at a Wayans Brother. Or throw a Wayans Brother at a Jonas Brother! Who cares after $200 million in domestic box office, right? In fact, if your last picture made some serious box office, why not save time and HIRE AN INTERN to throw phones and stuff at your assistant? Fun! And then why not give a couple other kids COLLEGE CREDIT to FILM your intern throwing things at your assistant? And then: ENTER

THAT FILM IN SOME FESTIVALS, GET DISTRIBUTION, WIN SOME AWARDS. And get this: you as producer will ACCEPT THOSE AWARDS! Fun!

The recipe for a great producer:

> Two parts artiste,
> Six parts sideshow barker,
> One part serial killer.
> Stir.

WHAT DOES THIS MEAN TO YOU, AS A WRITER?

When you've perfected your spec script or pitch, you'll try to sell it all over town. You take it to executives at studios, you might take it to some directors (who might get you in the door to higher-ups at the studios), and you'll also take it to a few PRODUCERS. If a producer likes it, you'll then go around to studios WITH the producer.

The upside to taking your script to a PRODUCER: With a producer attached, the studio isn't JUST buying your script, they are ALSO buying a producer who's going to develop your script with you. A good producer (who's smart and who's been around awhile) can make a script much better. And if the studio greenlights your movie, that producer will produce it for the studio: hiring the director, etc. A BIG-NAME producer might give the studios more confidence to buy your movie, knowing that the odds of it turning out good are better with a producer who's made a lot of good movies. Good producers also know the town—who at the studio to pitch to, which studios have loose bags of cash lying around.

The DOWNSIDE: The producer also comes with a HEFTY PRICE TAG. The producer gets a FEE and a percentage of the profits. So—your movie, with this extra chef, will also be less profitable to the studio. But if you get a producer attached who has a reputation for earning hundreds of millions at the box office, they're worth the price. Even if they ALSO have a reputation for throwing phones at people.

91

HERBIE: FULLY LOADED
WTF happened?

Herbie: Fully Loaded was a total piece of s#!t. We agree. We don't blame the director. Under the circumstances, she did the best she could. We don't blame Lindsay Lohan, bless her troubled little heart. We don't blame any of the other screenwriters who changed the script after we were fired. (There were twenty-four of them.) That piece-of-s#!t movie was not their fault. The reason *Herbie* sucked was the fault of one lone executive. Beware, young writers—THIS WILL HAPPEN TO YOU!

All it took was one (very highly paid) person to ruin that film: to ruin the opportunity of reviving the Herbie franchise, to waste all of Disney's cash, and to inadvertently start the domino chain that would lead to the tragic death of Lindsay Lohan.*

GETTY IMAGES

*As of this printing, Lindsay Lohan is NOT DEAD YET.

Was this executive evil? No. The sad fact is that this person was just genuinely incompetent.

Rule 5: There is more incompetence than evil in Hollywood.

For every genuinely evil person we've met in Hollywood (and we've met three*), there are dozens who are simply idiots. (NOTE: We did not say "harmless idiots." In Hollywood, there is no such thing.)

HERBIE—THE RIDE

(Don't forget your lube, and wear a poncho—you will get wet.)

We are both very big fans of the old *Love Bug* movies. We grew up in the seventies, and we saw them at the drive-in (not together, obviously). But yes, we both separately saw the *Herbie* movies at drive-in theaters. It was a kinder, gentler world back then, kids. Children weren't raised by the internet, raping each other's avatars and bitching about *Herbie: Fully Loaded* on IMDB. KIDS USED TO GO OUTSIDE, read books, fish in creeks, and yes—whole families would go to the drive-in to watch Disney movies.

We said to ourselves, "We should pitch a new Herbie movie. We should make it great."

We attacked the movie the way we approach everything: we looked at the central idea first. Herbie is a car with a personality that can drive by itself, and which, like Mary Poppins, comes into people's lives and helps them fix their own problems.

But the old Herbie movies are corny in a way you can't get away with today. In the real world, if a car drove itself, people would call the news. They'd put it on YouTube, the story'd be all over the world in a day. And a real car that could drive itself with no explanation would also scare the shit out of people.

So the first big thing we decided was: Herbie's magic needed to be

*Billy Crystal was not one of them. He's not evil. He's just a dick.

subtler. For example: Maybe it wouldn't start itself when it didn't want to go somewhere. Instead, maybe it would get stuck in a left turn and take you somewhere it wanted to go—like the big race. Maybe when it was mad at you, its horn would get stuck behind a cop car. Stuff like that. Subtler than a car that drives itself.

The second big thing was: We needed to put Herbie in a much more real world. Not some dopey, illogical, kids'-movie world, with characters like the crotchety old junk lot owner twirling his mustache and swearing "I'm gonna get that little car if it's the last thing I ever do!!!" Kids hate that kinda stupid shit as much as grown-ups do. We never write things for a "kids' movie." We wrote it like a real movie—THE WAY ALL GOOD MOVIES ARE WRITTEN. Only shitty kids' movies are written down to kids.

We set it in a very realistically portrayed world of San Fernando Valley street racing: a macho world, where an old, beat-up car would get laughed at—then be totally respected when it won some races.

We wanted the main character to be a girl from a stock car racing family. (When we wrote *Herbie*, there were NO women in Nascar.) So the fact that a dad preferred his son to race the family stock car, even though his daughter liked cars, made total sense.

- Act I: was about a girl who was forced to race in the world of *The Fast and the Furious*, even though she wanted to drive the family stock car.
- Act II: Herbie turned their lives around.
- Act III: The whole family pulled together, and Herbie won a Nascar race.

Simple, huh? So why did the movie suck so bad?

We sold the pitch straight to the president* of the studio. The president LOVED this take: putting Herbie in a totally real world, not a sappy kids'-movie world, and giving the movie a strong female character with a good love story and a legitimate, believable obstacle that Herbie could help her overcome.

We turned in the first draft, and the movie was greenlit. Off the first draft. The president of the studio agreed to pay Lindsay Lohan her very

---

*Nina Jacobson. Brilliant woman who tried to prevent M. Night Shyamalan from making *Lady in the Water*.

expensive quote and make her pay or play. (That means she would get paid whether the movie was made or not.)

They were <u>that</u> confident of the movie. <u>Off the first draft</u>.

She had one note: it was too sexy for Disney. We swear. It was set in the world of street racing, so . . . we had some bikini girls in there. And one of these "Red Bull Girls" had the hots for Lindsay Lohan's character because she thought Lindsay was a man. Pretty hot for a Herbie movie, we guess. Good call, Prexy.

We said great, done. We took out the sexier stuff, the "Red Bull Girls," etc. It took us a couple of days to do the tweaks. We finished and turned it back in—and here's where it gets interesting/horrible:

We were no longer dealing directly with the president of the studio. We were now dealing with a studio executive <u>under</u> the president. *This executive was not in the room when we sold the pitch. This executive was not there when the president gave us notes on the script.* <u>And this executive was dumb as a stump and mean as a rattlesnake.</u>

We did about ten drafts for this executive: dumbing down the plot, making everything cuter, taking out things that made the movie make sense. This executive had no agenda. This exec wasn't making a power play. This executive just genuinely didn't understand the movie and what the president had liked about it. This executive just didn't know good from bad.

Now, we knew we were doing some heavy damage to the script, and we tried to get the script in to the president, to run the changes by her. The executive wouldn't let us talk to the president of the studio. ("I speak for the studio.") When the exec wanted us to make Herbie smile, we re-fused. It was illogical to us. We know it seems like a dumb point for us to stick on, but . . . that's not "personality," that's a superpower. That was just WAY too cute and dumb—the opposite of why we wanted to write a Herbie movie in the first place and why Disney had bought it.

When this exec was happy with the script, the exec turned in the new draft to the president—<u>and the studio UN-greenlit the movie and fired us that day</u>. We begged the president: look, fire us, but at least let us leave you with a script that's not horrible.

We worked over a long weekend and gave the studio what was basi-cally our first draft with the sexy stuff taken out. We turned it in, they regreenlit the movie. Then they fired us.

BUT this bad executive was still in charge of *Herbie*. So the exec hired and fired twenty-four more writers to do all of the bad stuff that the studio had made us do. Then the studio made *Herbie: Fully Loaded*. <u>This happens all the time. It's why most movies suck donkey balls.</u>

We've had it happen to several of our movie scripts and to three pilots we sold to Fox: we sell something to the president, then some executive or producer comes in and wants to get his or her thumbprints all over it.

Sometimes it's because the executives or producers see themselves as writers; sometimes it's because they think they know better than the president; but more often than not, it's just because they don't understand the basic idea that the president liked and bought. They simply don't get it. They don't understand the script or pitch, so they change it.

<u>Let's make this analogy</u>:

You have a Volkswagen Bug. You sell it to someone. He says, "Deliver it in eight weeks. Make it pink." Then that person's underling says, "I know we bought a Bug, but all the other studios are buying SUVs this year, so let's make it a big SUV." Then: "I read an article about boats today and how they're going to be popular this year—let's make this thing kinda like a boat." Then they say: "*Terminator* made a lot of money, let's make this thing kinda like *Terminator*." Then: "Make it green." You go back to the person who bought a pink Bug, and they say: "What the hell is this giant green *Terminator* boat?"

WHAT WE LEARNED AND WILL PASS ON TO YOU!

Most times you're screwed! There's nothing you can do! Suck it up, cash the check (if you got one), move on, and hope it doesn't end your career!

But remember these things:

- Before you kick up dust, always try to incorporate the nimrod's notes first—but do it without doing any damage to the script. **We are not exaggerating when we say again: "If you can master this skill, all of Hollywood will be yours."** Not fighting the studio's notes but doing a version of people's notes in a way that actually works—that is the secret of success in the studio system.
- Making an enemy of the nimrod is a huge mistake.

Rule 6: Make no enemies. Ever.
If a writer picks a fight with the studio, they will lose.

If a writer picks a fight with his producer or executive, the writer will lose.

- *(When you've sold a few scripts, this one applies.)* We try to never attach producers to our projects. Producers mostly suck. We try to only deal with the Buyer—the studio. Producers are sometimes a huge added expense: their fees can be massive. And sometimes their notes directly conflict with those of the studio. And the studio is the Buyer. The studio's notes are the only things that matter.

- When some nimrod is trying to derail your script, do anything you can to talk to the Buyer directly. Try to get a meeting with you and the nimrod and the studio head at the same time, so you're all on the same page. If the nimrod TRULY IS SAYING THINGS THE STUDIO AGREES WITH, then do it. Suck it up. If they are NOT, get the studio to articulate what it wants, so the nimrod will hopefully shut up and let you write the script the studio wants. Remember: you're not writing the script for you—YOU ARE WRITING IT FOR THE STUDIO.

    Handle this meeting carefully—be superpolite and respectful to EVERYBODY. And remember:

Rule 7: Nobody likes a crybaby.

If you're the writer, nobody cares that you sold a great idea and someone is screwing it up.

And always remember: the nimrod screwing up your script has WAY more friends on the lot than you. You're a writer. If there was a way for the studios to generate scripts without writers at all—they would.

Suck it up. Walk it off. Move on. Sell another screenplay.

If you think we're saying this out of bitterness, you're taking it totally wrong. This is good advice. It's the way it sometimes is in the studio system, and if you can't accept that—go write novels on the moor.

TRUE HOLLYWOOD HORROR STORIES!

Part Two:

The After-Lunch Pitch!
The Producer Who Slept!

CUE SFX: THUNDER CLAP!

FADE IN.

EXT. ROBERTSON BLVD — DAY

Two young, straight, but kind-of-gay-looking SCREENWRITERS pull their crappy cars off of Robertson Boulevard, across from the fabulous Ivy Restaurant, where Lindsay Lohan once hit some dude's van with her car and where she later tragically died from a toxic mix of antianxiety pills and sugar-free energy drinks.*

The screenwriters park in the basement of New Line Cinema, a studio that pulled one of the greatest tricks in Hollywood history:

Making the *Lord of the Rings* trilogy and $2.9 BILLION at the box office, before home video. :)

And then: ALMOST WENT OUT OF BUSINESS. :(

"Wait, what?" you ask, "They made those movies and almost went out of business?"

Yep. That's *essactly* what happened. If this book has taught you anything yet, it's—that's how Hollywood works. You make the *Lord of the*

---

*At the time of this publication, Lindsay Lohan is not yet dead.

Rings trilogy, then you die, alone and unloved, in the parking lot of an Arby's, trying to trade your Oscar for a pack of Salem Menthols.

Hollywood has a SHORT MEMORY. Think of Hollywood as a sexy young CHEERLEADER with a great pair of legs and Alzheimer's disease.

(Note: there is an upside to Hollywood having a short memory: you can remake the same movies over and over! For example, you can make *The Pacifier* with Vin Diesel, then make almost the exact same movie five years later and call it *The Spy Next Door*! Fun!!! AND RECYCLING IS GOOD FOR THE ENVIRONMENT!!!!)

ANYWAY—*back to our chilling tale!*

The young screenwriters had come to New Line to pitch their movie about a schlubby young mall cop who lives with his mother in a retirement community in Florida and gets caught up in a web of intrigue and *Die Hard*–style action. The studio executive (someone we would come to know and respect) listened to the pitch and did something that no studio executive had ever done before:

She fell asleep.

Sound asleep. A gentle afternoon siesta like the ones our friends in Sicily and Madrid enjoy. She looked like an angel, head listing back toward Heaven in gentle repose.

The screenwriters did not know what to do. There was a long, awkward moment. They looked at each other, then back to the sleeping angel, and decided to do the only thing there was to do: wait it out.

(Note: if the person you're pitching to falls asleep, DO NOT WAKE THEM. They may wake up confused and angry and as a result hire Ganz and Mandel instead of you.)

The screenwriters waited. After a few minutes, the angel's eyes fluttered, and she refocused on the room, TRYING AS HARD AS SHE COULD TO ACT LIKE SHE'D BEEN "THINKING," UNAWARE THAT SHE'D BEEN ASLEEP FOR QUITE A WHILE. This is easier to do in a college lecture hall, where you're one of a couple hundred people in the room. When it's you, an assistant, and TWO OTHER PEOPLE WHO ARE TALKING DIRECTLY TO YOU, it's pretty awkward. Not quite as awkward as letting out a fart, but pretty close.

When the studio executive returned to the land of the waking, she turned to the screenwriters and said groggily, "I'm pretty sure Adam Sandler's already working on a mall cop thing."

And you know what . . . <u>he was</u>. It was made with Kevin James. It was called *Paul Blart: Mall Cop*. And it made $183,293,131 worldwide.

The moral of this story: A movie with a schlubby guy as a mall cop is a VERY GOOD IDEA.

REDLIGHTING

OR

HOW TO GET YOUR MOVIE UN-GREENLIT!

ROBYN VON SWANK

For starters: "Redlighting" is not an expression ever used by anyone in Hollywood. It's an expression that we made up for this chapter, meaning the opposite of greenlit. It is not trademarked, so feel free to use it! The fact is, movies get STOPPED, SCRAPPED, HALTED, and BAILED UPON all the time.

(Note to editors: BAILED UPON seems like the right grammar? BAILED ON? ALL BAILED UP ON?)

Movies can fall apart faster than a macramé bikini made by a Thai child-labor slave. PRETTY FAST INDEED. Especially when that macramé bikini is on, say, Tyra Banks.

There are a lot of dumb things the writer can do to help get the movie stopped on a dime, or rather *stopped on the couple million dimes that have already been spent* and the possible contractual penalties of the stars, director, etc. Stopped on LOTS and LOTS of dimes.

Here are some things to watch out for:

1. Table Reads

Yikes. They want to do a table read of the script. *Um . . . okay, sure.* Consider yourself lucky if you even get invited to the table read of your script. They often don't invite the writer. But if they do, it will be a fun opportunity for you to go to a fancy hotel conference room and see BIG-TIME MOVIE STARS butcher your words. It's not their fault—they've just NEVER READ IT BEFORE. In fact, they're only vaguely familiar with the fact that they're getting paid several million dollars to star in this movie. All they know is the concept. Let's say, for example, you're doing the production rewrite on *Starsky & Hutch*. Well, keep in mind that Owen Wilson might not remember if he's supposed to be playing STARSKY or HUTCH until he sees which part Ben Stiller reads first. This kind of thing happens all the time. Keep in mind that no matter what they do, <u>THEY</u> ARE THE MOVIE STARS—<u>YOU</u> ARE THE ONE WHO WILL LOOK LIKE A DOUCHEBAG WHEN ANY JOKE FALLS FLAT. This is a COLD READING for them; they're doing their best.

Your writing career is hanging on an actor's COLD READING of your script in a room with twenty-five very powerful people and their assistants. Yikes. Double yikes. Exclamation point. Every dud that happens in the reading: PEOPLE WILL LOOK AT YOU as if they've just been told you have inoperable brain cancer.

Before any table read: YOU should go through the script and do a pass where you TRIM EVERYTHING down to the BARE MINIMUM. If your table read goes long—that is NOT GOOD. Let's say your reading goes so long that a bunch of people RUSH to the bathroom the moment it's done: NOT GOOD. So trim, trim, trim. Let the draft for the table read be light and breezy. And trim dialogue too. Is anything said TWICE in your script? Unless it's a callback or the THEME OF THE ENTIRE FILM (e.g., "I never knew what was right under my nose until the genie made me change places with that basset hound"). Never repeat yourself. If it's said twice, cut the second time it's said. And descriptions of action can be cut WAY DOWN—you just don't need to say everything that happens, especially when it BREAKS UP A CHARACTER'S DIALOGUE. Less is more. Aim for WAY LESS.

2. Budget

We know what you're thinking: HEY, THE BUDGET ISN'T MY FAULT! *DIDN'T THEY JUST PAY THAT MOVIE STAR $25 MILLION TO BE IN THIS GODDAMN BASSETT HOUND SWITCHEROO MOVIE?*

103

True, not every aspect of the budget is in your control. But keep in mind, as the budget of your movie SPIRALS OUT OF CONTROL (the normal state of budgets), the studio's position becomes more and more difficult. Keep in mind this fact that people often forget: MOVIE STUDIOS DON'T GET EVERY PENNY IN TICKET SALES BACK. They SPLIT the profits with the movie theaters. And not evenly but on a shifting scale (short version: the longer a movie stays in the theaters, the more the theater owners make). AND, if the star or director are big enough: THEY'RE GETTING FIRST-DOLLAR GROSS. So the studio is splitting the pie with LOTS of folks *who loves themselves some pie.*

The studios have to justify every expense, and your script has to be a GUARANTEED HIT if the budget is high. Not only does it have to be a GUARANTEED HIT in the United States, it has to have INTERNATIONAL APPEAL TOO. (General note: any movie you're writing for a studio these days HAS to have international appeal. Your movie has to be a hit in GERMANY TOO. *Keep that in mind as you write, dummkopf!* I.e., *no jokes about how David Hasselhoff IS NOT THAT GREAT at singing.* That stuff may play here, but you'll be in Vierten Platz* in Hamburg.)

When it comes to the budget: DON'T BE PART OF THE PROBLEM, BE PART OF THE SOLUTION. If there are creative trims you can make to the action of your script or if you can reinvent a very expensive set piece to be LESS EXPENSIVE, do it!

Look at the most expensive sequences in the film, and ask yourself: *Is it either so awesome that it's going to be in the trailer or really necessary for the story I'm trying to tell?* If it's absolutely necessary, if it's very funny and good enough for the trailer—keep it. If it's not either one of those—BE

*German for "fourth place."

THE FIRST ONE TO RECOMMEND TRIMS TO YOUR OWN SCRIPT. YOU WILL BE APPRECIATED FOR IT. In general, the less "precious" you are about your words, the better liked you will be.

Remember: the less your movie COSTS to make, the more it can MAKE in profit. The short way to remember this is:

$$\$\$ > \$$$

Two dollar signs is greater than one dollar sign. BUT THIS SAD FORMULA HAPPENS A LOT IN HOLLYWOOD:

$$\$\$\$\$ = \$\$\$\$$$

This means the studio spent four dollar signs on your movie AND MADE BACK FOUR DOLLAR SIGNS. Bummer. *Shoulda considered what the German audience would think about the basset hound taking a whiz on the leg of Hasselhoff's lederhosen. Bad move, dummkopf!*

3. Act III Problems

As a movie gets closer and closer to production, Act III of the script seems to pretty much ALWAYS be a problem. Even more than Act I and Act II problems, this is the biggie.

You'll find that once the movie is greenlit, LOTS of people will come out of the woodwork and they will think you have ACT III PROBLEMS. And they'll hover their finger over the REDLIGHT button until they're resolved (or until they fire you). Sometimes they know what they want. Most times they just want the end of the movie to be . . . better. Whatever that means. So get ready to REWRITE and to try out a lot of different versions of your third act. In fact, be ready to REWRITE everything and anything in the script, and don't be a douche about it, be wonderful and accommodating. Remember, this is the act where you get the guy DOWN FROM THE TREE and he's changed for the better. It ain't brain surgery. (See Chapter 23, "If Your Screenplay Doesn't Have This Structure . . .")

4. Getting a Contemplative Star Attached!

Wait—isn't getting a star attached a good thing? Sometimes, yes: if it's the right star and one who likes to work all the time, yes.

But: BEWARE THE CONTEMPLATIVE STAR. This is the kind of movie star who likes to THINK for long periods of time about the kinds of movies he or she likes to do and makes only one movie a year. Sometimes, in fact, stars will attach themselves to your script because they like it *just enough to think about it, on a back burner. For years.* Or even worse, because they fear someone else will scoop it up if they don't.

Keep in mind what is required of a movie star who attaches himself to your script: ZERO

Yep! Nothing is required. Seriously. All that has to happen is that the star says, "I'M INTERESTED IN THAT, LET'S DEVELOP IT FOR ME." And that's it. They've taken it off the market for anybody else. They don't have to sign anything, they don't need to commit any further, they don't have to give you dates they're free. Nothing. In fact, if you push them to commit, they'll probably just give you a bunch of notes. So if you've got a star attached to your script and they're not shooting one movie right now, with another in preproduction and another animated movie that they're also doing a voice for: BE CAREFUL. You might have a "contemplative star." Years may pass while your star thinks about the script in an abstract way while gazing longingly out the window of his mansion in Beverly Park* while you sit applying Icy Hot to your carpal tunnel wrists in the Frolic Room.†

5. Marketability

Before your movie gets greenlit, or sometimes even bought, it will be run by the MARKETING DEPARTMENT of the studio. The folks there

---

*Beverly Park is a neighborhood you may not have not heard of. We hadn't, even after living in Los Angeles for ten years. It is, in fact, one of the fanciest neighborhoods in the world. It's a place for BILLIONAIRES, not millionaires. Just for fun, use your Google Map and search BEVERLY PARK (near Los Angeles, California), and make sure it's set on "Satellite." Then zoom in. WOWZA. Wait . . . *THOSE ARE HOUSES? They each look about as big as Versailles!* 'Cause they are!!! They are as big as Versailles, only not as tacky!!!

†The Frolic Room is a terrific bar for hard-core rummies, barfly types, and screenwriters on Hollywood Boulevard, next to the Pantages Theater. There's a jukebox, and the drinks are reasonably priced. The perfect spot to drown your suicidal thoughts or just spend the evening in a quiet knife fight. Charles Bukowski used to piss himself there!

will have two simple questions: Who is this movie for? And is that person SOMEONE WHO PAYS TO SEE MOVIES IN A THEATER ON A REGULAR BASIS? You should have already answered both of these questions before anyone else with the script, which simply has to have an inherent appeal to the largest audience possible. If all else fails: ADD THE WORDS "IN 3-D" UNDERNEATH YOUR TITLE ON THE TITLE PAGE. Yes, oddly sixtyish years after its invention, somehow 3-D is the thing that's getting people's butts into the theater seats! Let's hope SMELL-O-RAMA is next.

6. The Executive Who's Shepherding the Project Gets Fired

What the hell?!? Good ol' Gary got FIRED!?! BUT HE'S THE GUY WHO THOUGHT BASSET-SWITCH WAS A HOME RUN?!?

This happens all the time. Don't be surprised if you've been inching closer to a green light for months, only to wake up and read on deadline hollywood.com that your beloved exec is FIRED. (Although the studio will never really say "fired." They will say "departing" or "ankling," for some reason. Or that the person has just been given a "producing deal on the lot." All those are code words for "fired.") Well, WAY TO GO, DUMMY. IT WAS *YOUR* JOB, AS THE WRITER, TO HELP THE STUDIO EXECUTIVE KEEP HIS JOB. WE ALREADY TOLD YOU THAT! He hasn't failed you—you have failed him (or else he got busted doing something fishy in the copy room).

If the executive who's been spearheading your movie got fired— chances are your movie is DEAD. No new executive will pick up Gary's mantle. Why not? If the movie bombs, they will get fired. And if the movie succeeds, everyone will give good ol' Gary the credit.

There's lots of ways the movie can fall apart. But you need to be a rock that everybody can count on. This is not the Sistine Chapel ceiling you're painting here. You're a contractor, making the best public bathroom you can make! But still, you can make it a wonderful bathroom. One fit for "the King" to die in.

TRUE HOLLYWOOD HORROR STORIES!

Part Three!

We got to pitch legendary comic Billy Crystal!

Dick.

TURNAROUND

What happens after the studio has developed and redeveloped your movie, fired you, hired other writers, fired the other writers, then hired you again—then decided they're NOT going to make your brilliant script into a movie anyway? Is it dead? Probably!

But—not always. There is also the possibility of TURNAROUND.

Turnaround happens when a studio SELLS a script it's developed to another studio. Usually it's for not very much money—just the amount of money that the first studio has already spent on the thing.

This happened to us on *Reno 911!* Fox paid for the original pilot, then didn't pick it up. Then, years later, Comedy Central asked us if we had any good ideas for a TV show, and we showed them our Reno pilot. Comedy Central bought the rights to the pilot from Fox.

Two kinda odd stories about that: The Fox lawyers decided that Comedy Central could air the (improvised) SCRIPT of the Reno pilot but couldn't use the actual footage. So in 2003 we had to REENACT the improvs that we'd done back in 1999. There was a scene where the two of us had to make out by the side of the road—as Dangle and a personal trainer. We had to do that twice. And both times, we had to do it while two armed California Highway Patrol officers were standing ten feet away to stop traffic—glaring at us.

Odd story number two: The lawyer at Comedy Central in charge of buying the rights (we're DYING to tell you her name, but we might get sued) FORGOT to mention the movie rights in the contract. Just flat-out forgot. So when Fox wanted to make a MOVIE of *Reno 911!* it went to the negotiating table with Comedy Central . . . only to realize that it didn't need Comedy Central at all. In the end, they did it in partnership together, for a lot of reasons. The character Clemmy wasn't in the Fox pilot, so we would have had to cut her from the movie. Plus, we wanted Comedy Central as a partner, for promotional reasons—and it would have been a sticky ugly fight to do the movie without Comedy Central. BUT—that f@*k-up cost Comedy Central millions.

There are some wonderful stories of studios selling a movie that it thought stank to another studio, then the other studio making the movie and that movie turning out to be, say—*E.T.*, which Universal bought from Columbia, *Speed* went from Paramount to Fox, and Warner Bros. sold *Forrest Gump* to Paramount. Ha ha.

When does this happen? Usually, the writer or producer has to aggressively sell the movie to the other studio. And sometimes it's a hard sell, since a studio is willing to let it go. (No one wants to date the girl who can't get a date.)

HOW TO PIMP YOUR MOVIE

By "pimp your movie," we don't mean bedazzle it like a jewel-encrusted goblet. We mean pimp in the old-fashioned sense: *Sell it like a whore, out on the streets and in the back alleys, for cold hard cash and sometimes rock cocaine.* The way pimps USED to sell young ladies. In the good old days . . . wait, sorry, lost our train of thought there . . . scratch that last part, about the good old days.

If you are smart or lucky or both, there is a possibility that you will get to stay involved in the MARKETING of your movie.

FACT:
<u>THE MARKETING OF YOUR MOVIE IS ONE BILLION TIMES MORE IMPORTANT THAN THE SCRIPT</u>.

A MOVIE CAN SUCCEED WITH A TERRIBLE SCRIPT. BUT NOT WITH TERRIBLE MARKETING.

So get your ass out there and pimp that movie, and if the movie comes in crying, trying to shortchange you on the night's take—you tell her not to mess with you again, or you'll mess up that pretty face of hers. . . . *Sorry, pimp train of thought again. Scratch that part about her pretty face.* You know what? We're gonna stop saying "pimp." Let's just go with "promote" from here on. PROMOTE your movie. The world of movie promotion is evolving all the time, as people's attention shifts from TV to the internet. Your movie will need its own Twitter account, for sure. And a Facebook page.

If you are lucky enough to be asked to be involved in the marketing: do everything you can. Here are some examples of stuff you might be asked to do.

- The star of your movie might be presenting at a televised awards show—and she is NOT HAPPY with the banter that the show writers have provided (they almost never are): YOU MAY NEED TO WRITE SOME OPTIONS FOR THEM. If they call and ask you to do that—do it. Do everything you can to make your star look more funny and charming than she already is.

- The studio may want to do a Funny or Die video featuring the cast of the film. This is very common these days. Even if the film is not a comedy, some movies looking for the same AUDIENCE (teenage boys, usually) will search for those potential ticket buyers on Funny or Die. It's just a matter of *that many eyeballs* all in one place. You should offer to write it. A good Funny or Die video is more effective and cheaper than some TV spots. Also good for the "street cred" of your star.

- The studio might want a short presentation film for ShoWest, which is a trade show where studios present their upcoming films to the theater owners. Like a car show, with movie stars where the cars would be. If they'll let you write the promotional video—do it, and show everybody what a great team player you are. Hell, treat it exactly like a car show, and stand next to your movie in a bikini, if necessary. And if anyone asks you to. Which is unlikely.

- There might be other site-specific ads that need to be written. Say your movie's set at the Kentucky Derby and the marketing department is buying three TV segments during the event this year; somebody has to write those spots. It will be either the marketing department or you. <u>Make yourself responsible for this stuff, and you'll be less embarrassed by it</u>.

- And—this one some people consider a bit "icky"—you may need to include some product placement in your script or write some tie-in-type stuff in the run-up to the film's release. This stuff is just a reality of the movie business these days. You can either gripe about it and how it's ruining your "artistic vision" or get involved in it and try to make it seem as organic as possible. You can bitch all you want about it, but MOVIES ARE EXPENSIVE

TO MAKE. And if a main character holding a Mr. Pibb Zero* in his hand makes it less expensive—then figure out a way to make that work. You may then be asked to write some tie-ins later with Mr. Pibb Zero. Remember, movies are like playing roulette, and it's THE STUDIO'S you're playing with, not yours.

- The studio might be presenting at Comic-Con, which is the largest gathering of smarty-pantses in the known universe. Every studio presents movies there each July, at the San Diego Convention Center. (If you've never been, you should go. It's flat-out wonderful. We once saw a fully dressed Chewbacca riding in a pedi cab. And identical twins BOTH dressed as Slave Ship Leia.) The studio may do a panel at Comic-Con—*which you need to be on and have great, smart things to say about the movie.* Or they may create a short film specifically for the Con, if footage is not ready to be shown yet (because the CGI isn't done, usually). The tone of what happens when your movie is presented at Comic-Con is *enormously important.* DON'T MESS UP AT COMIC-CON. LOTS OF BUZZ can be created there in just a few minutes, with the right clips. Buzz can also be UNCREATED. The presentation hall in the San Diego Convetion Center holds six thousand movie/sci-fi/comic-book fans. They're VERY OPINIONATED. And they love to tweet. And blog. If the studio needs help with a script for its Comic-Con video presentation—offer to write it. And keep in mind at Comic-Con—*bring your A game.* Everybody at Comic-Con tends to be REALLY SMART. And their questions might not be "softball" questions. *They might be the real, hard questions that showbiz reporters never ask.* Be ready to "get your pimp on."

And remember, there's always other pimps out there on the streets gunnin' for you. You're not safe on these streets anymore. These streets that you MADE . . . now the good times are gone. Lil' Johnny dropped a dime on you, and you had to knife his punk ass. But the cops know it was you . . . now's the time to save that rainy-day Cheddar, take that young trick Lily off the streets, and start over on a farm upstate . . . outta the mean pimpin' streets of North Philly. Fresh air, yeah, that's the ticket. Pull up

---

*Mr. Pibb Zero is not a soft drink that exists at the time of this printing. It is rather the authors' vision of a great, zero-calorie Mr. Pibb that might exist one day, in a brighter, better future. Imagine the great taste of Mr. Pibb, with none of the guilt. Hopefully, there are teams working on this idea as we speak.

stakes now, no more pimpin' . . . DANG, I'VE BEEN SHOT. BY A CROOKED
COP, RIGHT AS I WAS ABOUT TO GET OUTTA THE PIMPIN' GAME!!! DON'T
TELL MY MAMA. DON'T TELL HER HOW I WENT . . . Sorry. Anyway—

The most important thing: *Meet the marketing department at your stu-dio.* Get to know them. It's the same as with the studio executives: <u>Help them keep their jobs</u>. Marketing is tricky. Sometimes movies that SEEM like surefire hits get lost between the sofa cushions of cinema history, and nobody really knows why. The marketing department wants, and needs, your help. The better they like you, the better shot your movie has.

NAYSAYERS

When you get a movie made, you'll notice something: there are suddenly a lot of morbidly obese shut-ins with internet connections who have come out to hate you!

There's only one thing to keep in mind: every critic, whether he works for a newspaper, a TV station, or—like 90 percent of internet critics—isn't a professional writer in ANY way (he just started a website in his mom's basement) . . .

They ALL want to be screenwriters
—and they're not.

You're doing what you love to do, and they're not—so they're mad at you. Don't sweat it. No matter how badly they hate you, they hate themselves worse. Some of your movies may suck, some may be great, but just because some dude can work a mouse, that doesn't mean his opinion matters.

Remember:

It is not the critic who counts: not the man who points out how the strong man stumbles or where the doer of deeds could have done better. The credit belongs to the man who is actually in the arena, whose face is marred by dust and sweat and blood, who strives valiantly, who errs and comes up short again and again, because there is no effort without error or shortcoming, but who knows the great enthusiasms, the great devotions, who spends himself for a worthy cause; who, at the best, knows, in the end, the triumph of high achievement, and who, at the worst, if he fails, at least he fails while daring greatly, so that his place shall never be with those cold and timid souls who knew neither victory nor defeat.

—Teddy Roosevelt
(the guy from all those shitty *Night at the Museum* movies that grossed $987,587,011 worldwide)

THE SILVER LINING

The Upside to Writing a Crappy Film

Pound for pound, *Taxi* with Queen Latifah and Jimmy Fallon has to be one of the worst movies ever made.

—Adam Carolla

If you haven't seen (and chances are you haven't) the notorious Jimmy Fallon/Queen Latifah "vehicle" (yes, intentional use of the word "vehicle"!!!) *Taxi*, which we wrote, let us give you a bit of background about it. It's an almost shot-for-shot remake of a French film by Luc Besson called *Taxi*. The French version was wonderful. It featured a young, completely-nude-at-one-point MARION COTILLARD and lots of awesome car chases through the streets of Marseilles, France. It was a huge hit over there and spawned three sequels. It's just the kind of fun/dumb movie we love, and did we mention: MARION COTILLARD IS COMPLETELY NAKED IN IT? Just for a moment, but that's why God gave us a pause button.

We saw the original film, loved it, and were hired to rework it for an American audience. So what did we do? Not much. Luc Besson wanted the bank robbers in the American version to be superhot women. We didn't hate that idea; in fact, it seemed kind of fun. So we did that and made all of the locations New York instead of Marseilles, which was easy, because we had lived in New York for ten years, eating ramen noodles and cockroaches and living in apartments that were not fit for humans. (See Chapter 1, "Getting Started in Hollywood.")

Then our buddy Jimmy Fallon got cast as Detective Washburn. Awesome! Way to go, casting people! We love Jimmy Fallon, and he's perfect for for the part. And as the tough-as-nails taxi driver who's spent her life creating a hot-rod SUPERTAXI that could win Daytona . . . QUEEN LATIFAH. Hmm? This seemed a little odd to us. In the French film, the role was played by the world's toughest living human man: SAMY NACERI, who has, no joke: BEEN CHARGED WITH ATTEMPTED MURDER. That's how tough he is. ATTEMPTED MURDER-CHARGES TOUGH.

But could we make Queen Latifah work? "OF COURSE WE CAN MAKE IT WORK."™ (This trademarked sentence is the one you need to be saying to studio executives when they ask you if you can do stuff. Because if you can't: it's back to the Coffee Bean & Tea Leaf fer you, smarty-pants!)

So we did several drafts, then off they went to shoot it. Then, when it was done, came the dreaded TEST SCREENINGS (where they show your movie to an audience in Orange County who tells you what they think of it).

And it "tested" great! The film *Taxi* tested OFF THE CHARTS! GREAT! Wait, what? Yes. Not a typo. People loved *Taxi*. Couldn't get enough of Fallon/Latifah hotfooting it through the Big Apple, while Gisele Bündchen totes an Uzi and changes outfits. There's also a scene where Gisele Bündchen FRISKS Jennifer Esposito that might be the best girl/girl frisking scene in history. It can be viewed on YouTube or, GOD FORBID . . . BUY THE DVD.

The test screenings were SO GOOD, in fact, that we made what was (at the time) our BIGGEST PAYDAY EVER to write the sequel: *Taxi 2*. Yes, this is how crazy things in Hollywood can be. One of our biggest deals EVER was for *Taxi 2*—cue the silly punctuation marks!?!?!!?!?

Then, of course, *Taxi* was released, and not only did it pretty much end the film career of our friend Jimmy Fallon, it was also so WIDELY HATED that, for a while, it was held up as an example of EVERY-THING THAT SUCKS. Even people who actually suck balls for a living didn't want to be compared with *Taxi*. *Taxi* currently holds an 11 percent rating on the (very dubious) website Rotten Tomatoes. Sheesh—we were TOTALLY WRONG about this one, gang. Bob Simonds, the very smart and funny producer of *Taxi*, left town the day before the opening, having read some early reviews and tracking numbers. He told us, "Sometimes when you've got a flop coming out, it's best to skip town, as you'll find you're radioactive for a little while." Good advice.

Boy oh boy, did people hate *Taxi*. But they didn't just hate *Taxi* . . . They hated US. Yes, we had turned radioactive. So what did we learn? Well, nothing really. Except that people who are willing to see a movie FOR FREE in Orange County aren't necessarily right 100 percent of the time.

No, we never got paid to write *Taxi 2*,* but the studio did convert our deal into another script, which led to us writing *Night at the Museum*, which at the time of this printing is the highest-grossing live action comedy of all time.

So, long story short: sometimes your movie WILL SUCK DONKEY BALLS, even when you try your best. We didn't set out to make a crappy movie: we just did. Gisele Bündchen robbing banks and changing outfits STILL seems like a pretty good idea to us. But in the midst of the turd storm that was *Taxi*, here are a few things that happened because we were working on the film:

1. We got to fly first class to Paris, then got to stay at the luxurious estate of Luc Besson, one of the most fun and funny men who's ever lived. Basically, it was equivalent to visiting the KING OF FRANCE. We got to hang out at his estate, eat maple syrup with him, and watch Formula One racing on the awesome forty-foot screen in his château.

2. We got flown by helicopter from Luc Besson's estate in Normandy back to Paris so we could have dinner at Luc Besson's restaurant, Market. Highly recommended, very tough to get a table:

Market

15 av. Matignon, 8e

8th Arrondissement (Champs-Elysées/Madeleine)

Métro: Champs-Elysées-Clemenceau

Reservations required

Phone 01-56-43-40-90

www.jean-georges.com

---

*If anybody wants to buy a treatment for *Taxi 2*, we have one, never used, still in mint condition.

3. We got to hug Gisele Bündchen. Yep. Check that off the bucket list, bona fide (or should we say boner fide), HUGS from Gisele Bündchen. Yeah, we wrote *Taxi*. Yeah, it sucked really bad. But yeah . . . we got hugged by Gisele Bündchen. So there.

Even the poop clouds that bring shit storms sometimes have a silver lining.

OUR LUNCH WITH JACKIE CHAN

GETTY IMAGES

It was a lot like meeting Santa Claus. Santa Claus who does kung fu on you. And who has very hot Asian models for elves.

So we're at a table in the Hollywood Canteen on Las Palmas. We know, it sounds like a cafeteria where Cary Grant would be horsing around with Clark Gable over USO donuts—it's not. It's a fancy-schmancy "nouveau California cuisine" place.

We're sitting there, waiting for our lunch with Jackie, and this incredibly hot, incredibly tiny model comes in, wearing a red plastic dress that looked like a stewardess uniform for a sex cruise to the moon in a Stanley Kubrick movie. She's grinning ear to ear. She's so happy she can barely contain herself, and she announces—to the whole restaurant—*"He is coming! He is coming!"* Three more models come in, and we swear to God they're dressed exactly like Josie and the Pussycats. If they'd been wearing cat ears and tails, it would've gone with their outfits perfectly.

Then Jackie enters. He's in a head-to-toe white Puma . . . we're not sure what to call it. It wasn't a track suit. It looked like . . . If Obi-Wan Kenobi did yoga at a place in Malibu, this is what Obi-Wan would wear.

We are both *huge* Jackie Chan fans. We'd worshipped him for years. And when we met Jackie, *Rush Hour II* was still in the theaters, it had already made a FORTUNE, and Jackie was probably one of the biggest, if not *the* biggest, comedy stars in the world.

So Jackie nods to us and sits down. He asks the waitress, "What are soups today?" She tells him there are two, cream of asparagus and tomato/basil. Jackie says, "Yes." We all kinda look at each other, confused, and he says; "Yes. Two soup." That's what you have for lunch when you're Jackie Chan. Two soup. He drank his soups, holding the bowls like martinis. Drinking tomato soup with one hand in a white track suit—that's *balls*.

We pitch him a movie: a movie that ended up being *The Pacifier* with Vin Diesel. (The duck made WAY more sense when it starred Jackie Chan. In the Jackie Chan version, he bought the duck and presented it to the kids as a present. They all cheer: "Yeaaaah!" Then he raises a meat cleaver to chop off the duck's head, to cook it. The kids scream and stop him, and he's stuck with the duck as a pet. The studio cut all of that stuff but kept the duck.)

So we pitch him *The Pacifier*, and after the pitch he nods and says, "Script very good." He had two ideas.

When Jackie's supposed to be a tough guy ("Bad Jackie" is how he referred to it) he should have a toothpick. Jackie put a toothpick in his mouth, put on sunglasses, and made his "Bad Jackie" face. Yup. That's Bad Jackie all right. "Then"—and Jackie flicked his toothpick across the table, a half inch from Tom's nose. It hit the opposite wall of the restaurant so hard you could hear it. Okay. We wrote that down: *Bad Jackie flicks toothpick at . . . somebody.*

His second idea: Later in the story, when Jackie is teaching kung fu to a bunch of Girl Scouts, Jackie told us, "No offense. All evasive. I show. Come at me."

Ben stands up in the middle of this nice restaurant, and he's supposed to take a swing at Jackie Chan. We have no friggin' idea what Jackie's gonna do. Is he gonna throw Ben through a window? We've seen all of his movies, and Jackie throws a shitload of guys through windows. In

Jackie's biography it says that when you break your arm doing a stunt in Hong Kong, you're supposed to walk it off. Is that what's about to happen? Is he teaching a lesson to everyone in this restaurant about "walking it off"?

Ben takes a swing at him. He says, "No. For real." Ben takes a *for real* swing at him—and he takes off Ben's jacket and wraps it around Ben's arm so fast he didn't even see it. We have no idea how he did it. The restaurant applauds. He bows, says good-bye, and leaves.

Josie and the Pussycats, smiling ear to ear, bow and head out after him. Now we know why they were so excited. Tom went and found the toothpick and put it in his scrapbook, and Ben has never had that suit jacket dry-cleaned.

Rule 8: The movie may not ever happen, so—
carpe per diem. Seize the lunch.

TRUE HOLLYWOOD HORROR STORIES!

Part Four!

We got to meet legendary performance artist, movie actress, and diva— Sandra Bernhard!

Dick.

CREDIT$

Yeah beyaaatch, we used a dollar sign where an "s" would have been far more appropriate. Because your royalties on a film are based on the credit you as a writer receive on it. Note: The more writers credited on a film, the crappier the Lamborghini you are going to be able to buy with your residuals. Or, as we call them in the industry, "'zids."* Let's face it, there's hardly anything more embarrassing than a <u>used</u> Lamborghini. THAT'S LIKE A VICTORIA'S SECRET MODEL WHO'S THIRTY. (Yuck!)

Here's a handy reference for how credits work and how to read them.

Written by
This is the Cadillac of screenwriting credits, if American cars didn't suck. To put it in terms we can all appreciate: this is the topless Helen Mirren of writing credits. Classy and wonderful. "Written by" means that *you and you alone* are entitled to both "Story by" and "Screenplay by" credit. (Ka-ching!) This means you came up with the Story, which the WGA *Screen*

---

*No one in the industry refers to residuals as "'zids," except for total douchebags. And occasionally cool stunt guys who get bumped up to a speaking role on the day of the shoot. In this case only, the use of "'zids" is totally acceptable. For example: COOL STUNT GUY: "Thanks for letting me yell that line of dialogue as I get my bell rung off that air mortar . . . the 'zids will help with the pain a little."

Credits Manual defines as "NARRATIVE, IDEA, THEME, CHARAC-TERS AND ACTION" of the script. And SCREENPLAY, which the guide describes as all of the "SCENES AND DIALOGUE." Way to go! This credit rules. If this movie doesn't tank, you're going to make some money. It's hard to calculate how much money. But (after the studio has recouped its investment) it's about 1.5 percent of the profits. It's such a good credit that the WGA named their FAIRLY BORING magazine after it!!! *Written By*—the magazine for writers that no one seems to read. Not even writers. You can even follow *Written By* magazine on Twitter: @written_by (but we're not sure why you would).

Story by

Way to go! Story by! This is a pretty solid credit to get. And here's what it means. You get this credit if you did <u>not</u> write enough of the movie to get a "Written by" credit, after all the other writers who rewrote the movie worked on it, but you <u>DID</u> CREATE THE STORY. That means, per the *Screen Credits Manual*, that your work is "distinct from screenplay and consisting of basic narrative, idea, theme or outline indicating character development and action." This can mean you wrote an outline that some-body else used to write the movie or even that you wrote A WHOLE DRAFT OF A SCREENPLAY and some other writer threw out every-thing you wrote but kept just your story.

Way to go. Nice job on that. Pretty good cred', homey. But you will be sharing your residuals forever with whoever got "Screenplay by." So . . . you get about half of that 1.5 percent of the profits.

Note: "Story by" cannot be shared by more than two writers, ever.

Screenplay by

This means that you wrote most of the script, but you still have to split your residuals with the writer who got the "Story by" credit.

Screen Story by

This is an interesting bird, the old "Screen Story by" credit. It means that there was SOURCE MATERIAL for the movie you wrote, BUT—THE STORY IS "SUBSTANTIALLY NEW AND DIFFERENT IN THE MOVIE FROM WHAT IT WAS IN THE SOURCE MATERIAL." For example, if you were to adapt *Goodnight, Moon* and create an entirely new story line about the Old Lady Whispering Hush and how she goes off to fight sexy teen vampires in the hot back alleys of Future Detroit, it's quite likely that the credits for the film would read:

Based on the Book by
Margaret Wise Brown

Screenplay by
Lowell Ganz & Babaloo Mandel
(At some point you got fired and they got
hired and they won the arbitration.)

Screen Story by
YOUR NAME HERE!!!

In this last scenario, the movie has to be a PRETTY HUGE HIT for you to start dating even a, let's say, THIRTY-FIVE-YEAR-OLD VICTORIA'S SECRET MODEL. (Yeccchh. Sorry. Better luck next time.)

Narration Written by

Wait, what? Seriously—we've never seen this credit used, like . . . ever. Apparently it exists. We're guessing it means you, um . . . wrote the narration. So the stuff that, let's say, Morgan Freeman says offscreen while the movie is happening. For example:

> MORGAN FREEMAN (V.O.)
> Ellis Island, gateway for the
> tired, the hungry, the poor, and
> some very sexy Italians. Hello, I'm
> Morgan Freeman. And I'm wearing
> just a swimsuit because I'm in a
> voice-over booth in Burbank.

Pretty weird that there's a whole credit for this kind of stuff, but seems like there is. Just for fun, Google the words "Narration Written by." It will only ask if you mean something else. "Narration Written by" won't make you rich . . . at least as far as we know. Hard to say when we've NEVER SEEN THIS CREDIT USED. EVER. Hmm. If you get this credit for some of your hot narration, let us know how it turns out, and we'll try to include a photo of you in the next printing of this book. (Also, this narration for Morgan Freeman is free with purchase or theft of this book.)

Based on Characters Created by

This means you have Separated Rights (see the end of this chapter) to the characters in the film. Which could mean that the movie is a SEQUEL to a movie you wrote or that the characters are from some kind of SOURCE MATERIAL that you wrote. A great way to get this one (and a great way to get your movie made) is to WRITE A COMIC BOOK FIRST. No joke. This is sometimes faster than writing a script first, in terms of selling your movie. Especially if the idea is "high concept." This term is often misunderstood. High concept does not mean "art-house-fancy idea" but rather an easy-to-understand idea, like "what women want." Or almost any Wayans Brothers or Rob Schneider movie. It means "a very simple concept." *30 Days of Night* is "high concept." Vampires in Alaska, where the sun doesn't come out. *30 Days* was taken out to Hollywood as a movie pitch by its authors, and it received little interest. THEN—they made a comic book of it and started a BIDDING WAR* for the movie rights!

Adaptation by

Another credit that pretty much never happens. This means you "shaped" the script, but you didn't qualify for "Screenplay by" credit. Boo. Cue the sad music. This credit and "Narration Written by" are like the ugly stepsisters whom you keep up in the attic and don't mention when nice people are around. Fighting for "Adaptation by" credit is like measuring to see which Smurf has the biggest schlong. At the end of the day, *they're all just Smurf schlongs.*

& and AND

This is a very specific little detail that you've seen on movie posters a hundred times but maybe not noticed: the use of the ampersand symbol or the word "and." There's a BIG difference when **&** or **AND** appears between writers' names:

---

*WE REPEAT: A BIDDING WAR IS THE BEST THING IN THE ENTIRE WORLD.

> **&** means the two named writers worked TOGETHER, as a team (Robert Ben Garant & Thomas Lennon).
>
> **AND** means that they very specifically DID NOT WORK TOGETHER, but have been forced to share credit (Robert Ben Garant & Thomas Lennon AND Lowell Ganz & Babaloo Mandel).

Keep an eye out on movie posters; you'll see lots of interesting examples of this one. (It's our little inside way of letting people know that THE PERSON ON THE OTHER SIDE OF THE WORD "AND" came up with all the stuff in the movie that nobody liked!) Whew. Thank heavens for that "AND," 'cause some of that stuff was awful!

Separated Rights!!!

Separated rights are a truly wonderful thing, and they're hard to get. If you can ever get them: GET THEM! And then quickly scurry away with them before the studio attorneys pry them away from your weak, carpal-tunnel-ruined hands. Separated rights means you have your own copyright-style RIGHTS to the characters or material and that the studio CANNOT MAKE A SEQUEL or do really anything with the material WITHOUT YOUR INVOLVEMENT (*pronounced: paying you*). To get these, you must either:

Create an original story and receive "Story by," "Screen Story by," or "Written by" credit.

Or get one of those three credits off of assigned material (source material or someone else's script), where you create a SUBSTANTIALLY new and different story.

With separated rights come a lot of perks and a little bit of empowerment, which ALMOST NEVER HAPPENS TO SCREENWRITERS. Cool stuff, like the first option to write sequels, stuff like that. (See Chapter 31, "Sequels!") Hurrah for separated rights! Now, quickly! Scurry down into your burrow with those rights . . . everyone HATES when writers have power. Hide those rights in your warren beside your precious nuts and those shiny things you found out by the farmer's digging machine!

There are a few other aspects of credits that are boring but important. For example, the **ORDER** of the names of writers is in order of who did the most work to who did the least—and the Arbitration Committee (three people) decides that. (See Chapter 30, "Arbitration or Who Wrote This Crap?" *If you have the nerve!*)

Oh, and if the movie COMPLETELY AND UTTERLY SUCKS, you can, if you want, use a PSEUDONYM. But here's the catch: to use a pseudonym, you have to have been paid LESS THAN $200,000 TOTAL (so in this scenario, you're going to be dating a Victoria's Secret model in her <u>midseventies</u>) and . . . you have to register that fake name with the Guild, so it has to be "reasonable." You can't use "Guillermo St. Farts," for example.

LIVING IN LOS ANGELES

DAVID MICHEL LINCOLN

Downtown L.A., where nobody goes 'cause it's full of crack zombies.

Living in L.A. takes some adjusting to. It's not like other cities. Some would argue that it's not a city at all but a big sprawling suburb with no city attached.

> **FACT:** People who live in Los Angeles spend more time stuck in traffic than in any other city in the United States. We average seventy hours a year in our cars—that's DOUBLE the time in the next worst city. You know where we learned that? Listening to NPR, stuck in traffic. So . . .

When you move to L.A., you will need a few "CAR HOBBIES": valuable, time-filling hobbies you can pursue for the several hours a day that you're stuck in traffic.

Tom listens to NPR (89.3 FM), listens to books on tape, and has learned two foreign languages, all in his car, since he moved to L.A.! Ben listens to NPR and the right-wing radio station KFI (640 AM) and has figured out five different positions for having sex in a Jeep Sahara while driving! Take that, Kama Sutra!

Other people fill their traffic time by texting, getting REALLY good at karaoke (which is almost as big as Scientology here) or smoking marijuana! (Which is practically legal in L.A.) But whatever you do, no matter what you've heard, do NOT shoot at other people on the freeway. It's so '90s.

So—what do you do with the *several* hours in the day when you're NOT in your car?

MYTH: You can go out to some nice quiet beach, park, bar, or coffee shop and get a little writing done.

FACT: If you write in public here in Los Angeles, everyone will assume you are a douchebag. Sure, in other cities you can sit quietly in a Starbucks or a bar with your notebook or laptop and write all day. <u>Not in L.A.</u> If you do that here, one of two things will happen:

1. One of every four people will come up to you and ask, "What are you writing? A screenplay?" They will then tell you about *their* screenplay or their goals as an actress or talk for an hour about some up-and-coming project they're working on (which DOES NOT REALLY EXIST).
2. The other three out of four people will assume you're a douchebag who's writing in Starbucks to meet girls.

Writing in L.A. is like cocaine: do it in private unless you want to share.

There are only two bars in L.A. where we write:

The Village Idiot
7383 Melrose Avenue
Los Angeles, CA 90189
(323) 655-3331
Great drinks, great food, great owners, and if you sit by the window, watching girls walk by on Melrose is like watching a never-ending magic trick. It's like you died and went to filthy teenage girl heaven, sponsored by Ed Hardy and Pilates.

And . . .

The Cat and Fiddle
6530 Sunset Boulevard
Los Angeles, CA 90028
(323) 468-3800
Nothing fancy, but a great patio. It's where Morrissey drinks when he's in town. GO UP AND SAY HI! He's as friendly as pie!

Just warning you, BOTH of these bars get packed at night, with hipsters and hotties. We usually go during the day, when it's mostly rummies and aging soccer hooligans.

OTHER STUFF TO DO IN L.A.
L.A. has the best Mexican food in the world. MUCH better than Mexico. Plus, unlike in real Mexico, you won't get your face sliced off and sewn onto a soccer ball!

Our Favorite Mexican Restaurants

Casa La Golondrina
17 Olvera Street
Los Angeles, CA 90012
(213) 628-4349
The best Mexican food in L.A. Period. Try the margaritas! It's on old Olvera Street, downtown. Fantastic food, good ambiance, and a great place to people-watch tourists,

Angelenos, and scary Mexican dudes with shaved heads who just got drunk at the Dodgers game. Olvera Street is a great place to take people from outta town too, especially if they want to pick up a framed poster of Tupac or of Tony Montana playing poker with Tony Soprano.

El Cholo
1121 S. Western Avenue
Los Angeles, CA 90006
(323) 734-2773
The OTHER best Mexican restaurant in L.A. Period. Maybe we shouldn't have said "period" before. This is the oldest Mexican restaurant in town. Bing Crosby used to eat here. Try the margaritas!

Don Cucos
3911 W. Riverside Drive
Burbank, CA 91505
(818) 842-1123
Right across from Warner Bros. Try the margaritas!

Las Fuentes Mexican Restaurant
18415 Vanowen Street
Reseda, CA 91335-5312
(818) 708-3344
WAAAAAAAAY out in the valley, but the make-your-own-salsa bar is worth the drive.

La Serenata de Garibaldi
1842 E. 1st Street
Los Angeles, CA 90033
(323) 265-2887
Don't be scared by the neighborhood. Actually, DO be scared by the neighborhood: valet park, and run in and out as fast as you can. Once you're inside, it's a very romantic spot, the most unique Mexican menu in town. Incredible seafood. Try the margaritas!

And while you're stuck on the 101 driving home, why not have sex in your Jeep! Or listen to Patt Morrison on NPR! OR BOTH!!!

OTHER STUFF IN L.A.

Best Comic Book Store
Golden Apple Comics
7018 Melrose Avenue
Los Angeles, CA 90038
(323) 658-6047
If you don't like this place, you're not a nerd!

Hippest Clubs

Inapplicable. By the time you're reading this, they will have changed. With one exception—if you want to GUARANTEE you will see at least one or two BIG-TIME movie stars, the best bar is just a short three-hour plane ride north to:

The Gerard Lounge
Sutton Place Hotel
845 Burrard Street
Vancouver, BC V6Z2K6
Canada
(604) 682-5511

or

Tallulah Wine Bar
155 S. Bates Street
Birmingham, MI 48009
(248) 731-7066

Yes, the best L.A. movie-star bars in Canada or Michigan. Both which give big film tax breaks.

Best Cheap Thing to Do
Drive up the coast, stop at a beach, then eat lunch and drink a beer at:

Neptune's Net
42505 Pacific Coast Highway
Malibu, CA 90265
(310) 457-3095

Cold beer, fried seafood, local surfers, and German yuppies pretending to be bikers. This is as close to culture as we get in L.A., and we couldn't recommend it highly enough. It's where Lori Petty's character worked in *Point Break*! Lori Petty works there now, for real!

Best Neighborhood

DAVID MICHEL LINCOLN

The Grove
189 The Grove Drive
Los Angeles, CA 90036
(323) 900-8080
Sure, it's a make-believe neighborhood—but then, isn't all of L.A.? Take a stroll down the "street," catch a movie, dine at the historic Farmers Market, and watch Angelenos in their natural habitat, doing what they do best: walking around in thongs and spending a fortune on Baby Gap and iPhones.

And—

THE BEST THING TO DO IN LOS ANGELES?

Get the hell out of Los Angeles—with all the buckets of money you've made screenwriting!

We recommend these very easy, *extremely* expensive weekend getaways!

The Halekulani
2199 Kalia Road
Honolulu, HI 96815
(808) 923-2311
An exquisite hotel right on Waikiki beach, with majestic views of Diamond Head. Beautiful pool. Fantastic restaurant. VERY, VERY expensive—but that keeps out the riffraff.

Or why not helicopter over on . . .

Island Express Helicopters
1175 Queens Highway
Long Beach, CA 90802
(800) 228-2566

to . . .

The Inn on Mount Ada
398 Wrigley Road
Avalon, CA 90704
(310) 510-2030
This private inn overlooks Avalon Bay and was once the mansion of William Wrigley, Jr., who owned Wrigley gum, the Chicago Cubs, and 99 percent of Catalina Island. The rooms are awesome, the views are romantic, the place is incredibly private, and oh my God, is this place overpriced! The chopper will get you there in fifteen minutes. What's the rush? Well—pretty soon you're gonna run out of things to talk about with the dazzling young starlet you're whisking away for the weekend! Better get that champagne flowing!

One and Only Palmilla
Km 7.5 Carretera Transpeninsular
San Jose del Cabo
BCS, CP 23400
Mexico
(866) 829-2977

If you can afford this place—you should be in jail! Or you're in SHOWBIZ! Perfect private beach for a dinner for two, perfect drinks mixed by your own bartender, and it will cost you only one week of a *Starsky & Hutch* punch-up.

And, most important . . .

137

IN-N-OUT BURGER LOCATIONS

Arcadia
420 N. Santa Anita Avenue 91006

Azusa
324 S. Azusa Avenue 91702

Baldwin Park
13850 Francisquito Avenue 91706

Brentwood
5581 Lone Tree Way 94513

Burbank
761 N. First Street 91502

Canoga Park
6841 N. Topanga Canyon Boulevard 91303

City of Industry
17849 E. Colima Road 91748
21620 Valley Boulevard 91789

Covina
1371 N. Grand Avenue 91724

Culver City
13425 Washington Boulevard 90292

Diamond Bar
21133 Golden Springs Drive 91789

Downey
8767 Firestone Boulevard 90241

Glendale
119 Brand Boulevard 91204
310 N. Harvey Drive 91206

Glendora
1261 S. Lone Hill 91741

Hacienda Heights
14620 E. Gale Avenue 91745

Hollywood
7009 Sunset Boulevard 90028

Huntington Park
6000 Pacific Boulevard 90255

Inglewood
3411 W. Century Boulevard 90301

La Mirada
14341 Firestone Boulevard 90638

La Puente
15259 E. Amar Road 91744

La Verne
2098 Foothill Boulevard 91750

Lakewood
5820 Bellflower Boulevard 90713

Lancaster
2021 W. Avenue I 93536

Long Beach
4600 Los Coyotes Diagonal 90815
6391 E. Pacific Coast Highway 90803
7691 Carson Street 90808

Newhall
25220 N. The Old Road 91321

North Hollywood
5864 Lankershim Boulevard 91605

Northridge
8830 Tampa Avenue 91324
9858 Balboa Boulevard 91325

Norwalk
14330 Pioneer Boulevard 90650

Palmdale
142 E. Palmdale Boulevard 93550

Panorama City
13651 Roscoe Boulevard 91402

Pasadena
2114 E. Foothill Boulevard 91107

Pico Rivera
9070 Whittier Boulevard 90660

Pomona
1851 Indian Hill Boulevard 91767
2505 Garey Avenue 91766

Porter Ranch
19901 Rinaldi Street 91326

Redondo Beach
3801 Inglewood Avenue 90278

Rosemead
4242 N. Rosemead Boulevard 91770

San Fernando
11455 Laurel Canyon Boulevard 91342

San Pedro
1090 N. Western Avenue 90732

Santa Clarita
26401 Bouquet Canyon Road 91350
28368 Sand Canyon Road 91387

Santa Fe Springs
10525 Carmenita Road 90670

Sherman Oaks
4444 Van Nuys Boulevard 91403

Studio City
3640 Cahuenga Boulevard 90068

Temple City
10601 E. Lower Azusa Road 91780

Tujunga
6225 Foothill Boulevard 91042

West Los Angeles
9245 W. Venice Boulevard 90034

Van Nuys
7220 N. Balboa Boulevard 91406
7930 Van Nuys Boulevard 91402

Westwood
922 Gayley Avenue 90024

Woodland Hills
19920 Ventura Boulevard 91364

West Covina
15610 San Bernardino Road 91790
2940 E. Garvey Avenue 91791

If you haven't had it yet, **In-N-Out Burger** is the best fast-food place on the planet. ON THE PLANET. They serve burgers, fries, shakes, soft drinks, AND THAT'S IT. It's fast, cheap, and you should go eat one right now.

And Angelenos ("Angeleno" is the douchebag NPR term for "people who have to live in L.A.") know how to order stuff to be prepared in "special" ways. These secret ordering terms are not on the menu.

Here is a complete list (as far as we know) of those secret In-N-Out items—yours free with the purchase of this book. The knowledge, not the menu items.

The In-N-Out Secret Menu Is:

If you order your burger "Animal Style," you get extra pickles, extra secret sauce, with grilled onions.

"2x4" Burger: You get a burger with two beef patties and four slices of cheese.

"3-by-Meat" Burger: Three beef patties, no cheese.

"Double Meat" Burger: A Double Double without the cheese.

"The Flying Dutchman": Two beef patties, two slices of cheese. No lettuce. No onions. No bun. Ew.

"Protein Style" Burger: Burger wrapped in lettuce instead of a bun. For if you're on Atkins.

"Veggie Burger": Burger with no burger and double tomatoes.

"Grilled Cheese": Cheeseburger without the burger. It's good.

"Extra Toast": They toast your bread on the grill longer, so your buns are crispier.

If you order your fries "Animal Style," you get french fries with secret sauce, onions, and cheese on top.

Order your fries "Light": They cook 'em a little less than normal. Ew.

Fries "Well Done": They cook your fries a little longer. They're crunchier. IT'S AWE-SOME. <u>We recommend it highly</u>.

Choco-Vanilla Swirl Shake: Chocolate and vanilla swirled together, not blended.

Neapolitan Shake: Strawberry, vanilla, and chocolate all swirled together, not blended.

TOM AND BEN'S GUIDE TO AWARDS SEASON!

YOUR WHO/WHAT/WHERE (AND WHAT NOT TO WEAR) GUIDE TO THE OSCARS, EMMYS, AND GOLDEN GLOBES!!!!!!!*

*Note to Editor: This page is intentionally left blank, for future editions, pending the authors' being nominated, or even accidentally invited to any awards ceremonies.

★ ★ ★ **FREE MOVIE IDEA** ★ ★ ★
Yours Free with the Purchase of This Book

"BOBO & ME"

Approximate Budget: $35 million
Estimated Gross: $93 million worldwide
Shoots in: Georgia, for the tax rebate
Rating: PG
Awards Potential: Zero

Tracy Morgan stars as DWAYNE, a lovable janitor at NASA. Beyoncé Knowles costars as FELICITY, NASA's top primate zoologist. Felicity has spent the past nine years training BOBO, a brilliant CHIMPANZEE,* for a mission to Mars. Bobo is the most brilliant chimpanzee of all time, genetically engineered by NASA. Bobo can speak sign language, pilot a rocket, and, most important, <u>learn</u>. *Bobo is a fast learner.*

Felicity learns that her sinister boss, DR. APPLETON (Will Arnett) has planned to send Bobo to Mars—*with no intention of bringing him back to Earth.* (Equipping the rocket to bring him back would be too expensive.) It's a one-way mission for Bobo . . . a suicide mission.

Felicity sneaks Bobo out with Dwayne's help and plans to set him free at the San Diego Wild Animal Park. So . . .

Felicity and Dwayne hightail it across country on an action-packed, family-friendly ROAD TRIP—sneaking the genius chimp into hotels, camping with the chimp, etc. When Dwayne finds out Bobo is a math whiz, *he uses Bobo to beat the pants off of a VEGAS CASINO.*

All the while, Dr. Appleton pursues them, using NASA's limitless resources, including a team of NAVY SEALS *(who will be the victims of LOTS of hilarious physical comedy as they try in vain to capture Bobo.* Think *HOME ALONE* with a chimp, versus NAVY SEALS). The MOB is after them too when it learns that Bobo broke the bank at its casino.

Dwayne and Felicity find that despite SEEMING like total opposites, they are drawn to each other. Felicity will, in fact, tell Dwayne this in

142

* Note: Could be an adorable dog instead of a chimp.

some kind of simile related to primate zoology. Eventually, Dr. Appleton is ARRESTED FOR SKIMMING FROM THE FUNDS FOR PRIMATE RESEARCH. Dwayne and Felicity win. Bobo is set free at the San Diego park, where, in a touching scene, he meets the female monkey of his dreams.

PART TWO
WRITING A SCREENPLAY

If you're so smart, why don't *you* write a blockbuster?

IF YOUR SCREENPLAY DOESN'T HAVE THIS STRUCTURE, IT WON'T SELL, OR ROBERT McKEE CAN SUCK IT

Every single Hollywood studio movie has the same structure.
Repeat:

EVERY SINGLE HOLLYWOOD STUDIO MOVIE HAS THE SAME STRUCTURE.

From *Casablanca* to *The Matrix*. There are many, many books explaining this structure. We have no idea why you'd need a whole book. Okay:

Every studio movie has three acts.

ACT I: You get a likable guy stuck up a tree.
ACT II: You throw rocks at him.
ACT III: You get him down out of the tree.

Aliens arrive on Earth. They kick our ass. We kick their ass.

Bruce Willis gets stuck in Nakatomi Tower. He gets the shit knocked out of him. He throws Hans Gruber out of Nakatomi Tower.

Now—within those three acts, <u>things **ALWAYS** go down like this</u>:

Pages 1–10: We meet your hero and the world he (or she or they) live in.

Welcome to Kansas, here's Dorothy, she wishes she wasn't in Kansas. Welcome to Old Detroit, here's Officer Murphy, and it's a creepy high-tech world where they're looking for KIA cops to make into Robo-Cops.

If you have created a character or situation that can't be explained in about ten pages: <u>It is WRONG</u>. Repeat:

If you've created a character or situation that can't be explained in about ten pages: <u>It is WRONG</u>.

If you can't explain it in ten pages, you're making an art movie or an independent, or it's just too confusing. <u>The studios will not touch it with a ten-meter cattle prod</u>. Unless you're James Cameron. James, if you're reading this book, we're very flattered. And *Terminator* was awesome.

In *Casablanca,* pages 1–10: The voice-over guy tells us all about Casablanca, and then every single character tells us how cool Rick (Humphrey Bogart) is. In *Die Hard,* the first ten pages teach you everything you need to know about Nakatomi Plaza and the McClains.

In *The Matrix,* pages 1–10: We're in a world where people can almost fly. We meet Neo, who senses that there's something odd going on and who has an itch to find out what the Matrix is.

Page 10: The "inciting incident." (That's fancy talk for "Something out of the ordinary happens to your hero.")

This is Joseph Campbell's "call to adventure." Something happens to invite your hero into the adventure of his (or her) lifetime. Luke Skywalker sees Princess Leia's hologram cry for help. Bruce is trapped in the Nakatomi Tower when Hans Gruber takes over. **BUT WAIT! Your hero doesn't dive in yet**. Luke's gotta stay on the farm. Bruce Willis calls the cops and lies low.

On page 10, Neo meets Trinity. She tells him she knows what the Matrix is. Neo—does nothing. He goes to work the next day and acts like it didn't happen.

Page 25: Your hero is launched into the story.

Here is where your hero dives in. Between pages 10 and 25, the plot has thickened, and now our hero has no choice but to get involved. Uncle Owen and Aunt Beru are dead. Rick's ex shows up at his gin joint and needs the letters of transit. A mugger kills Spider-Man's uncle, and Spidey's the only one who can catch him.

Neo has seen unexplainable shit for the last 15 pages: they erased his mouth and put an android shrimp in his belly button, for God's sake. On page 25, he takes the red pill.

Around pages 45–50: Things get worse.

For 20 pages, Neo gets hit with bad news: The world was destroyed, and he's never really eaten noodles. And worst of all: HE is the Messiah that's supposed to save the world—talk about pressure. On page 45 he makes the GREAT LEAP off the building to prove he's The One . . . and he falls on his face.

149

Around pages 65–70: Something even worse happens.

On page 65, the Oracle tells Neo <u>he's NOT The One</u> and Cypher turns traitor and tries to kill them all. Tough day.

Around pages 70–80:
Things get as bad as they can possibly get.

We got the Death Star plans too late, it was all for naught! Vader's gonna blow up the rebel base at Yavin 4! Claude Rains outsmarted Rick—now the Nazis'll get the letters of transit! Spider-Man's lost his powers, and Dr. Octopus is gonna blow up Kirsten Dunst! Hope is lost!

The agents have Morpheus. Neo has to choose, his life for Morpheus's—even though he knows it's impossible because he's not The One.

So. You've spent the last 80 pages setting up how impossible it is to beat Hans Gruber/destroy the Death Star/fight the agents. Now . . .

You use pages 80–90 to show the audience
that WINNING IS GONNA BE EVEN HARDER
THAN WE THOUGHT IT WAS GONNA BE.

Neo fights Smith—and he's no match for him.

150

The Death Star is approaching! It's gonna take a one-in-a-million shot to destroy it, and Han Solo just split with his reward money.

Around pages 90–100ish:
The Climax! Your hero wins! Hooray!

Rick shoots the Nazi, and Claude Rains turns nice! Hooray! Han Solo comes back, and Luke shoots the Death Star. Hooray!

Neo kicks Agent Smith's ass, dies, and comes back to life. Hooray!

Final pages: Your hero walks off into the sunset/ James Bond screws Dr. Goodhead on a raft.

The world has been changed for the better by your hero. The bad guy's dead (unless you need Darth Vader for the sequel). It's a new beginning. Rick walks off with Claude Rains; it's "the beginning of a beautiful friendship." Everybody gets medals. Ewoks dance around.

And Neo flies off into the sunset—he is The One.

<u>The most important thing about this structure is that you ALWAYS USE IT</u>.

Always.

GETTY IMAGES

Wong Kar-wai, making some wonderful "art-house" movie.*

*"Art house" is Hollywood talk for "movie a studio wouldn't touch with a ten-foot pole."

In EVERY SCRIPT THAT HAS EVER SOLD, the inciting incident is on page 10 and the twists happen EXACTLY WHEN THEY
ARE SUPPOSED TO. Wong Kar-wai movies are great. They don't make
those in Hollywood.

Screenwriting Tip!

Hey you lil' William Goldman, you!
Wanna speed up your screenwriting?
Then why not try this helpful,
professional screenwriting tip?

When naming your characters, try to make sure that NO TWO CHAR-ACTERS' NAMES START WITH THE SAME LETTER OF THE ALPHABET.

For example: Do not have characters in your script named: GRETA, GAY BIRTHDAY CLOWN #1, GREG BEHRENDT, GANDHI, and GHOST OF GIUSEPPE.

"Why?" You may ask. "Who cares?! I'm not cutting Gay Birthday Clown #1—he sets up all the other Gay Birthday Clowns!"

Well, while those are all terrific names—and Greg Behrendt is a great guy who will be terrific in the movie—when you're writing in FINAL DRAFT, there's an option called SmartType, which will add the name of the character in the CHARACTER SLUG LINE, just by your typing the first letter of the character's name.

By not having two character's names that start with the same letter, you could save up to five minutes an hour by NOT HAVING TO PICK which of the "G"-named characters you mean each time you type.

It seems like a small thing, but trust us. When you're writing A LOT, especially in production rewrites, this little trick can save you a lot of time and wasted energy.

Now then, spend that five minutes you saved this hour by quietly reflecting on where it all went wrong, or just masturbate!

IN A FEW PAGES, WE'LL TEACH YOU HOW TO FORMULATE CHARACTERS IN A SCRIPT*

You may never be any good at writing. You may already be great at writing. But no one can teach you to write.

This chapter is just PRACTICAL TIPS. Tips for creating good characters for your studio script.

Tip 1: The only way your movie is going to get made at a studio is if a MOVIE STAR wants to play your hero. Keep that in mind as you write your hero.

That means your hero needs to be likable, cool (and, by the end of the movie, EVEN COOLER), and attractive. YES, ATTRACTIVE.

---

*DISCLAIMER: We cannot really teach you how to formulate characters. No book can. How do you come up with good characters? Develop your imagination, read good books, watch good movies over and over again, meet interesting people and hear their stories, and meet boring people and hear their stories. Experience things! See the world! Live! Love! Feel pain and joy and loss and victory and defeat! And most of all—practice practice practice! Write! Write! Write!

Name one NON-ANIMATED studio movie with an ugly hero. Why? Because no movie star is going to pick up a script and read a character described as "a fat, ugly, unlikable loser" and jump at the chance to play that role. Actors are vain. EVEN FAT, UGLY, UNLIKABLE ACTORS.

Sure, sometimes an ACTRESS will play her one "ugly" role, to try to win an Oscar—but <u>if you're trying to win Oscars YOU BOUGHT THE WRONG BOOK, BUSTER</u>. We wrote that movie where the monkey slaps Ben Stiller.

And when we say make your hero *likable*, we don't just mean make 'im "guy with a nice smile who you see in the elevator" likable. You've seen movies, right? Make him HAN SOLO likable. INDIANA JONES likable. <u>Make him so goddamn likable that every single kid who sees your movie is gonna wish he was Your Hero for the rest of his life.</u>

<u>Don't pussy around</u>. Your Hero needs to be a **HERO.**

There's no simpler way to put it. Your hero needs to be a hero from from page 1. They were BORN a hero, they just haven't gotten a chance to be a hero yet—not until the adventure YOU'RE sending them out on (think Luke Skywalker, Strider). They just needed to be thrust into a situation (that you're gonna make up) that ONLY THEY CAN SOLVE. Only he can defeat Alan Rickman's evil scheme. Only he can blow up the Death Star. Only she can save Newt and kill the mamma alien.

Or maybe he got a chance to be a hero once, but he blew it. Maybe he used to be a gunslinger—but he "doesn't do that any more." BUT HE'S STILL A HERO on the inside. (Shane, Rick from *Casablanca*.) You get the point. Make your hero a silver-screen, movie-star-sized hero.*

---

*You know, like Batman, Zorro, Quint, James Bond, Harry Potter, Indiana Jones, King Arthur, Dirty Harry, Atticus Finch, Rick Blaine, Lieutenant Ripley, Captain America, Flash Gordon, Sergeant Kyle Reese, Tech-Com DN38416, Jackie Chan, Johnny Grey, George Washington, Abe Lincoln, Teddy Roosevelt, General Patton, Davy Crockett, George Gipp, Steamboat Bill, Jr., "Hawkeye" Pierce, Elvis, Rocky Balboa, "The Man with No Name," Snake Pliskin, Eliot Ness, John McClane, William Wallace, Spiderman, Captain Jack Sparrow, Captain Geoffrey Thorpe, Captain Horatio Hornblower, Sherlock Holmes, Robin Hood, Maid Marion, Trinity, Morpheus, Ferris Bueller, Jake and Elwood Blues, "Popeye" Doyle, Sonny Hooper, J. J. McClure, Sergeant Tom Sharky, Bo "Bandit" Darville, "Gator" McKlusky, Will Smith, John Wayne, Cary Cooper, Jimmy Stewart, Strider, Gandalf, all them lil' Hobbits, all those dudes with the Right Stuff, The Fantastic 4, the Magnificent 7, Neo.

TIP 2: Remember: YOU ARE NOT WRITING A NOVEL.

You have only about 100 pages to say EVERY SINGLE THING there is to say about your characters. Be succinct. You don't win points for being vague and cryptic and arty. And your MAIN character better be crystal clear in the first 10 pages. (See Chapter 23, "If Your Screenplay Doesn't Have This Structure . . .")

TIP 3: Write your dialogue with specific actors in mind.

For several reasons:

It will help you write dialogue. It doesn't matter if the movie star whose voice you're writing in will never be in your movie. But if you write your main character as, let's say BEN STILLER, he has a very specific cadence:

```
                BEN STILLER
    . . . What? Yes. No . . . I mean . . .
    sure.
```

Your dialogue suddenly has a model. You go beyond knowing WHAT your character needs to say to HOW your character will say it. You'll know if it reads right or wrong.

If you write the skeevy guy who's tagging along with your hero as, let's say, ZACH GALIFIANAKIS.

```
            ZACH GALIFIANAKIS
    You gonna finish that sangria?
```

Then you'll know what *his* dialogue should sound like. What it should read like. His dialogue will be very specific, AND it will read VERY DIFFERENTLY from that of your hero, Ben Stiller.

Your goal is to make the people reading your script picture the MOVIE in their heads. Leave as little to the imagination as possible. If they're already picturing BEN STILLER and ZACH GALIFIANAKIS before they even GET to the dialogue, how much does that help them picture your movie in their heads? ANSWER: <u>a lot</u>. Again, you're not writing a novel.

Which brings us to the MAGIC word in studio movie character development:

Think.

As in: Think Ben Stiller. Think Dwayne "The Rock" Johnson. Think Reese Witherspoon. That magic word will make your movie easier to write, easier to read, and EASIER TO SELL.

See the difference in the script samples below.

```
INT. THE PENTAGON — DAY

GENERAL SLATER (40) storms in. He's a tall,
tough, lifelong military man: he's been
through combat and came out hard as nails —
but something tells us that under all that
Kevlar and muscle he's not such a bad guy.
He's FURIOUS.

                    GENERAL SLATER
          What the hell's going on here? I
          want two things, pronto. I want a
          strong cup of coffee, and I want
          someone to tell me who the hell
          gave the go signal on my project!

A row of four-star GENERALS all turn toward
the end of the table, where we see: DR. MAX
FELDMAN (early 20s). A whiz kid, straight
out of MIT. He's skinny, precocious, and has
spent more time around test tubes than around
real people. He's about as military as Kermit
the Frog. He gulps.

                    DR. MAX FELDMAN
          Um . . . that'd be me, your honor.
          Sir. I mean . . . yeah. I did it.
```

Slater marches over to Feldman, to yell down
at him. But Feldman interrupts him, stopping
him in his tracks.

> DR. MAX FELDMAN (CONT'D)
> I outrank you. On this project, I
> mean. The Drone 208 was my idea,
> and, well . . . if you still wanna
> stick around — you're gonna have to
> follow *my* orders.

Slater looks around, stunned. The somehow
lovable SECRETARY OF DEFENSE shrugs: the kid's
right. Slater can't believe it. Slater gulps.

> DR. MAX FELDMAN (CONT'D)
> And I'll take a triple mocha frozen
> cappuccino with cinnamon. And if
> they have those little chocolate-
> dipped biscotti, I'll take some of
> them, too.

Slater looks around. He gulps.

> GENERAL SLATER
> Decaf or regular, sir?

Now see how much BETTER it reads THIS WAY:

INT. THE PENTAGON — DAY

GENERAL SLATER (*think Dwayne "The Rock"
Johnson*) storms in. He's FURIOUS.

> GENERAL SLATER
> What the hell's going on here? I
> want two things, pronto. I want a
> strong cup of coffee, and I want
> someone to tell me who the hell
> gave the go signal on my project!

A row of four-star GENERALS all turn toward
the end of the table, where we see: DR. MAX
FELDMAN (*think Jesse Eisenberg*). He gulps.

> DR. MAX FELDMAN
> Um . . . that'd be me, your honor.
> Sir. I mean . . . yeah. I did it.

Slater marches over to Feldman, to yell down
at him. But Feldman beats him to the punch.

> DR. MAX FELDMAN (CONT'D)
> I outrank you. On this project, I
> mean. The Drone 208 was my idea,
> and, well . . . if you still wanna
> stick around — you're gonna have to
> follow my orders.

Slater looks around, stunned. The SECRETARY
OF DEFENSE (*Paul Giamatti*) shrugs: the kid's
right. Slater can't believe it.

> DR. MAX FELDMAN (CONT'D)
> And I'll take a triple mocha
> frozen cappuccino with cinnamon.
> Ooh—and if they have those little
> chocolate-dipped biscotti, I'll
> take some of them, too.

Slater gulps.

> GENERAL SLATER
> Decaf or regular, sir?

. . . SEE?

Tip 4. Make your characters feel real.

Even if they have superpowers. Or live in space. Or are being played
by Dwayne "The Rock" Johnson. Even if they're already dead. Read them

out loud: Does the dialogue sound real? Are all of their actions and reactions logical? Real?

TRY THIS EXPERIMENT

Go watch the *Superman* movies—all of them.* We'll wait.

· · ·

· · ·

Now—which ones sucked, and which one didn't? The first one, *Superman: The Movie*, was pretty good, right? (The original cut. Not the crappy director's cut, where he added in all those terrible jokes.) The characters in it were written pretty real, right? Okay, Margot Kidder wasn't so great, we'll give you that . . . but you get the point.

Now, how about the other Superman movies? *Superman II, III, and IV,* and *Superman Returns*? They sucked, right? The characters are written for laughs, they're cartoony, and they say and do stuff that flat-out doesn't make sense. Real characters make the movie good, even in sci fi and comedy.

Tip 5: Forget that film school crap about "Create a cradle-to-grave biography of each of your characters."

*You can also try this experiment with the *Rocky, Rambo,* or *Jaws* films.

What did they eat for breakfast? How long did they suckle at their mother's teat, and how do they feel about it? Who cares?

If that helps you: GREAT. Do it. *If that's not how you write—don't worry about it.* We know a lot of people, and we know them well, and we have no idea what they eat for breakfast or how long they suckled at their mamma's teat.

Rick from *Casablanca* is one of the best hero characters ever created for the silver screen. <u>The writers who created Rick had NO IDEA what his entire history was.</u>

They didn't even know that he "ran guns to Ethiopia in 1935 and fought on the Republican side in the Spanish Civil War." That stuff was written later by two PUNCH-UP GUYS. (See Chapter 28, "Rewrites: You Want It When? And I'm Getting Paid What?")

If creating all that backstory helps you, great. Do it. We usually flesh out only the elements of a character's backstory that relate to our movie. It's worked for us.

Tip 6: Make sure that the big horrible life-changing and insurmountable problem your characters face is also kinda fun.

If Luke Skywalker had battled, say, a debilitating cancer. Or world poverty . . . the *Star Wars* movies would have probably been accepted into some very prestigious film festivals. They WOULD NOT have made more than $100 billion at the box office. *Guess which one of those two things 20th Century Fox cares more about?* Sure, Luke's aunt and uncle got killed— <u>but he didn't like them anyway.</u> Then he got to go rescue a smoking hot princess and destroy the Death Star.

Sure, being trapped in a museum overnight with a *Tyrannosaurus rex* would be scary—but every kid in the WORLD would LOVE to be trapped overnight in a museum with a *T. rex*. Remember: no one asks movies to be complicated or challenging or enlightening—

They just want movies to be entertaining. That's why they paid their 11 bucks.

Tip 7: Watch *Die Hard.* Many times.

Its characters are incredibly clear, they're introduced with shockingly efficient exposition, and they're a perfect combination of archetypal characters:

- The hero, John McClane, has one flaw: *he takes being a cop so seriously it's gotten in the way of his marriage.* (Pretty damn good flaw for your action movie's hero.)
- He has a slightly goofy good buddy to talk to—two of 'em, actually—who, in the end, are the smartest guys around.
- The villain is JUST AS SMART AND LIKABLE as the hero.
- The villain has a "sidekick" who's much more evil and hateable than he is.
- The hero and the villain each have tons of likable cohorts and supporting characters. And you understand all of the characters and their motives in about five seconds: The plucky limo driver, the Twinkie-chugging cop who once shot a kid, the prick tabloid news guy who you just want to see get punched in the face . . . etc., etc.

Again—you're not writing a novel. It's a movie. Be succinct, and make it as good as *Die Hard.*

Okay. A Recap:

Laurie Anderson (performance artist/smarty-pants) has a great quote:

"Paradise is exactly like where you are right now . . . only much, much better."

That's what movies are like: Your hero should be as real as your next-door neighbor—but as cool as Han Solo. Your heroine should be as real as your first crush—only she's carrying the plans to destroy the Death Star and she looks great in a bikini. And the problem your heros overcome should feel as real as a stopped-up septic tank. Only the septic tank should be guarded by robotic centaurs, and only a one-in-a-million shot with a proton torpedo can unclog it.

★ ★ ★ **FREE MOVIE IDEA** ★ ★ ★
Yours Free with the Purchase of This Book

"MANNIES"

Approximate Budget: $45 million
Estimated Gross: $137 million worldwide
Shoots in: Vancouver, British Columbia, for the tax rebate
Rating: PG-13
Awards Potential: .5% (Kids' Choice at best)

Danny McBride stars as RICKY, a party animal/free spirit who's never moved out of his parents' basement. He's a romantic, a philosopher, and a bongo player, and dreams one day of opening a store that sells only ROMANTIC MIX TAPES: yes, cassette <u>tapes</u> with awesome MIXES on them. He's made a special one for the GIRL AT THE STARBUCKS near his house but can't work up the nerve to talk to her.

Ricky spends his evenings cruising around in a van with the Tron logo on the side of it with his friends: DENIS, the "weird one" (Zach Galifi-anakis) and their cool black friend who actually gets the ladies, RAYBAN (Craig Robinson). The trio make what little money they have by recovering, cleaning, and reselling golf balls that they find in the bushes of the local golf course. Although they *seem high* a lot of the time, there <u>are no specific mentions of drugs</u>, so it's family-friendly.

When RICKY'S stuck-up, holier-than-thou sister, RACHEL (Elizabeth Banks), and her fruity/asshole husband, RON (Thomas Lennon), get injured on a heliskiing trip in France, Rachel calls on Ricky to babysit for their precocious eight-year-old son, RUDY.

Ricky then realizes that he can make DOUBLE what he was making selling used golf balls by working as a babysitter.

<u>Ricky, Denis, and Rayban open a full-service nanny business called MANNIES, for "Man Nannies."</u>

COMEDY "SET PIECES" INCLUDE:

RAYBAN cruises for business with hot mommies at the local grocery store.

Ricky, Denis, and Rayban take three girls to the AMERICAN GIRL CAFÉ—Denis asks the waiter: "What kind of draft beer you got?" Waiter: "We don't have <u>any draft beer, sir</u>, this is the American Girl Café." Denis: "Then a <u>bottle</u> of Bud and shot of Jaegie."

Ricky tells a few kids a scary BEDTIME STORY, with a flashlight under his chin: "And then Mr. Moon went into a terrible drunken rage. He crashed his brand-new sports car into the pool of the hotel. And Pete Townshend was very mad." <u>Yes, he's telling them GOODNIGHT KEITH MOON</u>!

Eventually, Ricky starts babysitting the son of the Girl at Starbucks, and a nerdy/sweet relationship starts to blossom. At one point, Rudy teaches Ricky a SIMPLE LESSON THAT HELPS HIM UNDERSTAND WOMEN IN A WAY HE NEVER DID, which allows him to overcome his fear. He gives the girl at Starbucks the mix tape he's made her. They kiss. End Credits.

AFTER THE CREDITS, we see that one of Ricky's MIX TAPES has fallen into the hands of Apple's STEVE JOBS. Jobs calls Ricky on the phone and hires him to work at iTunes!!!

Note: The sequel to this film, *Mannies 2*, will go straight to DVD and will feature <u>none</u> of the original cast members—except for Thomas Lennon as Ron.

Note: The TRAILER FOR THIS FILM features the song "The Boys Are Back in Town."

HOW TO WRITE A SCREENPLAY

PART ONE

Enough bulls#!t. Now you're actually going to sit down and write a screenplay. Great! (Go put on those fruity carpal tunnel syndrome gloves if you know what's good for you!) Here's the big secret no one tells you: writing screenplays is easy ~~and fun~~! And why is writing screenplays so easy ~~and fun~~?

BECAUSE WRITING OUTLINES IS HARD
AND TIME-CONSUMING!

Repeat this mantra to yourself in a Yoda voice: There is no "writing screenplays," there is only "writing <u>outlines</u>." If you write a good outline, the screenplay will write itself.

If you sit down with a blank Final Draft file open on your computer, cursor blinking at you, taunting you to write a 105-page screenplay with no map at all, <u>you will fail</u>. The process will soon become frustrating, and you'll end up giving up on what was once a great idea and squander the rest of the day watching funny cat videos on the internet.

Star of funny cat video on internet.
Jumps on ceiling fan. It's adorable.

You simply <u>have to</u> write an outline to write a screenplay. There is no other way. Maybe you can write an ART-HOUSE FILM with no outline; for example, most of the Andy Warhol films don't seem to have outlines. Let's take Andy's 1964 film *Empire*, which consists of eight hours and five minutes of slow-motion footage of the Empire State Building. *(LOOK, MA, NO OUTLINE!)*

Now let's compare Andy's outlineless movie to other skyscraper movies—<u>ones that DID have outlines</u>:

Die Hard, 1988 (outline)
Box office: $140,767,956

Empire, 1964 (no outline)
Box office: $0.00

The Towering Inferno, 1974 (outline)
Box office: $116,000,000

Eraserhead, 1976 (no outline)
Box office: $7,000,000

As you can see, the movies with no outline made MORE THAN TWO HUNDRED MILLION DOLLARS LESS than the ones WITH outlines.

Yes, writing outlines sucks, and it's not fun or sexy. Nobody sits at his Mac at Starbucks all day telling people he's working on an "outline." It doesn't sound cool.

But, along with STRUCTURE (see Chapter 23, "If Your Screenplay Doesn't Have This Structure . . ."), the secret to writing screenplays is the outline! And once you've worked out all of the problems in an outline, writing screenplays really is ~~fun and~~ easy. If you've written an outline and examined your story from every angle, all the writing you're doing is creating dialogue, action, and gags. That's the ~~fun~~ part.

So *how do you write a screenplay?*

> Remember (in YODA VOICE):
>   "You don't, foolish and reckless boy . . .
>   there is only writing outlines."

Now, when we say "outline," we don't mean a few notes on a cocktail napkin. Sure, that's a great way to write Charles Bukowski poems, but Charles Bukowski already wrote those. We mean write out the whole movie. Almost everything that happens, minus dialogue, should be in your outline. Your outline should be long. (Ours run around 20 pages.) It seems like silly mathematics, but the longer your outline is, the more problems you've worked out in advance and the less likely you'll hit a wall while you're writing the actual screenplay. Keep in mind, if you have an outline, there should be NO WRITER'S BLOCK. You know exactly where you're going and what the next scene is, and you never have to slow down (except to watch funny cat videos).

For the level of detail we're talking about, see the sample outlines in the appendix at the end of this book.

Of course, things will change from your outline to your finished screenplay; this is the nature of the creative process. But if there's a problem, it's way easier to remedy in the outline stage. When you're in the actual screenplay stage, problems that arise become a game of Jenga—undoing work in your screenplay is time-consuming and frustrating. Remember: always write an outline. Fixing a blueprint is a lot easier than fixing a skyscraper. Get the hard stuff over with in the outline. Then spend the time you save eating at

Jules Verne Restaurant
Eiffel Tower, Paris, France
www.lejulesverne-paris.com

It's a truly "special occasion" restaurant inside the Eiffel Tower. But when you're a wealthy screenwriter—*every day is a special occasion*!

PART TWO

Even when you're writing a spec, you must always:

HAVE A DEADLINE!

<u>You must have a deadline</u>. Exclamation point. If you don't have a deadline, you're not writing for a living, you're writing as a hobby. Deadlines are extraordinarily helpful. Make a deadline for yourself, and <u>stick to it</u>. As we said in Chapter 5, when you're writing for the studios, you get ten weeks to turn in your first draft. This makes writing for the studios supereasy, 'cause if you're not done in ten weeks—YOU'RE IN BREACH OF CONTRACT, AND THEY CAN SUE YOUR ASS. Yikes!

Now, then, can you have an outline and a deadline and still fail? Of course. Your film could have an inherent flaw you didn't think of. Or as mentioned previously, it might not be like the KINDS of films showing at the multiplex right now. But if it is and you have an outline and a deadline, the odds are stacked in your favor!*

---

*Somewhat!

WRITING ACTION AND DESCRIPTION

Our only advice about writing action and description in your script:

Keep it simple.

Now, if we had any sense of wit at all, we would have ended the chapter right there. But . . . we don't. (No surprise. You've seen *Herbie: Fully Loaded*, right? VW Bug follows Lindsay Lohan around? They win the big race against Jeff Gordon at the end? Oscar Wilde we ain't.)

To the point, when it comes to your descriptions in your scripts—about locations, characters, and action sequences: keep them brief. Don't get poetic, just tell people what they need to know. Describe things perfectly, yet economically.

For example, in describing your **locations**: After every slug line for a location . . .

```
EXT. WAREHOUSE — NIGHT
```

. . . you then need to describe the warehouse:

```
A dark, abandoned warehouse on a seedy pier.
An SUV is parked beside it, engine running.
```

THAT'S ALL YOU NEED. Just the KEY information. Don't go on and on and on about "the eerie moonlight dappled through the trees" or the "lonely sense of forboding that seems to emanate from the very timbers of the ramshackle yet somehow lovable old building." NO. If you do:

1. People will start skimming forward through your script, and they might MISS something that's actually important to the story. And—
2. People will think you're VAMPING—stalling, padding out the pages—because your story isn't any good. People don't go to the multiplex to see dappled moonlight. They go for STORY, ACTION, and great CHARACTERS.

GET TO THE POINT.

Keep your descriptions very brief and very clear. No one wants flowery prose. The point of your descriptions is not to look good on the page. The point is to describe things in a way that makes everything VERY easy to picture. Easy to picture for people who've already read ten terrible scripts that day BEFORE yours. People who might not be the brightest potato on the porch in the first place. There aren't a lot of actors and directors in Mensa—*keep it simple, stupid.*

If it takes longer than an hour to read your script—NO ONE IN HOLLYWOOD WILL HAVE THE FOCUS TO FINISH IT. Dialogue reads FAST. Your paragraphs of descriptions should read faster. Most of the movie stars you hope will read your script CARE ONLY ABOUT THEIR DIALOGUE.

When writing description in your movie,
Think Hemingway—not Joyce.

Yes, it needs to pop off the page with zing and style, but it needs to be SHORT, CLEAR, and VERY, VERY READABLE.

For your **character descriptions**: See Chapter 24, ". . . How to Formulate Characters in a Script," and remember, you have the first 10 pages of your script to introduce your character. You don't need to do it all in the first paragraph. Any paragraph that takes up a sizable chunk of the page is TOO LONG.

For your **action scenes:** No one can tell you how to CREATE a good action scene—you have to learn to do that yourself, through living your own adventures, studying action sequences in great films, reading good books, and perhaps some moderate to heavy drug use.

But—when WRITING AN ACTION SCENE DOWN, our tip is this:

Clarity clarity clarity.

If it's a car chase or a scene with a T-Rex drinking at a water fountain, then running after Ben Stiller, say it in as few words as possible. Say only what you NEED to say to set and describe the action scene.

If your scene has a hundred guys who AREN'T lead characters, all shooting at one another—DON'T DESCRIBE THE ACTION OF EVERY SINGLE GUY. That's maddening to read and impossible to follow. Write something like:

```
More GIs pour out onto the beach, as Nazis
mow them down from their concrete bunkers.
It's a MASSACRE: GIs drown in hails of
underwater bullets; a GI with a flamethrower
explodes in flames, killing the entire
platoon in his landing craft.
```

Then talk the audience through what HANKS and SIZEMORE are doing.

Don't get hung up in details. Don't get hung up in technical jargon or descriptions of "rippling biceps." Write only the things that the reader needs to know to PICTURE the action scene.

Oh, and if it's an action scene, it also needs to be:

AWESOME.

Action scenes are very expensive.

An interesting side note about action scenes: if you write an action scene well, it might end up being the one thing in the movie that actually resembles your script.

Why? Because it will most likely be directed by a second unit director and planned by the stunt coordinator and the CGI guys. And they don't read a script and automatically start figuring out how to change it. They read a script and figure out how to execute it.

Also, the big action scenes are usually planned FIRST, so that the CGI can be done in time. So sometimes the action scene you wrote is done before the director has even finished the OTHER projects he's working on. He hasn't moved to your movie full-time yet. And CGI is very expensive to change.

If you write a great action scene, there's a good chance it might end up in the final film, just the way you intended—only because it was started and planned while the director was still half asleep.

SCREENWRITING PROGRESS WORKSHEET
(Check all that apply)

1. Numb hands and tingling in the fingers? ❐
2. Weakness in the hands and wrists? ❐
3. Cold hands? ❐
4. Poor circulation/hands falling asleep? ❐
5. Loss of fine motor skills in the hands? ❐
6. Drinking too much? ❐

If you checked any, most, or all of these boxes—CONGRATULATIONS, you have carpal tunnel syndrome! (And possibly a drinking problem.) Your median nerve has become compressed at the wrist, and it's a sure sign that you're finally writing enough to make it as a Hollywood screenwriter! Well done, let's high-five! (You won't feel it.)

Carpal tunnel syndrome is a serious condition, and there are steps for minimizing the pain and damage done to the nerves in your wrist, but offhand we don't know what those steps are. You should probably ask a doctor or sumpin'. But it SEEMS like you're supposed to wear those fruity-looking carpal tunnel gloves. We SKIP THE GLOVES and treat it the old-fashioned way: with moderate to heavy drinking, or what the Irish call "pint lifting." Drinking puts your hand and wrist into a totally different position from writing and is the number one treatment for carpal tunnel syndrome relief that doctors recommend.*

For more information on carpal tunnel syndrome, Google it, like a normal person. And while you're at it, Google Helen Mirren > Images > Safe Search OFF.

---

*To our knowledge, no doctors recommend this.

ADVICE FOR WRITING WITH A PARTNER

We've been writing together for twenty years. We used to do it the hard way. Now we do it the ~~fun and~~ easy way. We would like to impart this ~~fun and~~ easy way to you. It took us a decade to figure it out. You will learn it by the end of these few pages.

The key to writing with a partner is: use the fact that there are two of you as an asset, not a hindrance. Some writing partners write together in the same room, taking turns who types while the other one paces or sits, quill in mouth, gazing dreamily out the window as the mist rises on the moor.

This is crazy. Nothing is worse than typing with someone looking over your shoulder. <u>Nothing</u>.

Plus, you know that little voice in your head that judges everything you write as you write it, that says, "That's wrong," "That should be a 'then' instead of an 'and,'" "*That should be in italics*," "Wait, no, it shouldn't." When you both write in the same room, you have TWO of those little voices in the room instead of one.

Instead of writing twice as fast, you're writing twice as slow.

So—how do you write twice as fast? Easy.

First, write an outline of your movie. (See Chapter 25, "How to Write a Screenplay.") Figure out the entire movie, and write it out in an in-depth outline. This you need to do together. We usually write our outlines in a bar so we can drink beer and look at girls. That takes the edge off—and you'll be shocked to find how many jokes are lurking in the bottom of your third or fourth beer. (See Chapter 33, "I'm Drinking Too Much. Is That a Problem?")

Then, when the outline is done, split it up into little sections. Usually a page or so of an outline will end up being between seven and ten pages of script. Split your outline up into page or so sized sections. Make sure that the sections have natural, logical ins and outs. (Don't split a love scene or an action sequence in half, for example.)

When your outline is divided into twenty or so sections, flip a coin; one of you does the ODD sections, the other does the EVEN sections.

Then go to your separate homes (Tom has a writing compound in Barcelona; Ben has a small writing isthmus in the French Marquesas) and write your first section.

Then e-mail it to your partner. Then attach their first section to yours. Then read the whole script (parts 1 and 2) and tweak it a little: make it better, faster, funnier. Cut jokes you don't like, or make them better.

Then write your next section, part 3. Attach it. Repeat, polishing parts 1 through 3. Etc., etc., etc.

Soon you will have the whole script written—in half the time it would have taken you to write it alone or working together, looking over each other's shoulders.

Not only that, but by the time you get to the end of your script, you will have done twenty passes of the script, polishing it. Your FIRST draft is really your twentieth.

Neat, huh?

People ask us, "But don't you argue when you cut out each other's jokes?" No. We don't. If one of us cuts a joke we like, we put it back. If it gets taken out AGAIN, we don't put it back. It's that easy.

For this to work, you have to follow these four rules:

1. You and your partner must trust each other.
2. You must have the same sense of humor.
3. You must be egoless (fight for something because it's good, not because YOU wrote it).
4. Don't be a dick.

Follow these rules and this strategy, and you will write twice as fast as you would without a partner. You'll BOTH have carpal tunnel syndrome, but you'll also both have Brazilian supermodels to massage your hands for you on your hovercraft.

SPELL IT WRONG ON PURPOSE!!!

Not sure how you can enter a funny spelling into FINAL DRAFT? For example, you're trying to write the French word for a wonderful, fluffy desert:

soufflé

But it won't give you an option for the accent aigu over the e? Stop tearing your hair out and do what the pros do: SPELL IT WRONG ON PURPOSE. Instead of typing: souffle . . .

Try typing: **souffleee**

Then hit SPELL CHECK ("Command" on your keyboard), and it will give you a list of great options, <u>including the correct version, with the accent aigu</u>.

You can have fun with some other foreign spellings of words, just try it out! Type the version that's ALMOST BUT NOT QUITE RIGHT— and see what those wonderful fellows at Final Draft have in store for you! You'll be pleasantly surprised!

Like . . . what's that great word for the front of a building:

façade

Try typing:

faacaaade

When all else fails: CUT AND PASTE STUFF OFF OF THE IN-TERNET.

And after that: WE'LL SEE YOU AT THE OSCARS!!!*

179

*We throw an Oscar-watching party every year, so if you are at the Oscars and the cameras catch you, we might see you on TV!!!

REWRITES: YOU WANT IT WHEN?
AND I'M GETTING PAID WHAT?!?!?!!?

Fixing a script that the studio HATES . . . but they're making anyway.

<u>*This happens about 90 percent of the time:*</u> A studio buys a movie. Then, because of the script the writer turned in and/or because of the subsequent "development" job the studio did, they now absolutely HATE the script. And the writer. But—*they're still gonna make the movie.* (See Chapter 10, "Why Does Almost Every Studio Movie *SUCK* Donkey Balls?") So—they fire the writer and put the word out: we're looking for another writer to fix the script.*

Now, the studio has already spent some serious bread on the previous (shitty) drafts of the script. The fact that they're hiring *another* writer means that they're willing to spend *more* money—so SOMEBODY at the studio still thinks there's an idea for a great movie in there somewhere.†

So they call the agents and managers of a few specific writers who they think will be able to fix this turkey. A lot of times these gigs go to writers who already have a relationship with the studio. Whom they trust.

OR—they may give the gig to a new writer. That's why it's okay to have pitched a movie to a studio that they didn't buy. (**Rule 4: If you don't sell a pitch, that's okay.**) They heard your pitch or read your spec—you

---

*The studio usually doesn't actually tell the writer they've been fired. You usually hear about it from a third party—that the studio has "moved on to fresh eyes" on your script.

†Again, this is a good reason NOT to be bummed that you got fired. If the studio is hiring another writer, that means your movie might still be getting made. You'll probably get some kind of credit, and that means a fat paycheck. (See Chapter 30, "Arbitration or Who Wrote This Crap?")

seemed professional and competent, and they liked your sensibility. They didn't buy your pitch or spec, but they might give you a shot at a rewrite.

So—this is your CHANCE to get a gig at the studio. A LOT of writers first break into the system by delivering a great REWRITE; because not only are you going to deliver a good script, *you're also going to SAVE the studio the money they spent on the previous drafts*. Until you came along, that was MONEY DOWN THE TUBES.

So the studio people called your agent to see if you're interested in the rewrite—then what?

They ask your reps, "Is your client interested in doing a rewrite of a script?" (Let's call it *The Banana Police*.) You say, "Let me read it."

SOMETIMES: They'll send you the script. Sometimes they'll want to talk to you first and tell you what they like about the script, what they *don't* like, why they were originally excited about the movie, and why they don't like it anymore. *Then* they send you the script.

SOMETIMES: They won't show you the script at all. Instead, they'll tell you; "The script is so bad, we don't even want you to read it." (This happens A LOT.) Then they'll pitch you what they think the movie *could* be.

You get the script delivered to your door (or some exec pitches you the movie). You read the script.

> **WARNING:** *Even though they told you how bad the script is—<u>it's going to be a million times worse than you thought it'd be</u>. It's going to be so bad it makes you mad. You're going to yell—at the script, at your spouse, at your roommate, at your cat—"Why the hell is this retarded writer selling scripts when my genius pitch didn't sell?!? This guy can't even spell 'Bannana' right!?!"*

Take a breath. Then organize your thoughts: *What can you do to fix this script?* You need to:

- Read the script more than once, and take notes.
- Organize your thoughts. In less than a week, you need to go in for a meeting and pitch the studio the changes that you're going to make to the script.

- Practice your pitch. (See Chapter 3, "How to Pitch Your Movie.") Make it great. Sometimes pitching a rewrite is harder than pitching a new script. It's more complicated. And the execs you're pitching to need to be able to understand your big changes, and your little changes AND remember the old script in great detail. It takes great organization and communication skills.

- Make your pitch short, clear, and awesome. You need to RESELL them on the movie. You have to wipe the slate clean and convince them that they should forget the old version and that <u>YOUR version</u> is going to kick ass.

When we go in to pitch a rewrite, we ALWAYS start the meeting by saying something like "We hope we don't offend anybody. Don't take this personally—but we're going to be 100 percent honest about this script." Because we're always BRUTALLY honest about the old script, while trying to be tactful about the writer. We don't say, "This writer is a retard who has no idea how to write dialogue." We say, "We're going to totally redo all of the dialogue. It's stiff, it doesn't sound the way real people talk, and it needs to be totally thrown out and replaced." You never know, one of the execs you're pitching to in the room might have WRITTEN the dialogue. So be honest, but be careful.

Tell the studio all of the changes you're going to make. Tell them what you're going to take out and what you're going to replace it with. You can be general: "Act II is way too long, I'm gonna shave off about ten pages." Or very specific: "I'm gonna make the plumber on page 10 into a locksmith." And keep your rewrite pitch short. Ten, fifteen minutes. They'll have tons of questions afterward, so do your homework.

What happens when you and the studio disagree about something that you HATE and they love?

Remember: <u>THE STUDIO IS ALWAYS RIGHT</u>. Just because the scene where the Banana Police teach a bunch of monkeys to do the "Cabbage Patch" is the worst scene you've ever read—<u>that doesn't mean you can't fix it</u>.

Ask the studio: "What is it about the 'banana scene' that you like? Do you like that they teach monkeys *something*? Or that they teach *someone* a dance?" If they like it JUST THE WAY IT IS—great! Problem solved. Less work for you. Those pages you don't have to touch. Remember, your name's probably never gonna be on this turkey anyway.

But mostly, just convince the studio that you can see what *it* sees in the script—its <u>potential</u>.

Why Rewrites Are a Good Gig

1. If you've never worked at this studio before, it's a great way for them to get to know your work. You can really prove you know how to write a screenplay.
2. If you pull off a good rewrite, you're a **superhero**. You came in and saved the day, and people will be thrilled. Pulling off a script that *you* pitched . . . that's expected of you. But fixing someone else's script **SAVED THE STUDIO MONEY.**
3. The money you get paid to do rewrites is GREAT. You get paid by the week. A lot of times, it's less work for more money than selling your own pitch, because the hard work is done. There's already a script (not just 100 blank sheets of paper). You usually start off getting paid about $10,000 a week—and that's just for your first rewrite. If you're good, your rate will climb very quickly. You can get rich doing rewrites. *Take that, America's schoolteachers!*

Or, if you wanna make SERIOUS bank, get a gig doing:

PRODUCTION REWRITES

Production rewrites happen when a film has been GREENLIT (meaning they're going to shoot the movie *soon*) and the studio STILL hates the script. *This happens ALL THE TIME. Herbie: Fully Loaded* had twenty-four different writers AFTER our draft was greenlit and we were fired. (See Chapter 14: *"Herbie: Fully Loaded."*)

Why does this happen?

Sometimes someone pitches a movie that's such a great idea that movie stars sign up to do it and the studio greenlights it before the script is even written. Then the script is turned in, and it sucks. Then, in "developing" the script, it gets worse.

Sometimes a writer turns in a script, and about 90 percent of it is AWESOME. It gets greenlit. Then the studio sets to work "fixing" the other 10 percent. And the studio and director and sometimes the movie stars screw up the whole movie. It's amazing how one botched pass of a script can create a domino effect—and the whole movie can fall apart like a house of cards.

Sometimes <u>even when everyone likes a script</u>, movie stars have their own writers come in and do a "little pass" of the script. Most directors do the same thing—and a lot of times that "little pass" totally screws up the script. Now, the studio can't just GO BACK to the *good* draft. (Which would seem to be the logical thing to do, right?) No, that would step on the movie star's or director's toes.

No—they have to move FORWARD, never back. So—they hire a writer to "fix it."

Again.

The studios usually hire pros for production rewrites—people they've worked with *a lot*. Whom they know they can count on, because honestly, the studio's balls are in a clam. They NEED to fix the script FAST.

Production rewrites are VERY stressful. The clock is ticking. They needed a new script YESTERDAY. The studio is in a panic, the producers are in a panic, the director's in a panic . . . and they're usually all ARGUING with one another about what needs to be done with the script (which is why the script is a mess to begin with).

The director will want you to put something into the script that the studio HATES, or vice versa—and rather than just discussing it with each other, they're BOTH calling you directly and telling you to *do it.*

But when the new draft sucks and has stuff in it the studio hates—guess who gets fired? YOU!

Your job is to make the script GOOD <u>and</u> TRY to do what they *all* want. Sometimes you can't do both.

We always try to make the script GOOD first, while doing what the studio wants. To us, the studio trumps the director. The studio is paying us, not the director. MOVIE STARS sometimes trump EVERYBODY. You have to put in their notes (then we show that draft to the studio and make THEM take out the movie star's stuff). (See Chapter 29, "Martin Lawrence Has a Few Thoughts or How to Take Notes from a Movie Star.")

Production rewrites are a TREMENDOUS amount of work. You're writing one scene while they're shooting another; then they'll call you and tell you to rewrite the scene they're shooting RIGHT NOW. We had to rewrite the first thirty pages of *Starsky & Hutch* three times in a week. We probably rewrote the entire movie ten times in less than a month. We'd write stuff, someone wouldn't like it, we'd rewrite it—over and over.

Agreeing to do a production rewrite is signing your life away, 24/7, for as long as it takes to fix the script or until they fire you. They'll call you at all hours. They'll expect to see new pages every day. They'll expect OPTIONAL versions of scenes. And every single person you're dealing with is tearing his hair out and screaming at you.

Oh, and you'll NEVER get screen credit. Never ever ever.

So why do it? The MONEY, for one thing. They really pay you a LOT of money. And if you get a reputation as a "closer"—someone who can make a script good in a pinch—they'll hire you to do it again and again.

And they'll probably think very seriously about buying your next pitch.

PUNCH-UPS

Punch-ups are production rewrites, but smaller and much more surgical. The studio has greenlit a comedy that's not funny. So they want you to go in and add jokes.

Or they've cast someone very specific for a particular role, and that person wants you to rewrite the role in their voice. ("GREAT NEWS! We've cast the Jonas Brothers as the Banana Police! Could you add a little "Jonas Brothers magic" to those scenes?") Ew. Just typing that made us feel icky.

ROUNDTABLES

Roundtables are fun and a good way for young comedy writers to get a foot in the door. Usually, an agent hooks you up with the roundtable, or some writer you've met socially calls you up and asks you to do it. Patton Oswalt (writer, actor, bon vivant) invited us to our first roundtable when we were starting out.

The studio sends you a comedy script (usually it's greenlit). You have the night to read it and scribble down any jokes you can think of in the margins. The next day, you and seven to twelve other writers sit around a table. The director is usually there, as well as someone to take notes. Then you go through the script page by page, and you all pitch your jokes (out loud). It's fun, and the studio buys you breakfast and lunch. They tell you you're going to get paid $1,000, but we swear to God we have never been paid for a roundtable. We've done at least twenty of them. Never been paid a dime.

BUT—do roundtables if you can. Especially when you're just starting out. It's a good way to meet directors, execs, and other funny writers. You laugh the whole day—sometimes for two days.

WRITING FOR MOVIES THAT HAVE ALREADY BEEN SHOT

Yes. A lot of times a studio SHOOTS a comedy and funny never happened. So—they need to do reshoots.

The studio will show you the movie in a little private screening and tell you what they want you to write. You get this gig the same way as a rewrite. Sometimes you pitch what you're going to do, but usually they tell you *practically every word* they want in the new scene or scenes.

You write the scene or scenes, they give you notes, you go back and forth MANY times, getting it to where they all like it. They pay you by the week.

ADR (ADDITIONAL DIALOGUE RECORDING) "JOKES"

Sometimes they want you to add jokes to a movie WITHOUT their re-shooting anything. Now, you're thinking—*how the hell do they expect you to do that?*

If it's an animated film, they might reanimate the mouth, but your line still has to fit organically into the scene. Tricky.

If it's NOT animated, they might want you to write jokes *that will fit into the mouths of the actors in the scene.* Then the actors come in and rerecord the dialogue, and they slip your jokes into their mouths. We're not kidding. It happens a lot.

Or they might want you to add jokes that some character supposedly delivers from <u>offscreen</u>. *Again, we shit you not.* You have to go in and write wisecracks that some character supposedly is saying OFF CAMERA.

Does this ever actually work and make a not-funny movie funny?

Nope. Never.

But they do it anyway. Needless to say, you will not get screen credit for this type of work.

AND YOU DO NOT WANT IT.

29

MARTIN LAWRENCE HAS A FEW THOUGHTS
OR
HOW TO TAKE NOTES FROM A MOVIE STAR

Ah, the movie star—as majestic and rare as the California condor! (Actually, there are 348 California condors known to be living. There are nowhere NEAR that many actors who can open a picture. So on second thought, screw those condors, they're not that rare.)

The movie star is majestic to behold in its natural habitat—which is on weekends in the summer, at the Golden Globe Awards, or at Cannes.

First of all, let's make sure we're not confusing the movie <u>star</u> with those other categories, the movie <u>actor</u> and that awful monstrosity the <u>celebrity</u>.

The term "movie star" describes someone who can OPEN a movie.

That means that almost no matter what happens, with this actor in your film, your film will be number one at the box office the weekend it comes out. Movie actors and celebrities cannot do this. Movie actors are just that: actors who act in movies. Celebrities are people who are in movies even though they cannot act at all. Here's a quick reference:

Tom Hanks, Sandra Bullock = MOVIE STAR

Mark Ruffalo, Sandra Oh = MOVIE ACTOR

Perez Hilton, Paris Hilton = CELEBRITY

It's easy to know if you've cast a movie star in your movie. The first way to tell is that they'll be REALLY EXPENSIVE. How expensive? you ask? Well, the ones listed up top should run you in the $20 million to $25 million range, plus a slice of the FIRST-DOLLAR GROSS. (*Which means they start making money at the same time the studio does, nice. FIRST-DOLLAR GROSS IS VERY HARD TO GET!!!*)

So you should do a quick price check to make sure you've got an actual movie star, because accidentally hanging your opening weekend on a JARED THE SUBWAY SANDWICH GUY (*celebrity*) or a SANDRA BERNHARD (*bridge troll*) will spell disaster.

Sure, there are some movie stars who cost LESS than $20 million, but you get what you pay for. You'll be lucky to open in second, third, or (gasp!) fourth place. And we're not exaggerating when we say that opening in fourth place is ten times worse than being in Auschwitz.

Where were we? Oh, yeah. So you spent the $25 million, and now you've got a big-time movie star attached! Way to go. Now comes the interesting part. Because by default, any movie star automatically knows much more about MOVIE WRITING than you. "But wait," you say, "that movie star has never written anything in his whole life! He doesn't have one single writing credit!"

PHOOEY!

EVERY MOVIE STAR, TO SOME EXTENT, WRITES THE MOVIE THEY STAR IN—even though they couldn't find the "CLEAR REVISED" button in Final Draft if their life depended on it. They write it because they are the star. The movie wouldn't be happening without them and they know that. They got approval over the director too. (That means the director is directing the movie only because the movie star said it was okay.)

Movie stars get to call the shots, have writers hired or fired, and often they bring in their own PERSONAL WRITER, or a team of writers, to give the script a little "polish" for them. Most movie stars have writers they like to keep around, strolling behind them like mariachis, singing ballads of their box-office victories and/or finessing awkward dialogue.

But sometimes, before they bring in their writers, you get a shot at putting in the movie star's notes. So if you've got a movie star attached— *and you haven't been fired yet*—congratulations! Now get ready for their notes! There is an art to taking them. Get good at it. Here's how it goes:

For starters, the notes meeting will usually be someplace strange— either a secluded part of a restaurant, their fabulous mansion in the Hollywood Hills, or possibly in their trailer on the movie they're currently shooting.

1. Don't act weird. Be respectful and cool but not "fan-boy-ish" around your star.

    In general, regular people tend to act WEIRD around movie stars; they get excited and SWEATY. Try not to be either, as it makes movie stars uncomfortable.

    For instance, if the meeting's in their trailer on set, DO NOT SAY, *"Jeez, this thing is bigger than my whole house."* Everyone says this whoever steps in their trailer. It's not funny to a movie star that their trailer is bigger than your house, it's just sad. So DON'T point it out. Don't act like the Make-A-Wish Foundation sent you there to meet the movie star. Act **professional.**

    BUT DON'T TREAT MOVIE STARS LIKE THEY'RE ENTIRELY NORMAL EITHER. Remember: they're NOT entirely normal. They make $25 million <u>a couple of times a year</u>. And every living American knows their name and what they look like in a swimsuit. SO WALK THE LINE between NOT treating them special and *treating them A LITTLE BIT SPECIAL.* We treat them sort of like they're the "down-to-earth" members of the royal family. It tends to work.

2. Unlike with the studio, you need to agree with movie stars ALL THE TIME. Period. And not just for show. <u>You really agree</u> with all of their notes. Or you're fired. Not only are you fired, the star WON'T EVEN HEAR ABOUT THE FACT THAT YOU GOT FIRED. It will happen before you even walk back to your car.

3. Be VERY FAMILIAR with movie stars' entire canon of work. Don't accidentally pitch something they've done before in another movie. Movie stars HATE repeating themselves. And, yes, they expect you to be VERY FAMILIAR with everything they've done. Save yourself some embarrassment by brushing up on your movie star. Know their hits, and even better: find GOOD THINGS about their flops. (Note: It's best not to discuss the flops at all. BUT, if they come up, YOU SHOULD HAVE ONE POSITIVE DETAIL ABOUT THEM TO DISCUSS.)

   For example: you've just sat down in the trailer of, say, JENNIFER LOPEZ (celebrity, singer, and movie actress—but not movie star).

> JENNIFER LOPEZ
> Wow. I can't believe how crappy
> *Gigli* turned out.
>
> YOU
> I dunno, I thought you looked great
> in those fight scenes.
>
> JENNIFER LOPEZ
> Ha, thanks. I worked really hard on
> those. Now here's my notes . . .

Whew! Nice save.

4. Don't be a chatterbox. Nobody likes a chatterbox. Especially movie stars who are used to talking to professional chat-show hosts like Craig Ferguson. Talk when you have something smart/clever/funny/interesting to say, and only then. Don't blab on and on; it makes you seem nervous, because you are. Mostly listen and nod.

5. Don't ASK FOR ANYTHING. Not even water. Seriously. Have everything you need before the meeting. Don't "need" things. Many movie stars are BUD-

DHISTS, or they at least "dig" Buddhist practices. They know that to WANT anything is to suffer—so don't be WANTING anything from them. PLUS, ALL DAY LONG, EVERYONE IN THE WORLD ASKS FOR THINGS FROM THEM. Autographs, photos, appearances at the bedside of their ailing grandchild. People never stop asking movie stars for stuff, so BE A BREATH OF FRESH AIR, and don't need anything from them. Even water—no joke. This establishes a tiny psychological footing for you. <u>Today: you're the one person in their life who doesn't need anything from them</u>. Keep this up, and they're more likely to keep you around. (Start picking out your mariachi outfit!)

6. Listen carefully, and incorporate <u>all</u> of their notes. (Some of their notes will likely be TERRIBLE or half baked. But guess what—you're gonna do those notes too. And guess what: YOU'RE GONNA GET BLAMED ON THE INTER-NET for this terrible idea. (See Chapter 18, "Naysayers.") But, that's why you're getting paid the big bucks! *C'est la guerre!**

Remember, if you can get a movie star to like your writing and even know your name, you become INFINITELY more powerful in Holly-wood. Being the first- or second-choice writer a movie star prefers to work with will present you with LOTS of opportunities—and put you into a better negotiating position. Movie stars, like agents, don't just want SCRIPTS; They want people around who can craft words and scenes and are willing to work tirelessly to get the script right and make them look better. If you get the chance to do ten free drafts of Act I for a movie star—DO IT. And make every one of them great.

French for "THERE'S A GORILLA!"

ARBITRATION
OR
WHO WROTE THIS CRAP?
(You did—if you know how to arbitrate!)

Unless you are a working screenwriter, this is a part of the movie industry you have most likely never heard of—and if you ARE a working screenwriter, it's one of the most important parts of the business.

"What the f@#k is arbitration?" you ask. Arbitration is the process by which the Writers Guild determines who receives CREDIT for a film, after the film gets made.

"Credit? So f@#king what?," you say. Well—with CREDIT come ROYALTIES. "Royalties?" you say. "You mean like cold, hard cash that can be traded for jet skis, Wii Fits, and sex acts?" Yes. That's exactly what we mean.

Now, we don't know how much clearer we can make this: If you don't receive credit for a film, you'll never receive the piles of money that the screenwriter gets. The credited writer of a film gets 1.5 percent of the film's profits (that's the film's box office, minus what the studio spent). Plus royalties every time the film plays on TV. Plus royalties for every DVD sold, plus a script publication fee, plus money when they write the "young adult novelization" of your script . . . it goes on and on. Credit on a successful film can be worth a lot of money. If you do not get CREDIT on the movie, you get ZILCH—no matter how much work you did on the script. And to *get* credit, you will almost definitely have to arbitrate. So . . . what's arbitration?

HERE'S HOW IT WORKS

You wrote a movie for a movie studio. You got fired. (And maybe rehired, then fired again.) Now—if your movie is being filmed and you're not the one writing on it: someone else is. If a movie is being filmed, there's a 99 percent chance it's being rewritten. It's not uncommon for DOZENS of writers to work on a project. Especially comedies.

You probably won't know who else wrote on the film until you get, in the mail, THE RECOMMENDED CREDITS: **after a film is completed, but before it is released, the MOVIE STUDIO submits their SUGGESTED CREDITS to the WRITERS GUILD.** They submit their suggestions, and then the Writers Guild almost always makes the studio's "suggestions" into the OFFICIAL CREDITS. (We know, that's kinda f@#ked up, huh?)

This is important and harks back to the "don't be a dick" section of this book—because the studio will almost always recommend that the credits go to the WRITERS THEY KNOW THEY'RE GOING TO WORK WITH AGAIN IN THE FUTURE.

Don't be surprised if some TOTALLY UNDESERVING DOUCHE-BAG is given credit for your movie. It's because the studio has other projects with him and they don't want to piss him off. They'd rather be the "good guy" to both of you and let you duke it out in the ARBITRATION PROCESS.

So—what is the arbitration process?

First, you have to write up a STATEMENT to submit to the Writers Guild ARBITRATION COMMITTEE, saying why you deserve screen credit and why the other writer or writers suggested DO NOT deserve credit.

To get credit, here's what you must prove
to the Arbitration Committee:

"Any writer whose work represents a contribution of more than 33% of a screenplay shall be entitled to screenplay credit, except where the screenplay is an original screenplay. In the case of an original screenplay, any subsequent writer or writing team must contribute 50% to the final screenplay [to also get credit]." (From the WGA *Screen Credits Manual*.)

BE READY TO PROVE NOT ONLY THAT <u>YOU DO</u> FILL THOSE REQUIREMENTS BUT <u>THAT NO OTHER WRITER DOES</u>.

Make no mistake: <u>This is war</u>, and the best thing you can do is to BE PREPARED. Other writers will be ruthless in their statements, and you have to be too. The Writers Guild will read your statement and the statements written by the other writers you're fighting against, and then THE ARBITRATION COMMITTEE will judge and decide who gets screen credit. *Who are the judges on the committee?* The Arbitration Committee is composed of <u>THREE OTHER WRITERS</u>, all of whom have received credit on some film in the past. They were RANDOMLY SELECTED to serve on the panel for YOUR arbitration (like jury duty for Writers Guild members). They alone will decide your fate. You need two out of three of them to agree that only you fill those requirements and deserve credit.

Will their decision be fair? Who can say? The Guild tries to ensure that the three writers on the committee aren't FRIENDS with anyone who's arbitrating (or enemies with them either). They do this by ASKING you, as a Guild member: "Do you know any of these writers you're about to judge, or do you have any prebiased opinion about them or their work?" <u>So it's totally up to the honesty of the three writers</u>. Do they ever lie? (We dunno. *We've* certainly lied to get out of REGULAR jury duty.)

<u>The committee's decision is final, and cannot be changed, ever.</u> Ever. If you lose, you can complain, but nothing will be changed. It's the rules.

(AUTHORS' NOTE: The arbitration process is completely f@#ked and is the cause of a great deal of discord within the Guild. There's no other creative union that pits its members against one another, and with such hefty consequences.)

Now . . . can you win? <u>Yes. We have.</u>

Here's What You Need to Do to Win

1. **Get help.** There are a few professional arbiters in Los Angeles who specialize in this field. They can help you with your statement, and, most important: <u>they can read all the scripts and tell you if you have a case or not</u> before you even start. These helpers are not widely known, but your entertainment lawyer will know of one. Get the best one available BEFORE THE OTHER GUY DOES. <u>They'll be expensive but they'll be worth it</u>. The good ones run about $5,000 to $10,000. If you win, you'll make a fortune in residuals. If you lose, you won't make a dime.

2. **Be scientific.** Read every draft of every script by every writer and make notes. Dissect the scripts, and find every single aspect of the **plot**, every **character**, every piece of **action**, and determine WHO IS RESPONSIBLE FOR IT (who wrote it first, in the earliest draft). And the answer better be: <u>mostly you</u>.

   (*Note: Name changes of characters and changes to dialogue are supposed to count <u>less</u> than plot, but these changes frequently FOOL the committee and bite you in the ass. Also, if you're doing a rewrite, it's in your best interest to <u>change everything you can</u>!*)

3. Write a statement that states your case <u>very clearly</u>, and convinces the committee that all other writers' contributions are INSUBSTANTIAL. Your statement needs to be AMAZING. A good arbitration statement can take as long to work on as a script itself. <u>No joke</u>. You should write this statement as though you're writing for your life: <u>because you are</u>. This is war, and there are douchebags lurking out there who did a few days of dialogue polish on your script who are trying to STEAL YOUR ROYALTIES. Spend A LOT of time crafting your statement. Hit all the facts, and also

reinforce your "emotional attachment" to the film. Remember: <u>only successful screenwriters will be reading this statement, so make it the best thing you've ever written</u>.

4. **Cross your damn fingers, 'cause arbitration is a crap shoot.** There is simply no science to it. It's an entirely vague, veiled, and f@#ked-up process. If you lose, you will very likely <u>never know why</u>.

And if you win, give a VERY NICE GIFT to the arbiter who helped you (so they'll take your case the next time, even if the writer you're arbitrating against asks first).

Then invest in short-term municipal bonds. (Those are the kind of bonds that are entirely TAX FREE, so a gain of 6 percent is really a gain of 12 percent!!!) We know a good investment guy if you need one.

SEQUELS!

So your picture made some money! Mazel bro—serious mazel on that, way to go. Now, then, when is it appropriate to discuss . . .

. . . the sequel?

Well, here's our simple rule:

NEVER DISCUSS THE SEQUEL BEFORE THE MOVIE COMES OUT! <u>EVER</u>!!! DON'T EVEN THINK ABOUT IT. THIS IS LIKE THE WORST JINX EVER. SERIOUSLY, KNOCK ON WOOD IF YOU EVER TALK ABOUT A SEQUEL BEFORE THE FIRST MOVIE IS A HUGE SUCCESS. The box-office elves that live out in the trees will hear your boastful comments, and they will smite the crap out of you.

For example: we remember standing in the lobby of the El Capitan Theatre, talking with the brilliant Nina Jacobsen of Disney moments before the premiere of *Herbie: Fully Loaded*. "Maybe in Part 2 she's in Japan!" is the kind of thing we're all saying. "How great would that be. Good ol' Maggie Peyton,* trading paint with Day-Glo neon Japanese Tuner cars! Woo-hoo! Let's do it . . . oh, wait. Crap. What's that horrible sound? OH, NO—everyone hates *Herbie: Fully Loaded*! And us! Run! Run

---

*Lindsay Lohan's character's name in *Herbie: Fully Loaded*.

for your lives!!! Oh God, no—they got Lindsay! Lindsay Lohan is dead!!*
SAVE YOURSELVES!!!!"

Did you read the part about how *Taxi 2* was one of the biggest deals
we ever made!?!?!?!?!!? No amount of crazy punctuation in the world can
properly express how befuddling that fact is. In fact, at some point somebody probably joked about *Speedracer II.* Speedracer and the mysterious
Racer X did not meet again.

Sequels are like the mythological MEDUSA. DON'T PISS OFF
THE MEDUSA, or she'll turn you to stone or something. Be sensible
and cautious. Discuss sequels only when your film has OPENED, won
its first weekend, and either HELD ON REALLY WELL or won ITS
SECOND WEEKEND. Let's face it, if you win TWO WEEKENDS,
your sequel chances go way up. IF YOU WIN THREE WEEKENDS, a
sequel is almost a guarantee. FOUR? FUGGEDABOUTIT. Same if your
box office goes UP from your first weekend to your second weekend, à la
Night at the Museum or *The Blind Side.* $200 million domestic is a pretty
good guideline, but not a guarantee. But for chrissake: DON'T JINX IT.
SHUT UP ABOUT THE SEQUEL, ALREADY. We shouldn't even be
talking about it here in this chapter called "Sequels." The box-office elves
are waiting in the shadows, ready to SWITCH our movie with an evil,
ugly changeling movie!

Of course, if your movie is a huge hit, it's likely people will talk sequel. Or even better: *threequel.* If you got "Written by" or "Screen Story
by" credit, you literally do not have to lift a finger on the sequel, and
you will still get paid. Of course, you'll make <u>more</u> with some finger
lifting—so go for it. If you wrote the first one, the studio <u>has</u> to offer you
the job of writing the sequel. So crank those sequels out until you have to
DIG YOUR WAY OUT OF ALL THE MONEY WITH YOUR BARE
HANDS. Like some kind of wonderful Scrooge McDuck scenario, where
ol' Scrooge McDuck is literally BURIED IN AN AVALANCHE OF
HIS OWN MONEY. Ah, Scrooge McDuck. That guy is great. (General
note: When you start to sympathize with the ULTRARICH characters
in your favorite cartoons, like Scrooge McDuck or Montgomery Burns
instead of, say Donald Duck or Comic Book Guy, you know you're on
the right path.) In short, sequels are all good news. The studio has to

*At the time of this publication, Lindsay Lohan is still alive.

199

pay you. They have to pay you more. And even if you pass, you still get paid!

So when they pull the trigger on the sequel, *Basset Hound Switcheroo 2: The Basset Case*, the only question is: WHERE SHOULD I CELEBRATE? Well, why not take your trophy partner to the Jade Mountain resort at Anse Chastanet in Saint Lucia? (www.jademountain.com.)

Think you've ever stayed in a nice hotel room? Well, you haven't. Not until you've stayed at the Jade Mountain resort. Seriously, these rooms will knock your socks off. They don't even call 'em rooms. They call them "sanctuaries." And they have only three walls because it's always nice there and so you can see the Pitons mountains—and they kind of look like boobs. The rates are probably really high, but so what? Let *Basset Hound Switch 2* worry about it.

THOMAS LENNON ARCHIVES

GETTING THE BOOK RIGHTS

So you read some book, and you think it'd make a great movie. Or a comic book or an epic poem or a magazine article or a short story . . . any work of fiction or true story. How do you acquire the screen rights?

Step 1: Tell your manager to do it.

Your manager will make a bunch of calls and tell you if the screen rights have been sold. If they haven't been sold, he'll negotiate a price for you.

Can you buy the rights yourself, without a manager? Of course—but this is one of the reasons you have a manager. You should be busy WRITING. Let them take care of this kind of stuff for you. Your manager will have one of their lackeys look into it for you.

If you don't have a manager, you're gonna have to do some Googling. Find the publisher who published the story, then contact the subsidiary rights department. Or, if it's a TRUE story, find a phone number for the people in the story. Or, if they're deceased, find their family. (But be careful. If it's a story with many people involved or if the deceased has a large family, finding out who actually OWNS the rights might be very, very tricky.)

When you've found who owns the rights, call 'em up, use your best phone voice, and say who you are and what you want. ("I'm a big-time Hollywood screenwriter, and I think your story would make a great movie! Can I option the rights to it?") Pretty soon, they're gonna ask you HOW MUCH YOU'RE GOING TO PAY THEM FOR THE RIGHTS.

So you need to have done some research. Usually when you option the rights to something, there's an up-front fee. Could be $50,000; could be a lot more, depending on how popular the property is. If it's an OLD book or story or one that's obscure, it might not cost much at all. Sometimes you can buy rights with NO up-front money—just an agreement that the author will get paid if the script gets made into a movie (then the studio would pay them).

But. It's complicated, and unless you LOVE doing this kinda homework and negotiations—have your manager or lawyer do it.

Step 2: If the rights are available, buy them or take the idea to a studio and THEY'LL buy them.

If you can afford it, buy the screen rights. If you control the rights, you'll be able to negotiate for back end and maybe become a producer of the project. Maybe.

When buying the rights, you need a lawyer. A lawyer will negotiate the price of the rights for you, as well as the conditions. They will draw up a contract so that you don't somehow get screwed.

Just remember: when you buy the screen rights, you usually won't own them forever. If you can't sell the movie in some prenegotiated amount of time—say, a year—the rights revert back to the book's author or the real person, if it's a true story (whoever owned the rights before). And they keep your money.

If you *can't* afford the rights, that's okay. Go pitch the book to the studio. If they like your take on the book, then they'll buy the rights. You'll still get paid to write the movie; you just won't share in the profits.

Adapting material to the big screen is a good business to be in.

Studios HATE to take risks. They LOVE to buy movies that are based on something that has already proven to be successful and already has a following. Even if the book isn't *Twilight* or *Harry Potter,* the fact that it's been published means that it has more of a following than your pitch or spec. And if it's a true story—that always has a good marketing angle.

I'M DRINKING TOO MUCH.
IS THAT A PROBLEM?

The short answer: no.

The longer answer: nope.

Not only is heavy drinking <u>NOT</u> a problem—it very may well *HELP WITH YOUR WRITING! Your health too!**

Writing and drinking go together like Oscar Wilde and little boys! Or Tennessee Williams and little boys. You get the picture. Hard drinking can lead to great writing (and sometimes weird stuff with little boys). But let's focus on the writing part!

The drinking of hard alcohol, wine, and spirits has a long-standing tradition in writing. Why? It's quite simple: <u>because there are certain</u>

---

*This statement has not been verified by a medical doctor.

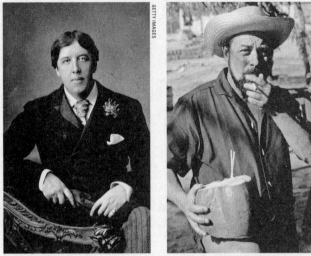

Oscar Wilde   Tennessee Williams

<u>ideas, themes, and tones that a writer simply cannot achieve without</u> <u>stepping outside of his "head."</u> Alcohol can help you do that. In every ancient culture, shamans and storytellers used herbs, fungi, and even fermented goat's balls to "take a trip" and see things in a different light—or, as Hemingway described it, "get tight." Think of booze as a Sherpa who can lead you outside your conventional mind: up a mountain of colorful ideas named ... Jägermeister Mountain. Sorry, we're actually a bit tipsy right now.

Daily, consistent use of alcohol (and/or 'shrooms) can open up the wonderful hinterlands of your brain! There are ideas lurking in the corners of your mind. TAP THEM—as you would tap a marvelous keg of frothy lager! Fight your writer's block with PLENTY OF FLUIDS. Ask the beautiful notions hiding in your mind to come out and dance with your fingertips across the keys of your MacBook Pro.

Writing and Drinking FACT

Number of times *Casablanca* was written during Prohibition: ZERO.

Number of times *Casablanca* was written *not* during Prohibition: ONE.

Alcohol wins—hands down!

Whether it's a "light buzz" or what we hard drinkers call "the shit-'n'-spins," it can be just what the doctor ordered* to get your creative juices flowing!

Let's look at more SCIENTIFIC EVIDENCE by comparing one of America's greatest writers, Ernest Hemingway, to America's NON-DRINKING AMISH COMMUNITY. Hemingway has <u>ten great novels to his credit</u>. Those Amish teetotalers: nothing but beautiful rocking chairs.

DO YOU WANT TO GET SERIOUS ABOUT YOUR WRITING, OR DO YOU WANT TO MAKE BEAUTIFUL ROCKING CHAIRS? Okay, maybe this is a bad example. But you get the point. <u>Hemingway loved to get drunk—and he could write like a mofo.</u> (And he was VERY POPULAR with the ladies. If you haven't read *The Garden of Eden*, it has a full-on three-way sex scene—nice job, Ernie!)

But what about William Faulkner? you ask. FORGET IT. Bill Faulkner would get hammered like a two-cent nail—and it led to some of the most beautiful and confusing novels our language has ever produced. As a reference, the passage below is from Faulkner's final draft of *The Sound and the Fury*, written, probably, during a drinking binge:

> Through the fence, between the curling flower spaces, I could see them hitting. They were coming toward where the flag was and I went along the fence. Luster was hunting in the grass by the flower tree.

AND A PASSAGE FROM HIS "SOBER" DRAFT, written when Faulkner was on the wagon:

> Through the fence, between the fence . . . sticks. You know—the sticks that you make fence out of . . . Anyway—through the fence poles, I could see them golfing. My name is Benji. My mom thinks I'm retarded.

GOOD HEAVENS, what a difference! Sometimes it takes a couple gin and tonics to come up with great things. Like making up a county called Yoknapatawpha County! *Yoknapatawpha!?!* That's not a word, Mr. Faulkner—*not in any language other than drunkish!*

---

*This statement also has not been verified by a medical doctor.

William Faulkner took a compulsion to write and a compulsion to drink and changed the American novel forever. And without hard alcohol, it's possible that Hemingway might not have ended up where he did: <u>with ten great novels to his name and on top of the world!</u>*

So go grab your writing glass by the stem (so as not to warm up the wine!) and remember those wonderful words of wisdom:

In vino, veritas! Which means . . . something in Latin.

---

*Ernest Hemingway blew his brains out with a shotgun in Ketchum, Idaho. Not technically "the top of the world."

FINAL THOUGHTS

The best part about being a professional screenwriter is—*being a professional screenwriter.**

---

*The SECOND BEST thing is the money. We can't stress this enough: HAVING LOTS OF MONEY IS REALLY, REALLY GREAT. There are TONS of fun things that you can do with money! Things like—create a Hybrid Lamborghini and fill it with candy. Be the first person to have sex with two stewardesses on the moon. Form a reenactment group that reenacts battles from *Lord of the Rings* and *Tron*. Create a HOAX. "Fix" an event in the Olympics. Hire a fifty-year-old stuntwoman to walk around with you dressed as your mother—throw her down stairs and through barroom windows! Hire Barbra Streisand to sing at your birthday party, then sit in the front row and yell "Booo!" Stage a coup. Sponsor TWO female roller derby teams and have them battle to the death. Build a TIE Fighter that really flies. (Dude—can you imagine how much tail you'd get at Comic-Con?) Go to Monte Carlo, put it all on black, and double it. Fly to New Orleans EVERY DAY for breakfast beignets. Sponsor your own "Batman"—you know, have some little kid's parents murdered in front of him, then supply him with the finest in martial arts training and crime-fighting equipment. "Gaslight" an enemy. Build a full-size catapult in your yard, just to keep your neighbors on their toes. Build a sex robot. Rent Disneyland for a day and play Most Dangerous Game with the dude who plays Tarzan. Buy a street in Paris and name it Jar Jar Binks Street. Go to Vegas, put it all on black, and double it. Build a UFO. Make your own Zhang Ziyi out of marzipan! Spend $10 million on outdoor Christmas decorations and keep them up ALL YEAR ROUND. Start a cavalry unit. "Gaslight" a friend. Buy the island RIGHT next to Johnny Depp's and do a giant outdoor Pink Floyd laser-light show every night. Put on a nonmusical version of *Cats*. Fake your own death, then jump out of your coffin at the funeral and yell "Boo!" Pay someone to break a world record—one of the gross ones that involves eating large amounts of something weird. Go to Laughlin, put it all on black, and double it. Open a Hotel for Imaginary Animals. Perfect teleportation. Stage a giant pie fight in Harrods' food hall (without telling Harrods). Build some kinda James-Bond-villain-y super

You're PAID to sit around and think up stuff. How cool is that? It's the most satisfying thing in the world. *If you're a writer, that is.* If you're a writer, <u>it's what you'd be doing anyway</u>, even when you were *supposed* to be serving lattes or flying a 747. And remember:

Hollywood will always need writers.

Actors can be replaced with CGI. Studio heads last two years. Without scripts, directors can't do shit.

Go west, young man.

Take your laptop, hop a freight car, and head out to the Dream Factory—where the streets are paved with gold! (Not true.) The last piece of advice we'll leave you with is this:

As a writer in Hollywood, there are many things that you cannot control. Decisions affecting your career will be made while you are not in the room, all the time. There will always be writers who are more connected than you. There's nothing you can do about that. *Don't worry about the things you can't control.* Worry about things you can. <u>The one thing you can control is this:</u>

You can always work harder than the next guy. So <u>DO</u>.

weapon. Buy airtime on local TV and start running attack ads on some random dude. Get your own *Island of Dr. Moreau* thing going. Throw a parade for yourself EVERY DAY. Put a bounty on somebody's head! Stage a giant bar brawl with 100 stuntmen at the Rainbow Room (without telling the Rainbow Room). Build the world's most expensive helicopter, INSIST on piloting it for its maiden flight, then CRASH on takeoff. (Think of the YouTube hits!) Buy $100,000 plates at political fund-raisers then show up in a KKK uniform. Buy a house in Beverly Hills, tear it down, and put up an Aerosmith-themed water park. Meet interesting people. Go interesting places. See the world! Live! Love! Feel pain and joy and loss and victory and defeat! Or—bite the bullet, be the guy who finally DOES IT: pour your money into science, get the best minds in the world together to work on it, and FINALLY be the guy who invents a device that lets us talk with mice.

Now—stop thinking about it, stop talking about it. Pull your head out of the bong and start writing a spec. What the hell are you waiting for?

—Robert Ben Garant, Thomas Lennon
(Dictated, but not read. On speakerphone
from their separate writing compounds in
Barcelona, Spain, and on Hiva Oa, in the
French Marquesas.)

APPENDIX

SAMPLE OUTLINES

1. *Reno S.O.S.!*
2. *Scouts' Honor*
3. *Instant Monsters*

We've included these three outlines so you can see how much detail we put into them and you should put into *yourself.* As you can see, we do all the heavy-lifting creative work in the outline stage. So when it's time to write the script, all that's left to fill in is the jokes and dialogue. With this technique, writing screenplays can be easy!

Reno S.O.S.!

Reno 911! fans often ask us, "Are you going to make a sequel to *Reno 911!: Miami?*"

The answer, in a word, is *no.*

Why? The answer, in a word, is *money.*

The answer, in twenty-two words, is—we are not going to make a sequel to *Reno 911!: Miami*, because *Reno 911!: Miami* didn't make enough money to warrant a sequel. (Also because we talked about the sequel beforehand, waking up the box-office elves.)

Oh, it made money. It only cost 9 million bucks to produce, and it made about $22 million. Tons more on DVD. If you make $12 million bucks in any other business, you're a genius. Not in the movie biz.

Why didn't it make more? The biggest reason is that we made an R-rated movie for a TV show whose fans are mostly fourteen years old. Big mistake. We can't tell you how many kids said to us, "I loved your movie, man. Me and my friends bought tickets to *Ghostrider,* and snuck in to see it. It was awesome." We have yet to receive a letter of thanks from Nicholas Cage. We assume it got lost in the mail.

But—expectations for *Reno 911!: Miami* were very high. It tested through the roof. So—we were commissioned to write a sequel, before the first one was even out in theaters. (See Chapter 31, "Sequels!" <u>And NEVER, NEVER, NEVER discuss a sequel until the first movie has opened. It's just bad luck.</u>)

So—with 20th Century Fox's kind permission, we have included, in this book, the complete "scriptment" for the Reno movie sequel: *Reno S.O.S.!*

This would have been as much of a script as we ever wrote—*Reno 911!* and *Reno 911!: Miami* were improvised, based on "scriptments" like this.

Read. Enjoy. And if you and your improv buddies want to go out and film this yourselves—20th Century Fox's lawyers will crush you.

RENO: S.O.S.!

The (never-produced) *Reno 911!: Miami* Sequel

Outline

by

Robert Ben Garant

&

Thomas Lennon

FADE IN:

EXT. RENO NEVADA — "SKYLINE" — MORNING

TITLE CARD READS: Reno, Nevada. 5:35 a.m. 1989.

"Simply Irresistible" by Robert Palmer blasts over establishing shots: We see the "skyline" of Reno, Nevada — a small, dusty town nestled at the base of the Sierras. We see posters for a Milli Vanilli concert; a newspaper taped over a broken window reports the fall of the Berlin Wall; TVs in a pawn shop window show ads for *The Arsenio Hall Show.*

INT. JIM DANGLE'S BATHROOM — CONTINUOUS

JIM DANGLE, young, fresh and optimistic, is pumping iron in front of the mirror of a large, elegant bathroom. He combs his mustache, checks his highlights. He likes what he sees and turns up his radio: "Simply Irresistible" plays even louder.

INT. JIM DANGLE'S BEDROOM — CONTINUOUS

Jim's wall is covered with medals and citations from the Arkansas State Police. Half dressed, in his uniform shirt and thong, he opens a small box and pulls out: brand new Lieutenant bars. He beams with pride and pins them on his collar for the first time.

Dangle's wife, DEBBIE DANGLE, enters, hugs him, and tells him she's proud — in a sultry bedroom voice. She's in lingerie, flirty and very physical, and about 150 pounds overweight. She tells him that her "Bad Lieutenant" is gonna get a special treat when he gets home from his first day at his new department. (Dangle is still very much in the closet.) He gives her a uncomfortable smile,

"growls" back, and tells her he can't wait.
He puts on his uniform pants — <u>long pants</u>,
and heads to work, giving Debbie a macho swat
on the ass.

EXT. JIM DANGLE'S HOUSE — MOMENTS LATER

A minimansion in a nice neighborhood. Dangle
climbs into a glistening new Miata and peels
out. His license plate reads: LADEZMAN.
Debbie "flashes" him from the door . . . <u>a lot</u>
<u>of flesh</u>. It's horrifying and causes a CAR
CRASH in the street.

EXT. RENO SHERIFF'S DEPARTMENT — MOMENTS LATER

The same old Reno sheriff's station, except
that its sign is sky blue neon. Dangle pulls
in, Wham blasting.

INT. MORNING BRIEFING ROOM — CONTINUOUS

There are several local and national news
cameras in the room, recording the meeting:
Other than that, it's the same old briefing
room, except for a few "JUST SAY NO" posters
and a large banner declaring a WAR ON DRUGS.

We see our Reno deputies circa '89: GARCIA'S
hair isn't grey. JONES has a Kid 'n Play
flattop. JUNIOR isn't wearing sunglasses or
Kevlar, and his hair is in a horrible mullet.
There is no KIMBALL and no WILLIAMS. And —
CLEMMY is a fresh-faced sexy blond 20-year-old
(played by a 20-year-old actress) . . . but she
is very hungover, drinking an Alka-Seltzer.
(We already can see where she is headed.)

Running the briefing — Sergeant TRUDY
WIEGEL. She's well spoken, intelligent, and
authoritative as she demonstrates how to
assemble a Glock in .8 second, expecting the
other deputies to be able to do the same.

They tell her with genuine respect: sir-yes-sir. Trudy's a total pro and not bad-looking, either.

Trudy announces, "As you know, the notorious serial killer known only as Dr. White, wanted for eating over seventy victims in Thailand, has returned to Washoe County, where he is still at large. So the Reno Sheriff's Department has brought in a new Lieutenant to head the case — a highly decorated supercop from Arkansas who most people think will one day be president. It gives me great pleasure to introduce their new fearless leader: Jim Dangle."

Dangle enters, gives Clemmy a macho slap on the ass, gives Jones a lingering hello, tells Junior to get a haircut, and starts the meeting. He gives a macho pep talk, mostly to the news cameras. He tells them that even though it's a high-profile case that'll no doubt get national press, for him it isn't about fame. He knows that years from now, after he's caught this killer, he'll look around his fancy office, no matter where it is — Washington, D.C., or Geneva — and he'll look back and say, "We did it. The Reno Sheriff's Department didn't screw this up. And that's why I'm where I am today."

CUT TO:

TITLE CARD: Present Day.

INT. DANGLE'S TINY, RUNDOWN TRAILER — MORNING

Dangle is woken by his alarm clock. He looks around his crappy trailer, depressed.

The trailer is tiny and ratty, with posters of Broadway shows and Bruce Lee with his shirt off.

The bright-eyed young Lieutenant is long
gone. He's startled to find JOE THE CAMERAMAN
filming him and accidentally fires off
a bullet at him . . . sorry. He lights a
cigarette and pops *Buns of Steel* into his old
VCR. He smokes, depressed, as he does a few
halfhearted butt-clench moves, then there's
a horrible CRUNCH as the VCR shreds the
VHS tape. He finishes his cigarette, makes
himself an Irish coffee, and squeezes into
his tiny shorts. It takes a few attempts — we
see the whole process. It's not pretty. He
grabs his bike (which is bike-chained to his
fridge) and heads to work, miserable.

EXT. VIRGINIA STREET — DAY

Dangle skids to a halt in downtown Reno, a
street lined with casinos and pawn shops,
underneath a neon sign that reads THE BIGGEST
LITTLE CITY IN THE WORLD.

Dangle confesses that even he doesn't know
what "biggest little city in the world"
means. He tells the camera that as a civil
servant (who is apparently gonna be stuck in
the Sierras until he dies, like the Donner
Party), he wants to show people the "good
side" of Reno and dispel a few negative
myths. First, that Reno is the meth capital
of the world. It's not — that's Mojave,
California. Reno's #2, and as number 2, they
try harder. He says that Reno isn't as crime-
ridden as people think; just as he says that,
a GUY runs out of nowhere and steals his
bike.

Okay, it's *Go Time*. He gives chase on foot
and is soon out of breath. He sees: a gang
of ten-year-old KIDS on little Huffy bikes.
He flashes his badge and commandeers a bike,
shoving a kid to the ground. He does a few

"fancy" bike tricks and gives chase. And as
he does . . .

He gives us a high-speed bike tour of Reno.
He points out the scenic Riverwalk (that you
should NOT walk on at night, unless you're
begging for a scenic Riverside rapin'). He
points out the friendly and not-so-friendly
LOCALS. He cuts through the Bowling Hall of
Fame. He points out the town's best Topless
Burger Hut (the waitresses are topless,
the beers are bottomless) . . . where he sees
KIMBALL, who'd called in sick that day. Huh?
Then he realizes that someone behind him is
shooting him with paintballs — the kid whose
bike he stole is after him, with a gang of
paintball gun-armed TEN-YEAR-OLDS on Huffys.

Junior, responding to his calls for backup,
pulls along side Dangle in a speeding squad
car and tells him, "Don't worry — we got a
roadblock up ahead — " CRASH. Junior smashes
right into the roadblock, leaving Dangle
alone in the pursuit.

He passes TERRY, who may or may not be giving
a tug job in an alley. He cuts through the
El Dorado casino (where Clemmy and Williams
are gambling) and through a strip club (where
Jones and Garcia are drinking). All of them
called in sick today . . .

The bike thief makes it across train tracks
JUST as a train goes by . . . shit. But Dangle
sees a perfect ramp to jump the train. He
gives up . . . but no — he backs across the
street, eyes the ramp, pedals as fast as
he can — and is hit unceremoniously by a
truck on the cross street before he even gets
to the ramp. The kids on Huffys take their
bike back and pummel him with paintballs. He
lies on the road in pain.

FLASH BACK TO:

EXT. DARK PARKING LOT OF A RUNDOWN
LAUNDROMAT — NIGHT — 1989

(All-in-one shot — à la The International
Inn's Romance Ballet in *Reno 911!:* Miami —
the Reno deputies go undercover on an all-
night stakeout. Passing the long hours, they
get to know each other for the first time —
and the seeds of their "romances" are born.)

Dangle has set up an all-night stakeout at
a Laundromat in the bad part of town, where
Dr. White has abducted two victims in the
past. They take turns, in pairs and in
civilian clothes, sitting in a car in the
dark parking lot, doing laundry in the mat,
and keeping watch on the Laundromat's roof.

Sitting in the parked car, Trudy and Dangle
get to know each other for the first time.
Dangle, playing "straight" (and *overdoing*
it a bit) talks about men and women on the
force — the chemistry, the sexual tension.
Wiegel is a true professional — but she's
intrigued by his theories and constant macho
advances. Eventually, she points out that
they look a little suspicious sitting in a
parked car. Maybe they should . . . pretend to
make out? They do.

In the Laundromat, Jones is pretending to do
laundry, and Young Clemmy is trying to get
him to fool around. He resists — not out of
professionalism but out of his "don't shit
where you eat" theory. Then a young mom from
the neighborhood comes in to do her laundry.
She's young and hot and slim — she introduces
herself to Jones: her name is RAINEESHA
WILLIAMS. Much to Clemmy's dismay, Jones
seems very into her. Even after she brings in

her two young kids. Clemmy leaves to check in with the deputies on the . . .

ROOF. Garcia and Junior keep watch. Clemmy climbs up the fire escape to join them — with a six-pack of beer. She comes on to Garcia, who is oblivious to her advances. He's too into the chase, the stakeout — he likes being a cop. Clemmy suggests that Junior should split and relieve the folks in . . .

The car. When Junior shows up, Dangle and Wiegel are making out hot and heavy. Dangle EAGERLY lets Junior relieve him and exits, to check out the laundry mat. Alone, Junior suggests that he and Wiegel make out. She jujitsus him.

In the Laundromat, Dangle sees Jones. Macho, bragging about making out with Wiegel — he strips in front of Jones — "to wash his clothes." Uncomfortable with Dangle's not-so-subtle advances, Jones soon escapes out, to the roof . . .

On the roof, Clemmy is playing strip "I never," but Garcia isn't biting. Jones climbs up onto the roof and joins in, and is followed by Williams, who's turned on that Jones is a "cop on a stakeout." Williams and young Clemmy compete for Jones's attention. Garcia leaves, still oblivious, to go relieve . . .

Wiegel in the car. Garcia and Junior sit in the car, staking out. Wiegel heads into the Laundromat, walking in on Dangle, nude. She thinks it's a play for her. She resists, briefly, then throws herself at him.

On the roof, Junior tries to join "I never" just as it's breaking up, and Jones and Williams head down. Junior tries to keep it going with Clemmy. Clemmy says SURE . . . But passes out drunk. Junior "keeps it going" anyway . . . until Dangle comes up, still naked, looking for Jones.

In the car, Jones and Williams are making out hot and heavy in the backseat, with Garcia, oblivious, in front. Jones is about to close the deal — when suddenly Raineesha has to leave. She's late, for work! She's a model and has a gig. She leaves before Jones even gets her name. The first time that's EVER happened to Jones.

Wiegel is all alone in the Laundromat. And she is ABDUCTED by a tall man in a raincoat. No one even sees it happen.

Dangle wanders in looking for her . . . And the phone rings. Terrified, he answers: a voice tells him, "I have your sergeant. She's across the street, at midnight — I eat her heart." Across the street — is the creepy DONNER PASS MOTEL. The voice on the phone laughs . . .

FLASH-FORWARD TO:

EXT. RENO SHERIFF'S DEPARTMENT — DAY — THE PRESENT

Establishing shot of the Reno Sheriff's Department.

INT. MORNING BRIEFING ROOM — CONTINUOUS

Tired and despondent, Dangle reads the day's briefings. Same old same old, until . . . he reads a bulletin from Carson, in shock: DR. WHITE, the serial killer, has finally been apprehended after seventeen years. He is going to be extradited to Thailand — and the

Reno Sheriff's Department is in charge of escorting him there to stand trial.

Dangle sees this as the chance to redeem himself — from whatever went wrong in '89. He vows that this time, Dr. White will not get away. The other deputies are psyched! They get to fly first class! And for some reason, Junior already has quite a selection of Bangkok sex slave brochures: "Be careful, though, my buddy T-Bone got a wife there, and found out six weeks later it was a guy." (The other deputies ask . . . how could he not know? Junior tells them — T-Bone only does it doggy style.)

EXT. AIRPORT — NIGHT

The deputies wait on the tarmac for the arrival of Dr. White. It looks like a scene from *Silence of the Lambs.* It is tense, and the deputies' eyes are filled with fear . . . we go in tight on Junior's glasses.

                                        FLASHBACK TO:

EXT. DONNER MOTEL — NIGHT — 1989

TITLE CARD: 1989.

Junior stands at attention in the parking lot, without his shades as Dangle gives orders: "Who here's the best shot?" Junior says, "Me, sir." Dangle tosses him a pair of NIGHT-VISION GOGGLES, incredibly sensitive to any light. Junior puts the goggles on and expertly assembles an ASSAULT RIFLE. Dangle says: "Let's move out, and remember, Dr. White is smart, so watch for traps!" They move in stealthily, like the *Mission Impossible* team. They kick down a door — nothing. Another door — nothing. They hear strange MOANS coming from a third door.

Junior kicks it down, and — <u>a blinding light FLASHES right in his face</u>.

Junior screams and <u>opens fire</u> into the room. When he's out of ammo, Dangle flips on the light. In the room is a sexy BLACK STRIPPER doing a show for two JAPANESE MEN in tighty-whities with a Polaroid. (Junior unloaded a full clip and missed all of them.) Not a trap. Just a stripper in a Josephine Baker banana skirt and fig-leaf pasties and two Japanese dudes in their underwear.

Dangle pulls the goggles off Junior and checks his eyes: he's blind. "Don't worry," Dangle says, "it's just temporary." They head out to look for Wiegel.

                    FLASH-FORWARD TO:

EXT. AIRPORT — NIGHT — PRESENT DAY

Junior tries to light a cigarette, but he keeps missing — it wasn't temporary. He can still barely see. The wail of arriving sirens snaps Junior out of his reverie. A motorcade pulls up, leading a white State Prison van.

Surrounded by well-armed GUARDS with M-16s, Dr. White is delivered by the State Prison OFFICERS, strapped to a gurney, in Hannibal Lecter headgear: We only see his creepy eyes, not his face. Dangle eyes him, scared but determined to do his duty. The prison officers tease Dangle, saying that he'd better not let Dr. White get away again this time.

The deputies escort Dr. White onto the plane in manacles.

CUT TO:

INT. AIRPLANE — NIGHT

The deputies fly first class — and love it!
They've never seen a hot towel, and they grab
handfuls of the free headphones and cashews.
Dr. White is immobile, manacled, still in the
protective mask. Since the prisoner can have
anything he wants, they order "him" a lot
of shrimp cocktails and Wiegel orders "him"
Beaches on DVD.

Dangle sits beside Dr. White, telling him
that he's glad he's finally caught and Dangle
can now close the book on the biggest failure
of his life — the one that got him stuck in
Reno. Now maybe he can move on.

As the lights go out for the night and the
stewardess passes out blankets — the idea
comes up: this may be the only shot they have
in their lives to enter the fabled "Mile
High Club." Wiegel gives Dangle the eye . . .
he shudders and tells her how unprofessional
that behavior is. Then he eyes Jones, who
eyes Clemmy. The Reno love octangle weaves
its creepy web. Finally, Jones sneaks out of
his seat and heads to the bathroom, signaling
into the dark, "Follow me."

INT. AIRPLANE BATHROOM — MOMENTS LATER

Jones waits in the bathroom — and a moment
later, Clemmy joins him. They try to figure
out how to get romantic in such a tiny little
room; then Williams squeezes in. She thought
Jones was signaling *her*. Jones and Clemmy try
to explain that they *accidentally* came in
together. Then Dangle enters, excited. Then
he says he also came in by mistake.

The plane hits turbulence, and the pilot announces that he has lit the fasten seat belts sign. "Please return to your seats." Then Wiegel comes in, after Dangle. Garcia enters, thinking Clemmy was waiting for him. Kimball comes in to legitimately go 10-200. Finally, Junior enters — he was going to try to enter the Mile High Club "flying solo." (That counts too.) The plane is shaken by turbulence, but they're all so packed together they barely budge, like the Marx Brothers' "stateroom" scene.

They realize — "Who's watching the prisoner?" SUDDENLY they're shaken like a cocktail shaker as the jet hits horrendous turbulence. They hear screams and the whine of the engines — they are rattled up and down. There is a JOLT — and all is still and silent. What happened? They slowly open the bathroom door . . . and blazing SUNLIGHT streams into the bathroom.

EXT. BEAUTIFUL TROPICAL BEACH — CONTINUOUS

It's like the Kansas-to-Oz transition in *The Wizard of Oz* — outside the bathroom is a fantastic, sunlit beach. They step out — it's like a dream. They look at the sun, the surf, the palm trees . . . it's a picture-perfect paradise . . .

. . . until the CO-PILOT of the plane runs by, <u>completely on fire</u>. The deputies try to put him out and finally wrangle him into the sea. He sighs, relieved, and thanks them . . . and is immediately CRUSHED by a piece of fuselage that falls down out of the sky, obliterating him.

In shock, the deputies look around the beach. The plane actually made a pretty good emergency landing. It sits almost intact, halfway on the beach. The steward and stewardess help passengers off the plane, down the INFLATABLE SLIDE/RAFT, trying to be cheery, through their forced smiles. Other passengers are picking up supplies from the surf.

Dangle looks at the cameraman and tells him, "You know what this means, don't you? This documentary's probably gotta get an Academy Award." The deputies lend a hand, and we . . .

DISSOLVE TO:

EXT. BEACH — HOURS LATER

The rattled, tattered SURVIVORS are gathered on the beach. The supplies are stacked in a pile. The pilot, CAPTAIN RICK (Chris Tallman) is a macho, no-nonsense all-American type with a *can-do attitude*. He bosses everybody around, and people tend to do what he says. He tells the assembled survivors that there's no need to panic: they were on course, they sent a distress signal, they're in the flight path for Bangkok. Rescue should be coming soon. The best thing to do is stay calm, and honestly enjoy ourselves. Think of it as an unscheduled vacation, courtesy of FunJet Airlines.

We meet the other survivors:

FLIGHT ATTENDANT STEVE AUSTIN (Jack Plotnick): A bitchy flight attendant who's aware that he has the same name as TV's Six Million Dollar Man. He remains reluctantly attentive to the travelers, even though they've crashed, seeing if they want any nuts, etc.

He is assisted by TWO SEXY FLIGHT ATTENDANTS (Irina Voronina and Verina Marcel), whose uniforms were severely *abbreviated* in the crash.

They also are lucky enough to have a doctor: DOCTOR JOHN WELLS. A brilliant surgeon with movie-star good looks. And as a veteran medic from both Gulf wars, he's pretty sure he can get the survivors though this.

And 15 assorted PASSENGERS: men and women, Asian and white tourists, a cute girl with a yappy poodle, etc. Everyone's in tatters and bruised. There's only one serious injury:

EXT. FUSELAGE — MOMENTS LATER

. . . A. D. MILES: A chipper, Boy Scout-like passenger who has been impaled by a large piece of the fuselage. He's alive, but Dr. Wells says he can't be moved: a large piece of steel is sticking straight through the middle of him, pinning him to the plane. He's in remarkably upbeat spirits. He says he was going to China to scatter his mom's ashes — he clutches the urn close to him at all times.

Dangle takes charge and starts issuing orders: they need to explore the island, find food and shelter, and someone needs to figure out how to make coconuts into suntan oil, or they're all gonna burn and get all peely . . .

228

The captain asks, "Who the hell put you in charge?" *Captain* Rick's got a higher rank: captain to Jim's lowly *lieutenant*. Dangle points out that he's a captain on FunJet Airlines, not the *Marine Corps*.

They fight over who's in charge, and the survivors take sides. Captain Rick claims that as a captain in midjourney, he can even marry people (and possibly threatens to marry two of the survivors, against their will).

Captain Rick asks how they are on supplies: *A-ha!* Dangle already had his deputies gather them and take inventory. He announces, taking charge again, "The good news is — we have a doctor and enough fuel and food for a week, all stacked right over there." But — "we have only one flare." He holds it up. "So we have to be careful with it."

Then BLAM. Dangle accidentally fires the flare — straight into the pile of fuel, igniting all the food and the devilishly handsome Dr. John Wells in one HUGE blast . . . oops.

All eyes glare at Dangle. Captain Rick asks Dangle, "Where the hell's your prisoner, anyway?" The deputies realize — *Where is Dr. White?* They look for him . . . he's nowhere to be found. But they do find his "Hannibal Lecter" MASK, with his manacles — broken. He's escaped.

They come to a terrifying revelation: <u>They've never seen his face</u>. He was in a mask. No one knows what he looks like. He could be any one of them. They look around at each other. Any of the men COULD BE THE KILLER.

                                    FLASHBACK TO:

INT. DONNER MOTEL — NIGHT — 1989

Young Clemmy removes her T-shirt and tears it into bandages for Junior's eyes. She puts her uniform back on, losing a button: now her shirt's half open, showing off her leopard-print push-up bra — it's the look she'll keep later in life.

The sexy black STRIPPER in the banana skirt and fig leaf pasties rushes over to the officers.

"Don't arrest me. This is not what I normally do," she says, "I got a kid to feed." Dangle asks her name. "Williams, Raineesha Williams. Spelled the normal way, with two e's." Dangle says, "Show's over, sister. But we could use your help — we got a man down."

Raineesha says, "No, thanks." Jones enters. This is her "modeling" gig? It looks like fate is throwing them together.

                              MOMENTS LATER:

INT. DONNER MOTEL — HALLWAY

The deputies are creeping through the motel, Young Clemmy with her new cleavage look, Junior blinded, holding on to sexy, half-naked Williams. Junior keeps reaching out to feel Raineesha (as a guide, not to cop a feel. Raineesha asks, "Then why do you got boner?" Junior: "Adrenaline.")

Dangle's worried about Wiegel. Garcia says, "Don't worry, she's a law enforcement machine. If there's one person who can hold her own against this psycho — it's Trudy Wiegel." She's brilliant.

230

                              FLASH-FORWARD TO:

EXT. BEACH — PRESENT DAY

Trudy's trying to open a coconut with her bare teeth, knocking it against them like a brain-damaged chimp. Dangle takes it away from her before she hurts herself.

Dangle takes charge of his deputies,
determined to find Dr. White. He divides his
deputies into teams — and they'll start the
search in the morning.

EXT. MAKESHIFT CAMP — DAY

Captain Rick addresses the passengers. He
thinks the mainland is 15 miles west. With
no supplies, they decide to send someone out
on the plane's inflatable RAFT. The current
should take it straight there. They draw
straws: Jones and Garcia are chosen.

EXT. SEASIDE — LATER

Jones bids a tearful farewell to Raineesha.
"It's a big ocean, maybe I won't make it back
alive, maybe this is our last chance to get
freaky." She asks him, "How many girls have
you used this line on?" He admits — all of
them. "It worked every time. Honestly, I'm a
little exhausted." Williams almost goes with
him — but no. She'll save it — "until you get
back — with help."

Jones and Garcia take half of the survivors'
water and head out to sea on the inflatable
raft, with a makeshift sail.

EXT. THE SEASIDE — SUNSET

Junior is in the shallows spearfishing, like
a castaway. He concentrates . . . and he stabs —
his own foot. He holds it up, and the spear
has gone right through his foot.

                              NIGHT FALLS

EXT. AROUND THE CAMPFIRE — NIGHT

They sit around in silence, worried. But when
they look up, the stars are quite beautiful.

Some of the deputies talk — they always
wanted to take a vacation like this, but
they never could afford it. They spot some
constellations in the sky: real and imagined
(Orion, Dick Tracy, the Jackalope). Then
Kimball complains, "Doesn't it suck that it's
never peaceful? No matter where you go, some
loud jet ruins the peace and quiet." Then
they realize . . . that's a jet!

They rush to light the huge logs they'd laid
out on the beach to spell SOS. But they knock
the S as they light it — the logs roll out
of line, and they're blazing: too hot to
rearrange. They struggle with it, then look
at what they've formed. Instead of an S,
they've made a huge, fiery swastika. The jet
flies on, ignoring their Nazi message.

EXT. MAKESHIFT CAMP — NIGHT

They've made little shelters of blankets and
palm fronds. Under Dangle's orders, they're
gonna take shifts keeping watch, in case
Dr. White returns. Junior gets first watch.

Junior watches over camp. The sexy
stewardesses say good night as they turn
in. He turns to watch their tent. The
stewardesses go behind the makeshift barrier
made of blankets that gives them privacy.
But the torch they have lit inside, casts a
perfect, sexy silhouette on the sheet.

He watches as they strip. He goes away,
giving them privacy? No, he was just getting
his camera phone to film it.

In silhouette: one helps the other unzip
and take off her dress. Then one gives the
other a shoulder massage. Then one bends
down and "goes down" on the other. It's a
fun, giggly orgy in silhouette. Junior looks

around — EVERY GUY, and Kimball is sitting
with him, watching.

The action on the silhouette peaks. When
their blanket falls: the girls are actually
standing several feet apart; one is washing
her hair, the other is bent over packing.
They're not having sex at all. The guys are
stunned, embarrassed . . .

EXT. DANGLE'S SHELTER — NIGHT

Dangle sits and watches the jungle — he knows
Dr. White is out there . . . somewhere. He
tries to stay alert, he puts his inflatable,
U-shaped airplane pillow around his neck,
and . . . falls asleep.

As he sleeps, a wise VOICE speaks to him,
inside his head. It asks him, What are
you afraid of? Are you truly afraid of
Dr. White — or are you afraid of failing
to find Dr. White? Dangle says, yes — that
actually IS what he's afraid of. Then the
voice says, "What you're truly afraid of — IS
YOURSELF."

Dangle wakes up — and sitting across from him
is: a mysterious and wise Chinese man, who
looks like and is dressed like BRUCE LEE.
(JASON SCOTT LEE). Dangle isn't sure if he's
dreaming or not.

Dangle asks him what he wants. The Dream
Spirit tells him that *what he wants is not
important. What IS important is what Dangle
wants.* Dangle says he wants . . . *a box of
Girl Scout cookies. The minty ones. No, the
Samoas.* The Dream Spirit tells him he is not
here to grant three wishes. Besides, *the true
Samoas of happiness do not come from the Girl*

Scouts. They come from within, from knowing who you are.

Dangle's a little bummed that he doesn't get to spend the dream eating Girl Scout cookies with a hot Chinese dude. The Dream Spirit runs off into the jungle.

Dangle shrugs and goes back to bed. Then the Dream Spirit smacks him awake and drags him out of bed. "What part of 'I'm taking you on a Mythic Journey didn't you understand?'"

EXT. CLIFF — NIGHT

The Spirit leads him to a cliff for the first "Test of Character." Thus, Dangle begins his Batman-Begins-esque spiritual journey. The Spirit Guide hands him a bamboo staff and squares off against him, like a kung fu master. So — the Spirit Guide hits Dangle with his bamboo staff. Many times. Really hard. The Spirit Guide says, "When your mind has power over the pain in your body, then you can lead these people." So Dangle tasers his Dream Spirit, who drops unconscious like a sack of potatoes.

EXT. DANGLE'S SHELTER — SUNRISE

Dangle wakes up with a start. Beside him, under the airline blanket — is TRUDY WIEGEL. He screams. She wakes up and screams — they scream until . . . Dangle realizes that someone else in camp is screaming. Oh, no.

FLASHBACK TO:

INT. DONNER MOTEL — 1989

The deputies listen in the motel: Trudy Wiegel's SCREAMS are coming from the air-conditioning duct. From the sound of her

234

terror, Dr. White is doing something *horrible*
to her. The deputies hear Dr. White's
terrifying voice echoing through the ducts
too. (As well as Dr. White and Wiegel
arguing — it sounds like she's getting on his
nerves.) The deputies can't tell where the
screams are coming from.

Dangle has an idea: he and Jones will strip
down naked, oil up, and crawl through the
ducts to follow the screams. Jones doesn't
understand why they have to get <u>naked</u>? Seems
like they could fit in the ducts just fine
with their clothes on. Dangle checks . . .
well, yes, they do fit, but <u>just barely</u>.
Jones checks: no, not just *barely*, they fit
fine. Okay, fine — me and Jones will crawl
through the ducts <u>fully dressed</u> and find
Wiegel — the rest of you, stick together
and watch your backs. More SCREAMS flash us
forward . . .

BACK TO:

EXT. MAKESHIFT CAMP — THE PRESENT

Kimball runs out to tell the groggy-eyed
survivors: she sneaked into Clemmy's shelter
this morning, and — <u>Clemmy's missing</u>. Dr. White
has taken her into the jungle. Wait a minute —
"Why were you sneaking into her tent, Kimball?
And why do you have so much makeup on?"

EXT. MAKESHIFT CAMP — MOMENTS LATER

Dangle has assembled all of the white male
passengers for a Hercule Poirot-style
interrogation. He quizzes them all, to see
who might be Dr. White — it could be any of
them. One GUY'S alibi is that he's flying
to Bangkok to open the largest Hyundai
dealership in Thailand. Somewhere at sea,
he claims, is a 100-foot inflatable gorilla

that says "King Kong sized deals" that'd back him up. Dangle tries to trip them up, but he only manages to confuse himself and the other deputies.

EXT. JUNGLE'S EDGE — LATER

On Dangle's orders, the remaining deputies arm themselves and gear up to hunt Dr. White. They'll work in teams and meet up back here before nightfall.

After much debate about partnering, Dangle and Wiegel search together, as do Junior and Williams, and Kimball goes out on her own.

EXT. RAFT, OUT AT SEA — DAY

Jones and Garcia, crazed by sun and thirst, are at each other's throats: arguing about sailing technique, weather signs, you name it. They've been at sea — almost seven hours. Then they realize they're being watched. They look up — they are in a harbor, surrounded by boats. Tons of Thai FISHERMEN are staring down at them.

INT. CAVE — DAY

Clemmy has been chained to the wall. She's terrified. She screams for help — when a voice chimes out right beside her: "Hey, hot stuff!" It turns out she's not alone. She's chained up next to a crazed castaway who's been chained up there for years: "ISLAND MIKE" . . . left there to die by his ship's crew, who mutinied. He's gone completely insane, living off moss and "cave drippins." There's also a SKELETON chained up next to them, whom Mike refers to as Jimmy: "He's the brains of the outfit." He doesn't seem too pleased to be sharing his cave . . . but

he's glad it's a lovely lady. Clemmy hopes
Dr. White puts her out of her misery soon.

EXT. BEACH — DAY

Williams stares off to sea, looking for Jones
and Garcia. Junior walks up and asks why
the ladies are always so crazy about Jones.
Junior can't even get laid trapped on a
desert island. *I mean, what's he got I ain't
got? Other than charm. And height. And a
fantastic singing voice. And a huge cock.*

She's still holding out for Jones, though?
Jones has banged every chick in Reno. She
admits: she has horrible taste in men. They
keep talking and slowly justify — that since
they ARE literally on a desert island . . .
and they're probably gonna die. And they
MIGHT not ever get laid ever again, and this
humidity has 'em both horny as hell . . .
What the hell are they sitting around NOT
getting laid for? He points out — if you have
horrible taste in men — maybe I'm your guy.
They come to a gentlemen's agreement: what
happens on the island stays on the island.
And if we do die and we meet in Heaven —
pretend you don't know me.

Williams says she'll try anything at the
buffet once. "But if I'm doing this, I'm
gonna pretend you're somebody else."

EXT. JUNGLE — DAY

On the hunt for Dr. White, Dangle has lost
Wiegel. Perhaps on purpose. Then Wiegel runs
out, screaming that she just got bitten by a
snake in the bush.

There's some confusion as to whether she got
bit in her bush. "No, it was her ass, in the
bushes over there." Dangle suspects it's a

not-so-cleverly-disguised attempt to get
him to suck her butt. She swears she's not
faking it, even shows him the wound. He still
doesn't believe her. Then she falls over,
unconscious.

But Captain Rick has heard her cries. He
can't believe that Dangle can be so callous,
letting down a fellow deputy. He heroically
sucks the poison out as fast as he can.
Behind his back, Wiegel shows the two-pronged
fork to the camera that she used to make the
fake "snake bite."

INT. CAVE — DAY

Clemmy is coming up with an escape plan. The
only problem is — Island Mike. He's <u>nuts</u>.
He has a heated argument with the skeleton
chained up next to him and tries to lick
Clemmy's feet.

INT. WILLIAM AND JUNIOR'S TENT — DAY

We find Williams and Junior passing the
afternoon by engaging in a little . . . role
playing: Junior plays the role of a fine
southern gentleman. Williams . . . his sassy
and sexy . . . well, slave. "Lawdy goodness
gracious, Mr. Junior, Suh, you know miss Effy
don't allow me in the house alone with you
menfolk." They seem to be having a pretty
good time in between make-believe mint
juleps.

Captain Rick enters, interrupting just when
it's getting REALLY weird.

EXT. STREETS OF BANGKOK — DAY

Garcia and Jones rush up to a Thai POLICEMAN.
"We are so happy to see you!" They explain
the plane crash, the island, everything . . .

. . . Only to realize, the guy doesn't understand English. Or KNOW anyone who understands English. They see . . .

A PHONE BOOTH! Jones and Garcia rush over. The recording, they are thrilled to hear, is in English: Then it tells them — "Please deposit seventy-eight dollars." They have seven.

                                    NIGHT FALLS

EXT. BEACH — NIGHT

The deputies are frazzled. No help has come, and they've been without food for two days. Williams takes the first watch.

Quietly, as quietly as she can, she sneaks a bag of peanuts out of her pocket. She tries to tear it open . . . the TINY crinkle sound wakes up the whole camp.

The deputies fight over the last bag of peanuts. It turns bad fast. All guns are eventually drawn on each other, like a John Woo movie. Finally Dangle screams "Look what's become of us!" And dumps the peanuts into the sea. The deputies walk away, furious at him. More so when they realize — he was holding out. He had dumped only half the peanuts.

They jump him and wrestle until Captain Rick pulls him off — he knows where more peanuts are.

EXT. FUSELAGE — MOMENTS LATER

The plane's SNACKS are in a cabinet. Unfortunately, the cabinet is DIRECTLY BEHIND A. D. Miles, the guy pinned to the plane. To get to the food, they're gonna have to move him. That means surgically removing him from the plane.

They have a Dr. Wells medical book and kit. And so they all agree to perform one of those horrible "surgery without a doctor" scenes.

A cute Asian girl (the one with the poodle) — built like a bimbo and in a tattered swimsuit — steps up with an armful of tiny booze bottles. She tells them (in Korean with subtitles) that she's head surgeon in Seoul's largest hospital. Just stay out of her way, and she'll save the patient. The deputies take the bottles, all drink a shot, and talk to her like she's five years old. "Thank you. But never, *never* mix tequila and vodka. Now get her outta here, this is no sight for a girl." They get rid of her.

Before the surgery, Kimball asks A.D. where he wants his grandma's urn taken. He gives it to her, and she promises him to sprinkle the ashes in China and say a few words at the ceremony.

They operate . . . (A.D.'s "Body" is built to be realistic, graphic, and gruesome. As gross as the beached whale. It's a rough surgery, grueling and complicated — just as they close one artery, another one sprays in their faces. They have to take out and put back organs, trying to remember where things went in the board game Operation.)

It's intense . . . but it's a success! He lives! Until Junior smacks him on the back, congratulating him. That does him in with a cough of blood.

They look into the SNACKS cabinet. It's empty except for taco mix, taco powder, taco

shells . . . but no real food. They are out of
food.

They go to bed hungry.

INT. MAKESHIFT TENT — NIGHT

Dangle enters, exhausted. He climbs into his
sleeping blanket — only to find that Wiegel
is already there. She acts surprised: "I
think you must be in the wrong tent, Jim."
Dangle has had it. He explodes: "You know I'm
in the right tent, you knew I was coming,
how the hell many times do we have to go
through this charade?" He rants on and on
about how he's sick of her tricks and come-
ons. Wiegel lifts her airline blanket —
Captain Rick is there, glaring at Dangle.
Dangle leaves, embarrassed.

INT. WILLIAM AND JUNIOR'S TENT — NIGHT

We find Junior tied up and begging for his
life. Then we reveal: Williams, a proud
member of the Black Panthers, can't quite
decide how best to "Stick it to this man."
The poor scared honky begs for his life
— he'll do anything, anything, to make
"restitution." She says there actually
is *something* that her fine, strong black
brothers won't do. A place they won't . . .
go. Junior confesses: he's actually *from* the
dirty South. So he don't mind going there.

EXT. DANGLE'S SHELTER — NIGHT

Dangle lies there, confused, humiliated . . .
and *jealous*? When he is suddenly hit with
a bamboo pole. His Spirit Guide, laughing,
drags Dangle out to learn more philosophy and
kung fu. The Spirit Guide hands Dangle what
looks like a hard brown TURD.

The Spirit Guide explains, "This is a "dropping" from a rare island howler monkey. The monkey eats the seeds of a gingko flower, giving its feces psychedelic properties. Eat the turd, and you will find your spirit name."

Dangle eats the crunchy old turd. It takes a long time . . . he can barely choke it down. After he gets it all down, the Spirit Guide says, "Are you retarded? You just ate a monkey turd, given to you by a total stranger. It's not psychedelic — it was a test, to see if you were stupid enough to eat a monkey turd. Which you apparently you are. You've got to smarten up if you're going to lead these people." Jim collapses. The Guide asks him, "What are you afraid of, Jim?"

FLASHBACK TO:

INT. DONNER MOTEL — CRAWL SPACE — 1989

Dangle and Jones climb through the ducts above the ceiling, they can hear Trudy's tortured screams directly below them and Dr. White's evil laughter. Dangle signals to Jones, a complicated system of hand signals. They "hand signal" back and forth for a while, until they realize neither one knows what the other one is saying. Just then, CRASH — Dangle collapses through the ceiling below. Jones grabs his arms, catching him, but his lower half is hanging down into the room below — the one Dr. White is in. Jones tries to pull him up, but he can't. Dangle screams as Dr. White cackles from below. We hear the sound of a buzz saw or a blow torch . . . possibly both. Dangle screams, "Ah! He's got me! He's got me by the pants! DAMN THESE PANTS!"

Dangle screams, his lower half through
the ceiling below him, being attacked by
Dr. White. He screams, "He's got me by the
pants . . . cut me out of 'em, Jones, NOW!"
Jones pulls a knife from his ankle, reaches
down, and cuts Dangle out of his pants as
fast as he can. When he pulls him up: <u>Dangle
is now wearing khaki SHORTS</u>. His first ever.
Something about them just seems . . . right. He
grabs on to Jones, short of breath: "Thanks,
Jones, you saved my ass," says Dangle.

"Okay, sir," says Jones. "Stop hugging me,
and your balls are popping out." They drop
down through the hole in the ceiling, into
the room below . . .

FLASH-FORWARD TO:

EXT. OCEAN — DAWN

The sun rises over the island.

EXT. BEACH — DAY

Junior and Rick are spearfishing, with Rick
bossing him around, telling him "how it's
done." Junior spears a barracuda. Yes!
He pulls it out of the water, where the
barracuda on a stick bites Rick's face.
Junior tries to pull it off, it's a painful,
bloody mess. Then Junior steps on an urchin.
They hop, flail, and eventually fall into a
PATCH of urchin . . . it's horrible.

EXT. JUNGLE — DAY

Irina the flight attendant is taking a very
erotic shower in a waterfall. She's really
"working it." Posing, like she's in a *Playboy*
video.

243

We reveal: Kimball is hidden in the jungle, watching with binoculars. Dangle finds her. He asks what exactly are they doing? She explains: It's a trap for Dr. White "You know — he seems into blondes, this is good way to catch him." But it seems like she's set up this "trap" for her own enjoyment. *Why is she playing "Cherry Pie" on a boom box, for example*? While she explains, and it turns into an argument — Irina is yanked into the jungle by Dr. White, in his orange prison jumpsuit — they don't even see it happen.

INT. CAVE — LATER

Clemmy and Irina the flight attendant (nude and soapy) and crazy "Island Mike" are now all chained up in the cave. Island Mike can't believe his luck. After all these years, now chained between blondes, and one in her birthday suit! It's like Mardi Gras for him and Jimmy, the skeleton. Dr. White issues commands from the mouth of the cave above them (à la the "It puts the lotion in the basket" scene from *Silence of the Lambs*). Most of his commands involve making them do things that will make them more delicious when he eats them: He tosses down herbs and tell them, "It rubs the cinnamon and banana leaves on its skin." Clemmy is miserable — but her skin hasn't been this clear in years.

EXT. BUSY STREET IN THAILAND — DAY

244 Jones and Garcia walk down the street, exhausted. A sexy Thai HOOKER stops them with a friendly "Hello, Americans! I rock your world, seven dollars." Thank God, she speaks English. They explain things to her, but the only English she says is "I rock your world, seven dollars!" Or "You be so sex crazy you forget your own name, seven dollars." "You go round the butterfly and back, seven dollars."

Jones explains, exasperated, "Look, I have friends who need help. They are counting on me to save them." She says, "I understand. I feel bad for you. Six dollars." He says "Deal" and heads in with her. The hooker says, "But the Mexican can't watch — that's extra."

EXT. BEACH — DAY

Junior's fishing, and he finally spears a fish! He walks back to shore triumphantly — and halfway back gets stung by a man-o'-war. Dragged on shore, the jellyfish's tendrils all over him — someone says there's only one thing that'll stop the poison: Someone has to pee on the jellyfish. They try, but everyone who comes to his aid has a shy bladder — no one can pee. SEVERAL PEOPLE try for a while. He finally gets the jellyfish off — and *then* they all can all finally pee. He flees but gets peed on a fair amount anyway.

EXT. SEASIDE — DAY

Dangle hunts for Dr. White, when he notices, in the surf: a backpack drifts up, and he fishes it out. He looks inside — and his eyes widen, overwhelmed with joy . . .

It's RAMEN NOODLES! A whole box! Like a madman, he covets the box. He tries to eat them raw. He can't, they chip his tooth. He grabs the last water bottle and begins looking around for a pot to boil them in — his eyes light up when he sees . . .

The URN in Kimball's tent.

Dangle grabs the urn, but Kimball clutches it protectively. She made a vow to the dead passenger. He says he understands and respects that . . . then tries to snatch it again. She defends it — in what becomes an all-out *Cool Hand Luke*-style fistfight, punches fly. Eventually, Dangle gives up. But Kimball won't back off — she kicks the shit out of him, far more than is actually necessary.

A crowd has gathered to watch Dangle get his ass kicked. They ask him, what's he want the urn for anyway? Trapped — he shows them the Ramen noodles.

Their mouths water. Kimball eyes the noodles. "You know, I've been thinking . . . maybe she wanted her ashes to be sprinkled out in China. Maybe she wanted them in the China *SEA*. Which is connected to the sea here. Maybe if we had some kind of ceremony, and everybody said a few kind words . . . I could have half of your Ramen noodles." Dangle says, "Done."

EXT. POINT OVERLOOKING THE SEA — SUNSET

The survivors prepare to scatter the ashes from the urn. Kimball makes a nice speech and sprinkles the ashes into the sea. The breeze blows them back at the deputies. It tastes a little funny. The next deputy, as promised, takes a handful, says something nice about this old lady he didn't know, and sprinkles the ashes at sea. Then he tastes his fingers and rubs some of the ashes on his teeth.

As they go around the circle, passing the urn, we realize — A.D. was a drug smuggler, and the urn holds not ashes but pure, uncut cocaine. They pass the urn around and around — talking about Grandma, talking about life and death . . . by the end, they are taking "bumps" of Grandma. They eventually get some music going . . . everyone's talking <u>really</u> fast.

EXT. GUTTER IN THAILAND — NIGHT

Jones and Garcia sit, broke, frustrated . . .
and some Thai MEN in sailor uniforms step up
to them. The men say, in perfect English,
"We overheard what you were saying. You got
friends lost at sea, huh? We'll help you out,
We're the coast guard." Thrilled, they thank
the men and go with them. Jones and Garcia
hug them for joy and climb into their jeep.
Yes! It's finally over!

NIGHT FALLS

EXT. JUNGLE — NIGHT

The camp is out of leggy blondes, so Wiegel
decides to lure Dr. White as sexy cannibal
bait. She's covered herself in coconut milk
and a makeshift banana-leaf bikini. But it's
only attracted flies, which are surrounding
her, and she's having an allergic reaction
to the leaves . . . she's wheezing for breath,
swatting flies off of herself with a palm
frond which hurts every time she does it.

EXT. MOUNTAINTOP — NIGHT

Dangle is off in the jungle. His Spirit Guide
teaches him to walk on hot lava rocks and not
feel pain. He's barefoot, running across,
but he's getting <u>really burnt</u>. After much
torment, Dangle asks the Guide, "How? How
can he walk on the coals and not feel pain?"
The Guide says, "The answer . . . is shoes. You
should wear <u>shoes</u>. That's what a smart leader
would do. You've really got to smarten up,
man. Are you sure you're a lieutenant?"

Again he asks Dangle what is he afraid of?
Dangle blacks out from pain.

FLASH BACK TO:

INT. DONNER MOTEL — 1989

A creepy and dark basement. Sergeant Trudy
Wiegel has been stripped to her underwear,
gagged, and chained to the radiator, like
a scene from *Saw*. She looks like a totally
different person, twitching, shaking. She's
obviously been through a horrible ordeal. Her
eyes look a little . . . crazy.

Dangle and Jones rush to unchain her, but as
they untie her, Jones is knocked out from
behind with a steel pipe.

From the shadows, Dr. White's voice calls
out, "Time to make a decision, Lieutenant . . .
you can save Sergeant Wiegel, or catch me.
Which will it be? Because there's not much
time."

Dangle sees that a small EGG TIMER and
BATTERY have been taped to Trudy's head with
duct tape. It's counting down, it looks like
a little time bomb.

Dr. White smashes the window, and jumps out
of it. Dangle's about to follow, but he looks
at Trudy . . . terror in her eyes, only 30
seconds on the timer. He makes his decision —
he lets Dr. White go and goes to help Trudy.
He removes the little egg timer bomb from
her head and throws it across the room. He
bravely shields Trudy with his body as the
timer counts down . . . five, four, three,
two . . . then there's a tiny little DING.
Just the egg timer going off. Nothing else
happens.

Confused, Dangle pulls the gag out of Trudy's
mouth. She says, "*Hey, Jim!*" (In a voice that
sounds a lot more like the Trudy we know.)

248

"Hey, guess what, Jim — he tried to starve me and make me go crazy, but I survived by eating all these lead paint chips! I made up a song about 'em, wanna hear?"

Dangle goes to check the egg timer. Wiegel explains, "Yeah, that was just an egg timer, did he say it was a bomb? He's not a bomb maker, he's a cannibal."

Dangle checks out the window. Dr. White is long gone. Just then the door is kicked down. Dangle, Trudy, and Jones (who has just woken up) open fire — and shoot Junior in the torso. Junior falls to the floor, saying "Damn, and I got a bullet-proof vest on layaway."

FLASH-FORWARD TO:

EXT. JUNGLE — NIGHT

Dangle thanks the Spirit Guide for the vision quest. He usually just dreams about Greco-Roman wrestling with Orlando Bloom. The Island Spirit tells him, oh, this isn't a dream. His name's Scott, he's a *life coach*. He was on the plane. He gives Dangle his card and tells Dangle that he owes him 500 bucks for these "hero's journey" sessions.

EXT. BEACH — LATER

The survivors look over the supplies, nothing but *taco fixins*. And they're <u>very</u> hungry. If only there were something to put in the taco shells. They talk about their poor new friend A.D. and how bravely he hung on to life . . . how much his liver looked like a good cut from Ralph's butcher shop . . . but no! Then someone suggests: we could eat the poodle. They scoff: "That's disgusting." Then they look around and call for the poodle. It is nowhere to be seen: Unnoticed, the Asian chick casually kicks campfire ashes over a few little bones and picks something out of her teeth.

EXT. THAILAND STREET — NIGHT

Garcia and Jones climb out of the jeep with the sailors and head toward a police station, relieved. They thank the Thai sailors, who are happy to help and listen to all of the details about the crash and the location of the island. They head around the station, into an alley . . .

INT. WATERFRONT WAREHOUSE — CONTINUOUS

Jones and Garcia follow the sailors through a door. They look up and realize: they are in a huge, windowless warehouse, full of nefarious THAI MEN. In the middle of the room is a table with two chairs and one GUN. A Thai man puts one bullet in the revolver, spins it, and hands it to them. Shit.

DISSOLVE TO:

Garcia, full on *Deer Hunter,* aims the gun at his own temple and shoots.

We see a close-up of a Thai SPECTATOR as the GUN FIRES. The spectator flinches . . . then unflinches and says, "In twenty-eight years, I've never seen someone miss . . ."

EXT. BEACH — NIGHT

The survivors have gathered near the plane — and Captain Rick says a solemn prayer about the beloved departed A.D. MILES. Halfway through the prayer we realize that it's not just a prayer — he is also saying GRACE: thanks for the meal they are about to receive.

Tearfully, the survivors have made a "Make Your Own Taco" bar on the wing of the plane, heating the tacos with propane from a tank. Everyone cries as they eat the crunchy, delicious tacos they've made from their friend. Not a word is exchanged, the deputies just *crunch, weep, and "mmmmm"* at the apparently delicious tacos.

Then Dangle snaps, "Don't you see? We've become like Dr. White — we are monsters. What about duty?"

It's been two days. They think no one is coming for them. What happens when they're out of the crunchy tacos made from their dead friend? Dangle cries. They realize that he's right — until Captain Rick, always calm, is the voice of reason. There's only one logical thing to do, he says: draw straws to see who's gonna be the next taco. It's *Lord of the Flies*. They have lost all of their civility. Even the deputies are no longer listening to Dangle.

They ask Dangle, "Are you gonna draw straws to be a taco or not?" He says, "No, I won't become a monster."

Captain Rick calmly takes charge. He says — Dangle's right. "We shouldn't do this, drawing straws . . . we should just <u>eat Dangle</u>." Dangle scoffs. His trusted deputies would never turn on him like that . . . ?

To Dangle's dismay, <u>everyone is on Captain Rick's side</u>. Dangle runs for his life, into the jungle. He tells Joe the cameraman — if you're gonna document me, you better document fast. Joe runs with him into the dark.

INT. JUNGLE — NIGHT

It's *The Most Dangerous Game*, as Dangle is
the hunted. He can't trust anyone, even when
Junior offers to hide Dangle in his tent.
Dangle thinks it might be a trap! Dangle runs
away, and Junior is crushed: "You don't trust
me, I've been your best friend for years."
But Dangle is gone. Shit — the moment he's
gone, we see that Williams was waiting to
mace Dangle: to incapacitate him and add
flavor. It WAS a trap, and it didn't work.
Dammit.

EXT. MOUNTAIN CLIFF, OVERLOOKING THE SEA — DAWN

Dangle catches his breath; he can hear the mob
behind him. He climbs a small cliff and into
a cave, where he runs — SMACK into: CLEMMY.
Clemmy sighs in relief. Then screams: "Behind
you!" He turns to be face-to-face with a
crazed man in an orange prison jumpsuit. They
both SCREAM and run in opposite directions,
right into the walls of the cave. Dangle
starts to run — but he stops . . .

                                FLASH BACK TO:

EXT. DONNER MOTEL — NIGHT — 1989

The deputies stagger out of the motel,
limping, battered, looking like they've aged
ten years in one night . . . Clemmy's boobs
popping out, Wiegel crazed and twitching,
Dangle in makeshift shorts. A NEWS REPORTER
runs up to them and snaps a photo.

                                DISSOLVE TO:

A NEWSPAPER HEADLINE

Below the same photo reads: "CANNIBAL ESCAPES!
NEW LIEUTENANT A HUGE DISAPPOINTMENT!" We

pull back from the paper to see that it's in Dangle's hand. He's sitting in his kitchen, drinking Canadian Club right out of the bottle. Debbie, his morbidly obese wife, appears in the doorway, <u>completely NUDE</u>. "Come on, sugar, let me take your mind off it." Upon seeing her, Dangle jumps in his seat (and throws up a little in his mouth). He gets up, defeated, clicks off the kitchen light, and follows her into the bedroom.

BACK TO:

EXT. MOUNTAIN CLIFF, OVERLOOKING THE SEA — CONTINUOUS

Dangle turns around to face Dr. White, and the look in Dr. White's eyes changes — to fear. Dangle tells him, "It's all over. I'm not afraid anymore. I'm gonna finish this, right here and now." Dr. White backs away, afraid — and falls . . . off the cliff. He falls all the way down and lands on the rocky shore of the sea.

The angry mob of survivors arrives and sees the dead serial killer. Dangle dusts off his hands. "Got 'im. Nice work, gang." The stunned mob can't believe it. They can't believe what they were about to do.

EXT. ROCKY SHORE BELOW THE CLIFF — DAWN

They fish Dr. White out of the sea — he's snagged on seaweed or something. The deputies are back to normal, filing a report, back to their senses — acting like deputies again . . .

As they haul the killer out of the sea, they see that he is snagged on something HUGE. And . . . rubber. It's the hundred-foot Hyundai gorilla with "King Kong Sized Deals" written on it. It's intact. Someone suggests that maybe there's a way to make the balloon into a raft. They talk and plan until Dangle says, "Why don't we make the balloon . . . into a balloon?"

EXT. BEACH — DAY

The gorilla is inflated in all its glory. They have rigged it up for escape, using the last propane tank to fire it up with hot air, with a rickety bamboo basket. They soar upward, in their glorious and stupid escape balloon.

DISSOLVE TO:

EXT. BANGKOK — DAY

THAIS look up, utterly confused, as our deputies drift over the town underneath their giant, inflated gorilla. Dangle shouts down, "Excuse me? Can you direct us to the Sheriff's Department?"

INT. HOSPITAL — DAY

Local Thai police take the deputies' statement as they lie in paper backless hospital gowns getting shots for borderline malnutrition. Sitting next to them, also in paper gowns, are the flight attendant Steve Austin and Captain Rick.

The corpse of Dr. White is wheeled in. Dangle looks at the corpse and at his tired officers and tells them — now they can finally close the book on the biggest case in their lives. It's finally over.

A Thai POLICEMAN comes in and tells them that they are about to get a fax from Interpol: no doubt, congratulations. The fax comes through

with all of the vital stats of Dr. White —
along with a photo . . .

It doesn't look like the corpse at all. They
look closer, as flight attendant Steve Austin
peers over their shoulder. Dangle supposes:
What if that guy we killed was just another
passenger who Dr. White put into his jumpsuit
to throw us off? That means the killer's
still out there. Somewhere.

It's VERY obvious that the photo is of flight
attendant Steve Austin. He's Dr. White. They
all realize this at the same time. Steve
Austin smiles. "Well, I guess you caught me.
You — you're a better man than I thought. I
guess I'll turn myself in." Then he head-
butts Dangle painfully, runs for the window,
and jumps into it. It doesn't break, and he
slides painfully to the floor.

He jumps up and runs out the door and down
the fire escape. The deputies yell for the
police and tell them that Dr. White got away.
The Thai cops look at the corpse, totally
confused — there is obviously a language
barrier. Shit. So with their butts hanging
out of their tiny paper gowns, the six
deputies run out into Bangkok in hot pursuit.

EXT. HOSPITAL — DAY

Dangle stands in the doorway, facing
Dr. White. He grabs his IV stand like the
bamboo staff that the Dream Spirit has been
training him with every night. Cool "Dangle's
about to kick some ass" music swells: In an
incredibly fancy, badass move, he flourishes
it like the life coach taught him. Dr. White
takes a step back, terrified and cornered.
Dangle steps forward — barefoot onto the hot
asphalt. Ouch ouch ouch. He hops around and
goes back inside. Shit. Dr. White runs, and

Dangle and the other deputies run after him, hopping unheroically on the hot asphalt in their bare feet.

EXT. STREETS OF BANGKOK — CONTINUOUS

The deputies run after Dr. White in their paper half gowns, butts hanging out. The locals point and stare. Many people call after the ladies, "How much for the blonde? $50 American! $100!"

EXT. STREETS OF BANGKOK — CONTINUOUS

Junior tries a *Dukes of Hazzard* slide across the hood of a car. His butt SQUEAKS and stops him. And he hops off the hot hood in pain.

INT. DOUBLE-DECKER BUS — MOMENTS LATER

Dr. White jumps onto the bus, next to a Hindu DRIVER. He screams, "Step on it!" The driver yells at him, "Why would I do that? Do you have a gun, nothing to threaten me with? What the hell is wrong with you, why don't you put on some pants?" As he harangues, Dr. White gives up and climbs off the bus.

EXT. STREETS OF BANGKOK — MOMENTS LATER

Junior sees Dr. White running away. He turns and sees: a SPEAR, much like his fishing spear, at a vendor's stand. He takes it. Williams turns to him, and nods: "You can do it, Junior." Junior takes a deep breath, aims the spear at Dr. White in the distance — and throws . . . the spear PIERCES Kimball, who was JUST about to catch up with Dr. White. Oops.

INT. DOUBLE-DECKER BUS — MOMENTS LATER

Dangle and Clemmy jump onto the bus, and tell the Hindu driver, "Follow that guy — he's a serial killer!" The driver harangues, "Why would I do that? Do you have badges, some sort of identification? If he is a killer, why would I want to go nearer to him? Why don't you try just PAYING for the bus like a normal person? What the hell is wrong with you Americans, anyway?" They give up and continue the chase on foot.

EXT. BACK ALLEY — CONTINUOUS

Clemmy runs in pursuit. A handsome PASSERBY yells "$25,000! American!" Clemmy runs out of sight. Then comes back. "Um, exactly what do you expect for your $25,000?" The handsome tourist whispers to her. She nods. "You had me at handcuffs."

EXT. STREETS OF BANGKOK — CONTINUOUS

Travis and Williams run up to some COPS: "We need backup, pronto." They're, of course, arrested, as they try to explain what they're doing on the street half naked. Kimball trudges back to the hospital, speared.

EXT. STREETS OF BANGKOK — CONTINUOUS

Dangle runs, getting winded. His feet are hot and sore. Dr. White is way down the street, <u>about to hop on the back of a moving truck</u> — he's getting away.

Dangle can't run anymore. Then he sees: a brand new bicycle. It's a POLICE bike, almost the same model as his back home. It is chained to a bike rack. Dangle hesitates — then breaks the bike's lock. As he picks the lock, he tells the camera, "Never, NEVER do this at home, kids." He takes off the chain.

He leaps on the bike. "It's go time." Music swells, he takes off — and a SECOND chain

on the bike stops him in five feet. He
flies painfully over the handlebars, to the
concrete.

He looks down the street as Dr. White makes
it onto the truck. He turns and waves at
Dangle! "Good-bye, Dangle! See you in another
seventeen years!"

He laughs . . . and slips and falls off the
truck. Where he is run over by a bus. Then
another.

                                    CUT TO:

INT. MORTUARY IN THAILAND — DAY

Dangle enters in uniform with a medal on
his chest, his arm still in a bandage.
Dr. White is lying, dead, on a gurney.
Dangle smiles, covers Dr. White's face, and
nods to the MORTICIAN — who opens the doors
of the crematorium's oven, flips a switch
unceremoniously, and exits. A conveyor belt
slowly carries White into the oven. Dangle
smiles and whispers to White, "Who's laughing
now, bitch?"

SUDDENLY — Dr. White reaches out and grabs
Dangle. As he is sucked into the oven, Dangle
is being dragged too . . .

Dangle struggles to get away — but Dr. White
is strong. At last Dangle kicks free, but
White makes one last grab: for Dangle's
pants . . . Dangle smiles: there are no
pants to hold on to. Dr. White screams and
disappears into the flames. Dangle smiles —
and adjusts his shorts, adjusting a ball back
in that popped out in the fracas.

DISSOLVE TO:

EXT. RENO SHERIFF'S DEPARTMENT — ESTABLISHING

Title Card: Reno, Nevada: six weeks later

INT. RENO SHERIFF'S DEPARTMENT — CONTINUOUS

The deputies are back to normal: Wiegel is still a retard. Junior smiles sweetly, and he shows Williams a nice, romantic photo of the two of them from the island. She pays him $50, takes it, and destroys it. Dangle pulls out the old newspaper headline "NEW LIEUTENANT HUGE DISAPPOINTMENT!" He rips it up and lets the pieces fall into a garbage can.

Then someone notices . . . *Wait, where's Jones and Garcia?* Oh, shit. Guess we didn't really wrap everything up.

CUT TO:

EXT. THAILAND — DAY

Jones and Garcia are in their tighty whities in a cage in a traveling Thai circus. A circus WORKER sprays them with a hose, then throws in two heads of lettuce. They hold each other, crying and shivering.

THE END

SCOUT'S HONOR

Outline

by

Robert Ben Garant

&

Thomas Lennon

FADE IN:

DETROIT, MICHIGAN

We meet our heros: FIVE lovable INNER-
CITY KIDS, who are a scout troop. (Not the
official BOY SCOUTS OF AMERICA but a BSA-type
group.) They only joined Scouts to get out of
classes early. Their SCOUTMASTER is a weird
old loser; he's always drunk and doesn't show
up most of the time.

They're supposed to be learning BASIC AUTO
REPAIR, but by the time the car engine's been
taken apart, the master is drunk and the kids
have lost interest.

So they just goof around and play
basketball. They LOVE basketball. But they
SUCK at it, 'cause they all just wanna be
superstars (instead of being actually good
at basketball). *These kids could sure use
a little lesson in teamwork.* They worship
SOME FAMOUS BASKETBALL PLAYER. It could be
any player, any team. For the sake of this
treatment, we'll say it's SHAQ and THE MIAMI
HEAT.

The main kid is MIKE. When the drunk
scoutmaster yells at the kids for being a
bunch of no-good punks, Mike tells him: Why
should I even pretend I'm ever gonna be
something? (His dad was a con man who left
him and his mom to survive on their own. He's
got no hope, no goal for a better life.)

Mike, at home, lives with his MOM, DIANNE,
and their sick GRANDMA. She's a single
working mom and doing her best. Dianne wishes
Mike had something to give him hope. Mike
asks her, again, where Dad is. She says she
doesn't know. Grandma sees this and shakes

263

her head, and Grandma decides to write a letter — BUT TO WHOM?

Then they all see, on TV:

MIAMI, FLORIDA. A PRESS CONFERENCE:

The MIAMI HEAT, in association with the Boy Scouts of America-type group, have sponsored a national contest: the scout troop that collects the most aluminum cans will get to play the Heat, in a five minute HALF-TIME GAME, to earn their athletic badges. Plus cash prizes and team jerseys and stuff.

SO . . .

Dianne and Grandma (AND THE KIDS) think it would be great for Mike to win something like this. Mike and the other inner-city kids in the scout troop win the contest. Their parents and aunts and uncles all work in a Pepsi factory. The kids don't care a thing about scouting or the badges — they just want to meet the HEAT.

CUT TO:

PRISON:

WILL, prison convict, con artist, and MIKE'S DAD. When we meet him, he's playing basketball in the prison yard with the other convicts. Will is the coach, coaching as he plays: and they play mean, prison-yard basketball. Will plays for keeps; they play really dirty, really rough, and really well.

LATER, IN PRISON:

Will is working — sewing in the prison's factory — when Will gets a letter from back home in Detroit:

His MOM, Mike's Grandma, is dying. (Don't
worry — we will later discover that she is
NOT really dying. She's an old woman who's
frequently "dying," "recovering," and "dying"
again.)

So — Will breaks out of prison to go see his
dying mother.

                                          CUT TO:

DETROIT:

Will gets home, sneaks in to see Grandma —
and Grandma slaps him. (She's HILARIOUS and
not dying at all.) She's ashamed of Will.
She's ashamed that he's in prison, ashamed
that his 11-year-old-son, Mike, wouldn't even
recognize him if he saw him, ashamed that he
let Dianne, the best thing that ever happened
to him, get away. "If only you were a good
father, I could rest in peace and not be a
failure as a mother."

Dianne finds Will in her home and slaps him
too. He broke out of jail, and now they could
ALL get in trouble. Will finds out that Mike
has NO IDEA that Will didn't "leave them" of
his own choice — he's just been in jail for
eight years. And Mike has no idea what Will
even looks like.

Will tells Dianne he's really changed from
the selfish guy he was, a reckless gambler
and a con man. Will really wants to make
things up; to his kid, his mom, and Dianne —
the only good thing that was ever in his
life. She kicks him out — she DOES NOT want
Mike to meet his escaped prisoner father —
that's not the kind of father he needs.
Besides, Mike has already left — on the bus
to Miami.

MEANWHILE:

At the prison, they've discovered Will's
escape, and they are hot on his tail.
The main FEDERAL marshal is as tough as
nails . . . but he kinda sympathizes with Will
when he sees Grandma's letter — since Will
escaped to see his dying mother.

AT MAMMA'S HOUSE:

Will ducks out, "out of their lives forever,"
as Mike enters.

But he overhears:

Why hasn't Mike left? Their shifty old troop
leader, who was supposed to drive the bus,
flaked out. He spent all their traveling
money that the Heat sent them — and he can't
be found. Now they have no money, no driver
for their crappy old scout van . . .

They're not going to get to play the Heat
after all. Mike says, fine — "Good things
don't happen to people in this neighborhood,
anyway."

Will sees Mike through the window — sees that
his son is on the wrong path . . .

                              THEN . . .

Mike and Dianne get a call — the Scouts of
America has sent them a new troop leader to
drive them to Miami. (It's Will, doing a
voice on the phone — he's a very accomplished
CON ARTIST.)

Will makes his own SCOUT UNIFORM. He breaks
into the old scoutmaster's house, steals
the old man's uniform, and sews on tons of
badges.

The kids show up, to go to Miami . . .

TA DA! — Will shows up in the den leader's uniform as their new den leader. ("Sent from, uh . . . Boy Scout headquarters in, uh, Washington.") He's going to take them to Miami. He doesn't tell his son who he is, and Mike doesn't recognize him.

Will, driving a crappy bus, with the Scouts, makes it out of Detroit and heads south.

So with no cash, and no scouting experience, they make their way across the country.

Will sees what a cool kid his son has become but also sees that he's dangerously close to following Will's path, the wrong path.

The first night, he tries to pitch a tent in a campground — and fails. It's a horrible night, no tent, no food . . . The kids (no dummies) are suspicious of Will (he sure doesn't act like a Boy Scout). He doesn't even know what some of the badges mean, he wears his handkerchief like Tupac, his neckerchief clasps like rings, and there's something in his canteen that'll start a campfire.

The next night, Will shows them some "REAL-WORLD SURVIVAL SKILLS." When he can't set up a tent AGAIN, he says, "Okay, tonight I'm gonna teach you how to earn your 'check into a hotel with no reservation and no money' badge."

He pulls a con. He checks into a hotel, claiming he has a reservation and it should be paid for: "The scouts should've covered it."

267

Clerk says sorry, he has no record of a reservation OR a payment. So Will raises a huge stink, creating a scene:

>   WILL
>   This is how you treat OUR KIND in
>   Ohio.

>   MOTEL CLERK
>   Why don't we call the Boy Scouts?

>   WILL
>   Boy? Do I look like a BOY — to you?

Etc. They get free rooms. Next time they try the Four Seasons.

Will shows them how to earn a "how to siphon gasoline" badge. He can't tie knots, but he can break out of handcuffs. He teaches the kids CONS. It's delightful and hilarious, and they pay their way across the country and get out of jams.

MEANWHILE:

The marshal is on their trail. He asks Dianne if she's seen Will. She LIES and says she hasn't. Grandma thinks Dianne may still have feelings for him. Then the marshal finds out about Mike's winning the game against the Heat. Maybe Will would try to find his son and be at that game. "I know I would."

268

The cops are on the trail. With the search for Will widening and the GAME in four days, it's a race against the cops and the clock.

THE TROOP:

As the troop starts working together, they all start to bond. Will makes them brush up on their b-ball skills (wow — they suck).

How the hell do they expect to not EMBARRASS themselves against the Heat? They hadn't thought of that. Will tries to teach them regulation basketball — drilling, etc. Trouble is, even WILL has no idea how to play good clean regulation basketball. They continue sucking.

Mike begins to open up to Will. Will tries to get them to believe in themselves a little — the advice of a con on how not to follow in his footsteps.

HALFWAY THROUGH THE MOVIE: THE COPS ALMOST CATCH WILL.

There's a police ROADBLOCK looking for Will, and they'll never get through it. When this happens and Will turns back — Mike and the kids figure out that Will is on the lam. Will tells them who he is. Mike is furious. He's always hated his dad (who he's never known), then THIS is how he comes back into Mike's life — by LYING.

Will is crushed. Mike's right. But — he promised to get them to Miami, and he will. He needs money — so he does some kinda awesome three-card-monty scam on the street. The guy Will takes for $300 is a small-town off-duty cop — who makes the connection and reports Will.

Will BRAVES a bus station, as cops pull up and surround the station. He buys FIVE TICKETS TO MIAMI. Even though he's not going to make it to Miami, the KIDS will. He's truly risking it all for the kids, and the kids see that.

He gives the kids their tickets and says a teary good-bye. And the kids YANK him into the van and peel out.

When the cops try to chase them, NONE OF THEIR CARS WILL START. The kids stole all of their alternators. That's as far as they got in "BASIC AUTO REPAIR."

They've now BOTH risked their necks — for each other.

Will and Mike talk as father and son. Mike, who hated him before, because he thought he was selfish, sees that Will loves him, loves his mom — did everything he could for them. He wanted his son to go to college, have a better life — but he made a few mistakes, and he doesn't want his son to make the same ones. Mike says he wants to be just like him. Will tells him no, don't be a con man. Mike can be better than that. He can do anything he puts his mind to.

They call Dianne to tell her they're all right. Mike makes Will talk to his mom. She's furious, but when she finds out that Will's doing it for Mike — she's slightly less furious. She goes after them.

<u>NOW THEY'VE ESCAPED THE COPS</u>.

The kids ask Will — "Now what?"

> WILL
> Now what? Now — <u>we're going to BEAT the Heat</u>.

Will starts training them like a real basketball team, to beat the Heat the only way they could possibly have a chance — dirty. He teaches them how to draw the foul and how to make a big show, pretending to be hurt. <u>He teaches them how to get inside the Heat's heads</u>. Etc.

It's only going to be a five-minute

exhibition game, so here's the plan: When the Heat come out, they're gonna play up how cute they are, play to the crowd, play cutesy, friendly ball — the Scouts have to get as big a lead as possible before the Heat see what's going on.

Then — <u>foul Shaq, and work the clock</u>.

The marshal is on their trail.

He sees that Will only bought five children's tickets — he was going to send the kids to the game without him? Then the kids saved HIM? Hmmm.

They make it to Miami, stealing gas and eating with other people's credit cards. At one point, they play a bunch of WHITE GUYS in a game of street basketball, to try to hustle them for five hundred bucks. The Scouts LOSE to the white guys. (THEY HAVEN'T LEARNED TEAMWORK YET.)

Then, at the Florida State line, they stop at a casino, even though they're late. The Scouts are very disappointed in Will, who seems to be back to his old tricks — he sells their van and bets the money. Now they have no van. Will has to dress as a valet and steal a camper to get to Miami.

In Miami, the marshal is close on their trail. The marshal is WAITING for them at the game.

They make it to the AMERICAN AIRLINES ARENA. Will wants them to look GOOD, so he SEWS a bunch more badges on their uniforms from a pouch he stole from the old master: "Bird-watching — you see that bird over there, good, you got your bird-watching. Basket weaving??? You don't want that one."

GAME DAY:

Will knows that if he goes out as their
coach, he'll get caught. Mike and the other
scouts insist that he not go out — he's
brought them this far, they can do this
alone. They thank him for everything and tell
him to get away. Father and son tell each
other, "I love you."

The Scouts go out to face the Heat — and
Will comes out to coach them. The cops move
in to arrest him, but the marshal holds them
off — he wants to see the game. Dianne is
there, cheering the Scouts on.

THE GAME:

The fans LOVE the cute little Scouts. Shaq
greets the adorablest little Scout. The Scout
tells him, as tough as Clubber Lang,

"You're going down — you ain't twenty-three
any more, old man."

The Scouts play dirty, making a few masterful
shots and drawing <u>incredible</u> fouls, flinging
themselves across the floor in so much pain,
the refs and crowd start booing the Heat.

With a minute left, it's a tie game. The HEAT
call a time-out.

Angry and humiliated, <u>the Heat start playing
for real</u>. It's an amazing game, the adorable
Scouts are punching Shaq in the crotch and
getting technicals, Will is screaming in the
REF'S faces.

The game has only 45 seconds to go, AND IT'S
STILL TIED. The marshal wants to see the end
of the game.

In the end, Mike PASSES instead of shooting (he's learned teamwork) and his teammate scores at the last second and wins the game.

Dianne sees what Will has done for Mike and the kids. She and Mike admit he's got a lot of work to do — but she's gonna give him a second chance.

The marshal takes Will away, but, due to the extenuating circumstances, he'll see if he can pull some strings. Maybe they won't add any time to his sentence — he'll be out in a few years . . .

His son will be waiting for him. So will Dianne.

BACK IN DETROIT:

The Scouts are heros. A few are offered scholarships — but not Mike. Maybe next year.

Mike tells his mom that Will loves her as much as she loves him, and Grandma makes (another) miraculous recovery. He tells Mom that Will is a changed man, no more scams and cons — but then . . . a bookie comes to the door about a bet Will made while at the casino. "Oh, no — not again."

But when Will sold the van, he put the money — $2,000 — on the Scouts to beat the Heat. The odds were 1,000-1.

They're rich, and Mike's going to college.

Will's in prison, looking forward to their visits, biding his time, and forming a youth basketball team for troubled younger criminals. He's a new man.

THE END.

INSTANT MONSTERS

Treatment

by

Robert Ben Garant

&

Thomas Lennon

For the tone, think PG FUNNY/SCARY FAMILY
COMEDY, à la *Night at the Museum* meets
Gremlins.

FADE IN:

EXT. MARTHA'S VINEYARD — EARLY WINTER

The picture-perfect island in New England.

The LOCALS are salt-of-the-earth New
Englanders. A hundred years ago, they were
fishermen, trappers, and traders, now they
all work at COFFEE BEAN & TEA LEAF, YOGURT
STORES, ART GALLERIES, and SPAS. Most of the
homes on the island are MANSIONS, owned by
very wealthy SNOBS, newcomers/snowbirds —
who treat the ISLANDERS like "the help." The
LOCALS have to ferry to their homes on the
mainland — they can't afford to live on their
island anymore.

The harbor main street looks like ASPEN/
Disneyland — all galleries, coffee shops,
and overpriced tchotchke stores. One of
the only original things left is an old
LIGHTHOUSE, which is now A WHALING MUSEUM.
The rich/politically correct VACATIONERS want
it closed — because "whaling shouldn't be
glorified." The folks who work there respond,
"Um . . . we're celebrating whaling of the
1780s."

WE MEET OUR HERO, JOSH (*THINK JESSE EISENBERG*).

He's just graduated from high school, and he
works in a high-end TOY STORE in the harbor
shops, where SNOBS shop for way-too-expensive
toys for their awful, snotty kids. All day
he sells toys to rich SNOBS and their KIDS;
some of the kids even have their own American
Express BLACK cards. All day, Josh answers

questions like "Do you have those mini Hummers?" (Yes, we do.)

Josh is an ISLANDER, born and raised there. The toy shop where he works is across the street from the old lighthouse whaling museum. He's at a crossroads in his life, getting ready for college next year, in that awkward stage between being a teenager and being an adult. This will probably be his last summer on the island. His situation is complicated by being madly in love with:

SAMANTHA (20) works in the whaling museum. He's been her best-friend-but-never-quite-said-he-loved-her since the FOURTH GRADE. Josh knows every inch of the whaling museum by heart from hanging out with Samantha.

But he waited too long: She's now dating — a rich SNOWBIRD: KENT (30) (*think Ed Helms*), a wunderkind millionaire who owns a fancy HIGH-END TOY COMPANY.

Kent came here this past summer and swept Samantha off her feet.

THE RICH SNOWBIRDS ARE AWFUL.

They treat Josh like shit. They all drive little eco-friendly electric golf carts — they HATE Josh's beat-up old PICKUP TRUCK, with its huge, thirty-gallon gas tank and 1970s exhaust that shoots out plumes of smoke. The locals kind of wish the island could go back to the blue-collar place it used to be — but it's too late.

The only person Josh talks to much is the local sheriff: FREDDY "UPTOWN" WILLIAMS (*think Samuel Jackson*). Freddy USED to be a homicide detective in Detroit, for 30 years. But he's *seen and done way too many terrible things*, and he "*ain't never gonna do those things again.*" He took the job on Martha's Vineyard so he'd "never have to carry a gun, again. Or get shot nine times again, either." He's badass . . . or he was, 20 years ago. He's SHAFT in semiretirement, only with a fanny pack and helmet, riding around town on a Segway. He doesn't even carry a gun anymore. He zips around town telling mofos to "please respect our designated smoking areas."

AS OUR MOVIE BEGINS, SUMMER IS OVER — THE FIRST SNOW IS FALLING, AND THE LAST OF THE SNOWBIRDS ARE LEAVING ON THE FERRY FOR THE WINTER.

One lone man gets off the ferry: a mysterious GUY in a trench coat. He stumbles off the ferry and heads inland, unnoticed.

Josh is relieved that summer is over. Maybe with Kent gone, he can win Sam back. (Even though she has no idea Josh thinks he "lost" her.)

He's closing up his shop for the night, when a shipment of a dozen new toys arrives, new for XMAS — they are made by KENT'S toy company. They are . . .

"Instant Monsters." Supersmart robotic Monsters. Just switch them on, and they "come to life." Every one is different, some are cuter, some are scarier . . . but even the "scary" ones are kinda cute. They can hear, respond to noises, explore their environment, remember commands. They look awesome. Josh unwraps the VERY FIRST ONE, and turns it on. It's cool. Its advanced computer programming makes it SMART — it actually learns!

Without warning, it CHARGES him. Startled, he WHACKS it across the room, accidentally breaking it. Wires and chips pop out of its insides. *Whoops.*

Just then, Sam and Kent enter. Josh hides the smashed Monster. Kent tells Josh he is NOT leaving for the winter. He's staying in the new mansion he built on the hill. Kent says, "You should come check it out, Josh. We have a digital projector in the screening room." Josh, sarcastic: "Yeah, who watches prints anymore? Pfft."

Kent makes sure that Josh got the shipment of Monsters — he did, twelve of them. Prototypes. Kent's pleased: he bought the patent to the "Instant Monsters" from a small, family-owned toy company. Seems that Kent is just the "money guy" at his toy company. He's become so rich by BUYING UP other people's inventions, then putting the inventors out of business by moving the manufacturing of their toys to China. He did it again with these little Monsters, and he's gonna make a fortune.

Kent tells Josh they are expecting a delivery of 100 more prototypes, the last ones made in America. It was supposed to be here today. They are gonna sell out fast — they are VERY popular. It's gonna be a BIG Christmas for Kent's company — and he's gonna be rich rich richer than he already was.

Josh is miserable. Kent and Sam bop off, a happy couple, even though Kent is kinda a dick to her too. Bossing her around, telling her to "lay off the cookies, swimsuit season is only five months away."

Back at Kent's fabulous mansion, we meet BIG GEORGE, Kent's fulltime security guard and right-hand man. (*Think Craig Robinson.*) George spends most nights in the guardhouse at Kent's gate watching *Gossip Girl*. But that night, there's a little INCIDENT as:

The man in the trench coat arrives at Kent's gate. It's MARVIN DALY, the toy maker who invented the Monsters. He's a little drunk and VERY MAD. Kent promised Marvin he'd be making THOUSANDS of these Monsters but just took the prototypes and put his family-run company out of business. Marvin came with a MANIFESTO that he videotaped for Kent to watch.

George won't let Marvin in. Big George hates to do it, but he tasers him. Marvin skulks off, yelling "YOU DID THIS, KENT. THIS IS YOUR FAULT!" *Hmm. That's odd.* George throws the manifesto away.

Back at the store: Josh unwraps another "Instant Monster" and puts it in the window. The new one looks somehow not as friendly — his expression is somehow . . . *sinister*.

Josh locks the other ten "Instant Monsters" in the storeroom and puts the BROKEN Monster back together. He fits almost every piece back in. (Except for one little leftover fuse. Huh?) When he turns it back on, it works slightly differently. It's now kind of cute, less hostile — it nuzzles his foot and becomes his friend.

It's really cool and cute — like Gizmo, the good Gremlin. It has personality and puppy-dog eyes. He plays with it with a LASER POINTER. It can't resist chasing it, on the floor.

The toy is AWESOME: which REALLY bums Josh out — "Kent's gonna make a fortune."

Josh names his Monster . . . "Something cool? How about: Pierre?" The Monster seems to

like it, wagging his tail. Josh examines the
little fuse. Looks kind of like a computer
chip? Must be part of their little "brain."
Huh . . . Pierre accidentally knocks over a
glass of water. His foot SPARKS a little
when the water spills on him. He seems to be
afraid of it too.

Josh looks out the window to see:

Marvin, glowering at the Monster in the toy-
shop window, with the Monster staring back at
him. The sheriff asks Marvin to move along —
he's creeping out the customers. Marvin,
in his rage, tells the sheriff and Josh
"You'll all be sorry." He pushes a BUTTON on
a remote control, then heads to the ferry
pier, telling them, "The end is nigh!" What a
weirdo.

WE SEE: The remote started a COUNTDOWN on
the little chip that fell out of Pierre.
It's counting down to midnight. But — at the
ferry dock: Marvin MISSES the last ferry out.
Whoops. He was reading the summer schedule,
not the winter schedule. He's VERY UPSET that
he's stuck there. He panics — *but why*?

Then, at the stroke of midnight . . . we see why:

The COUNTDOWN reaches 0 — and the "Instant
Monster" in the window turns ON by itself.
And he looks MEAN. The Monster in the window
ATTACKS Josh. Josh fights him with toys,
which is all he's got. Bats made of NERF,
guns that shoot Ping-Pong balls . . . yelling
"Dammit, isn't there anything in this store
that's dangerous? Thanks, Ralph Nader!"
It's *Die Hard* in a toy store, against a
tiny Monster. The Monster is smart: he locks
it in a closet — and it finds its way OUT
though the air ducts, like *Alien*. The Monster
seems to HATE Pierre too, snapping at the

cute little guy. The Monster bites Josh, tearing his pocket off. He gets Josh's keys and unlocks the storeroom, letting out — the other ten very mean and very alive "Instant Monsters."

Josh barely escapes with his life and with Pierre.

The window Monster seems to be the ringleader; he's bigger and "scarier" than the others (but he's still only 12 inches tall). Let's call him SPIKE. He and the ten other "Instant Monsters" chomp and chew anything in their path, like little Tasmanian devils. They wreak havoc on the store. JOSH runs to get help.

MEANWHILE, ALL OVER TOWN — THE "INSTANT MONSTERS" START TO WREAK HAVOC:

One by one, the Monsters attack the rich snowbirds: They pounce on them, on their way to their hot tubs. They lure them out by rummaging through their recycling: "Is that those raccoons again?" They go out with a flashlight — and get mobbed by the tiny Monsters. They act like cute little toys to lure the rich, spoiled children (who gave Josh crap) closer. "Look at that cool toy, Dad! Buy me it!" Spike POUNCES.

It's like a funny horror movie — only the Monsters are tiny.

JOSH GOES TO SHERIFF UPTOWN WILLIAMS FOR HELP . . .

. . . who of course, doesn't believe him: "Little toy Monsters, like that cute guy you're carrying?" Josh tells him it's true and that Sheriff Uptown needs to get his guns. Uptown gets an intense look in his eyes, saying "Josh, I don't do that anymore. I'll never touch a gun again . . . I've seen too much craziness . . . do you know that one time in Detroit I found a HEAD. And wasn't even nobody looking for it. That was the real sad part."

Josh SLAPS Sheriff Uptown out of it and drags him to the window, showing him:

That the "Instant Monsters" are devouring Main Street like a flock of TINY GODZILLAS.

Sheriff Uptown downs his coffee with resolve. He opens a locked box and pulls out his huge, dusty gun. He whispers to it, "I swore we'd never dance like this again, Betty, but we got some miniature Monsters to mess up." Sheriff Uptown also gets his lucky BRASS KNUCKLES. And his sawed-off shotgun. And NUNCHUCKS: "I've seen and done some terrible things, Josh."

Josh: "Yeah, you mentioned that."

Sheriff Uptown tells Josh to stay put. He struts out to the street — and IS IMMEDIATELY EATEN. In, like, seconds. Oh, well.

SET PIECE: The Monsters DESTROY Main Street. They are eating all of the horrible snobs and stores we came to know and hate. (The cheap, corporate new stores seem to get devoured MUCH faster.)

284

Josh and Pierre barely escape the insanity. They manage to knock Spike, the Alpha Monster, into a snow blower — where he's chewed up and spit out into the snow in pieces. But then . . . the Monster puts itself back together. Its rubber skin now shredded in places, it looks like a ripped-up Terminator. You cannot kill these things.

JOSH AND PIERRE GO TO SAVE SAMANTHA AND FIND KENT.

He must know how to stop the Monsters — right?

Josh and Pierre get to Kent's supersecure, state-of-the-art mansion. It's awesome. With a movie theater and ALL KINDS of security — cameras everywhere, motion sensors, metal shutters that lock in case of a hurricane, etc. Kent's also a major art collector. He's got an astonishing collection: a Picasso, a couple Jeff Koons, Remingtons, a Warhol, Chagall, it's amazing. <u>Millions of dollars worth of art</u>.

Sam and Kent and Big George don't believe Josh. Kent says it doesn't make sense. They CAN'T go berserk. They're programmed to be safe toys. And then:

THE "INSTANT MONSTERS" ATTACK KENT'S MANSION.

They see them coming up the driveway: "There's no time to lose!" Then Kent notices . . . "Well, they're pretty small, it'll actually take them a couple minutes just to get up the driveway . . . still, let's hurry."

The Monsters chew through the power lines, so all the high-tech security doesn't work at all. Luckily, part of Kent's theater is still under construction: there are plenty of boards and nails around. The humans have to nail boards up over windows, like in a zombie movie.

While they're holed up and the Monsters attack . . . Kent FREAKS OUT. We see his true colors, and he's an icky scaredy-cat. And he's freaking everybody out, yelling, crying. He admits he "wet his pants, just a little, but I'm not gonna change 'em, because it will very likely happen again."

BUT . . . BAD NEWS: KENT FORGOT THAT HE HAS THREE PROTOTYPES IN THE HOUSE.

Prototypes of UNRELEASED "Instant Monsters 2.0." And those can FLY. And they are now NAILED in with them.

SET PIECE: They battle the Flying Monsters in the mansion, using the only weapons available: ART. Millions of dollars worth of art. Josh seems to be having fun, wrecking millions of dollars of Kent's art. Kent: "Come on, man, if you're gonna throw a Jeff Koons sculpture, at least try to AIM!"

They just barely survive. Destroying all but one Picasso, which, Kent points out, "was a print anyway. Only worth, like, ten grand."

Pierre takes out the last Flying Monster, saving his friends.

Kent is mortally wounded during the fight. Now they're gonna be dragging his ass around.

GEORGE WANTS TO KILL PIERRE.

He doesn't trust him, if the others went nuts, so will Pierre. It takes all Josh's efforts to save Pierre from George and convince him Pierre is okay. George makes it clear that he will NEVER trust Pierre.

Kent has no idea what's making the Monsters act like this; no one had access to their programming . . . EXCEPT — Marvin?

George tells Kent — yeah, he was here today . . . WHAT?

THEY DIG THROUGH THE TRASH TO FIND MARVIN'S DVD.

They watch it. It's his MANIFESTO. He explains, "This is what happens when you steal everything from small-business man Marvin Daly." It's a really LONG video manifesto, explaining how he programmed the Monsters to destroy EVERYTHING at midnight, to ruin Kent's company, like Kent ruined Marvin's. "By the time you see this, I'll be safely off the island, sipping a mai tai and toasting your demise." Our guys FAST-FORWARD through LOTS of the DVD, as Marvin rambles on and on . . .

Josh remembers: he saw Marvin as he was closing up the store. There's no way he made it off the island — he missed the last ferry. If they can find Marvin, maybe he knows how to shut the things OFF!

THEY REALIZE THEIR ONLY HOPE IS TO GET TO MARVIN.

Josh drags injured Kent along as they make their escape. Even as Josh saves him, Kent is kind of a jerk: "Wow, I wouldn't think a guy as weak-looking as you could carry me."

They flee in Kent's eco-friendly golf cart — that goes only 15 mph (where we re-create the "objects in mirror are closer than they appear" *Jurassic Park* joke). The Monsters are faster than the cart — so they have to ditch it.

They make it to town — which has been devoured. We see some mayhem as the Monsters chew up the town and eat some of the SNOBS we hate so much (the folks who were protesting the whaling museum, bitching about Josh's gas-guzzling truck, etc.). They call out for Marvin.

They find him, holed up in town. Marvin tells them, yes — there is a way to shut them down . . . BUT MARVIN IS DEVOURED BEFORE HE CAN TELL THEM. "Great. That's just great."

THEY HAVE TO GET OFF THE ISLAND!

By now it's just before dawn and the first ferry is due! They've almost made it through the night! They need to make it through the mayhem. They realize they can ride in Josh's old truck — but they need the keys.

PIERRE SAVES THEIR ASS AGAIN:

He braves the mayhem and gets Josh's keys from the toy store. He does this by pretending to be an Evil Monster — acting vicious. It works. He gets Josh's keys, and they make it to the ferry in Josh's old gas-leaking truck.

THEY GET TO THE DOCK JUST AS THE FERRY'S ARRIVING.

The ferry arrives — but it doesn't stop . . . it CRASHES into the dock, and we see why: it's full of the 100 more "Instant Monsters" that were getting delivered. The CREW is DEAD. The Monsters got loose on the boat, broke out of their boxes, and ATE everyone on the boat.

BIG GEORGE HEROICALLY HOLDS THE MONSTERS AT BAY ON THE PIER WHILE THE HEROES MAKE AN ESCAPE, BUT THE MONSTERS SWARM HIM.

And the unthinkable happens: Pierre gets a nasty BUMP and goes bananas. He growls at them — and HE attacks Big George, pushing him off the pier . . .

The others can't believe it. The other Monsters leave George and rush after our heroes.

SAM AND JOSH RUN FOR THEIR LIVES, SAM DRAGGING KENT ALONG — THEY HOLE UP IN THE LIGHTHOUSE MUSEUM.

They grab hold of the NOT-MODERN weapons on display in the museum (that still work w/o power or ammunition): WHALING WEAPONS! Harpoons! Hooks! Clubs!

They use ancient whaling weapons to fend off the Monsters. They make it to the top of the lighthouse, surrounded, and fending off the Monsters — like *Dawn of the Dead.*

Then — Josh gets an idea:

HE USES THE LIGHTHOUSE'S <u>LIGHT</u> TO DISTRACT THE 100 "INSTANT MONSTERS" (<u>LIKE HE DID IN THE STORE WITH THE LASER POINTER</u>).

<u>All of the Monsters chase the light</u>, outside in the snow. With the Monsters distracted, they can make it to the ferry and get off the island. But — <u>one</u> of them has to stay up here, distracting the Monsters, so the other two can escape.

Kent, who looks like he's going to die from his injury anyway, does the heroic thing. He says, "I'll do it. This is my fault, anyway. This is karma for me stealing from that guy . . . I get it. But Samantha would NEVER go with you unless I were bleeding to death, 'cause you're douche, Josh."

Samantha bids Kent good-bye. He's a hero — kind of a dick but a hero.

And Kent, with the last of his strength: operates the LIGHT, heroically, giving them time to escape.

Samantha and Josh get into Josh's truck and make for the ferry. (Halfway there, the light from the lighthouse turns bloodred, then goes OUT — the Monsters got Kent.) With the light out, they turn their attention to Josh's truck.

It looks like they might not make it. Sam asks Josh why he came for her. Josh breaks down and tells her, "Because I've loved you since August 28, 1984. Fourth grade." There's sparks between Josh and Sam.

They are cut off from the dock — and Josh seems to snap: he taunts the Monsters to follow as he JUMPS his truck onto the crashed boat. They follow him onto the ferry, and when they're all on . . .

Samantha floors the ferry's engine and heads out to sea, and . . .

Josh blows up his gas-guzzler truck with a flare. The ferry sinks, the "Instant Monsters" chase our heroes to the very end, as they race to stay above the freezing water, all the while chased by the Monsters. But soon the last of the Monsters hits the water and fries. It's over.

290

Josh and Sam swim to shore, shivering. She explains that to fight hypothermia, they're going to have to take off all their clothes and warm each other under a blanket.

And then — Pierre and George emerge from a DINGHY under the pier. Pierre didn't kill George. He *pretended* to, to SAVE HIM. Pierre wags his tail like a puppy. AND . . .

The Alpha Monster, Spike, pounces on Josh.
didn't get on the boat. And in midpounce,
slow motion: Pierre knocks him into the sea
The Evil Monsters are all gone.

As the sun comes up, the survivors come out
of hiding. The surviving snowbirds say,
"Well, we're certainly never coming back
here again." The locals say, "You know what
That's okay."

And it looks like Josh is gonna stay here
on the island — with his new girl. Well,
not new — they've known each other for 20
years . . .

The camera cranes up, and we see that all
of the destruction wreaked by the monsters
took out most of the corporate CHAIN STORES.
The Jamba Juice, the Coffee Bean . . . they're
all wrecked, while most of the old structures
are STILL INTACT. Except for some rubble and
a few fires, Main Street looks like it might
have looked a hundred years ago.

FADE OUT.

THE END

THE TREASURE OF THE SPACE INCAS, CONTINUED

Your heart is racing and your legs are burning as you LEAP from the burning rope bridge to the hatch of SPACESHIP 44-7. "Well done, my young friend," shouts Professor Kirby as he slams the hatch behind you, "I thought I'd lost you forever to Zo-Kochal and his henchmen!" The THUNK-THUNK-THUNK of arrows hitting the hull of the ship echos through the chamber as the ship's jade/magnetic engine kicks in and your stomach drops.

You catch a glimpse out the porthole—below you, the Nasca Lines, stretching out in sun-bleached stone for as far as the eye can see. Eagles, tortoises, shapes that only can truly be understood from a mile above. "You were right all along," adds the professor. "No one believed that these really were landing strips for these spacecraft, until your wonderful book report—the same one that brought you to my attention and started us off on this adventure."

"Thanks, Professor," you say as your hand meets his for a hearty handshake, "but I think my next report might be even more controversial: the one about where we're going!"

"If you've learned anything about the Space Incas, my young friend," says the professor with a wink, "you know that a better question might be—*when* are we going?"

Your laughter is interrupted when your cell phone buzzes in your pocket. You answer it and hear the familiar voice of Gary, the vice president of production at the studio.

"Hey, my young friend!" Gary from the studio yells over the din of jade spinning in the engines. "We've all been over the last draft of your book report about the Nasca Lines and how they're landing strips for Inca spacecraft, and we've decided we need some FRESH EYES."

You hang up the phone, stunned, gasping for breath, and yes: **YOU ARE FIRED.**

Turn to page 59.

GLOSSARY

THE CREDITS AT THE END OF A MOVIE—and what they mean.
(If you write movies, you should know this stuff.)

DIRECTED BY: The movie is "their vision." They are in charge of EVERY creative decision on set. They are the captain of the ship. Even when the person who hired the DIRECTOR (the STUDIO) wants something done on set, they can't just say, "I want Lindsay Lohan to bowl here." The STUDIO has to tell the DIRECTOR to say, "I want Lindsay Lohan to bowl here." Then the DIRECTOR makes Lindsay bowl, or they're fired.

WRITTEN BY: Low man on the totem pole. Often not even allowed on set. Even if the movie you wrote is YOUR life story, when THE STUDIO, THE DIRECTOR, or LINDSAY LOHAN tells you to write a bowling scene—you better write a bowling scene. Or they'll hire some new guys to write your life story.

PRODUCED BY: Usually the one who hired EVERYBODY. The star, the DIRECTOR, the writers. After shooting begins, they remain on set as creative consultant—a VOICE-IN-THE-MIX. However, they are the VOICE-IN-THE-MIX-WHO-MUST-BE-LISTENED-TO. They usually sit by the monitors, watching every take (either knitting or Googling showbiz gossip, depending on their age and sex). When they see something they want to change, they tell the director. The DIRECTOR has to either do it, talk them out of it, or quit.

EXECUTIVE PRODUCERS: Tricky one to define. Technically, they are THE BOSS. The EP is usually the one who got the ball rolling on the project, conceiving it, finding the source material, hiring the DIRECTOR and/or star and even the other producers. Some EPs oversee every aspect of every single production. And there are EPs on the *Night at the Museum* movies we never even met. Never even met.

DIRECTOR OF PHOTOGRAPHY: He decides how the movie is going to be filmed—the camera angles, the lenses. He conceives the lighting of the movie. Either the DIRECTOR tells the DP what he wants or the DP tells the DIRECTOR what he's going to do.

PRODUCTION DESIGNER: Creates the look of the movie, from the design of the set to the design of the hair, wardrobe, everything. They usually have to PITCH their looks to the producer and the DIRECTOR, through blueprints and designs.

Because without their approval, the production designer doesn't get the money to BUILD anything.

EDITOR: Takes the footage and puts it together into a movie. They usually do a pass themselves, then the DIRECTOR comes in and reedits it with them, until the DIRECTOR thinks it's perfect, then the STUDIO comes in and either HATES the cut and reedits it (sometimes firing the editor) or LOVES the cut and wants it to be an hour shorter.

COSTUME DESIGNER: Designs the costumes, then is in charge of the costume department. But everything has to be approved by the DIRECTOR, STUDIO, and sometimes the MOVIE STARS.

MAKEUP AND HAIR DESIGNER: Designs the looks of the makeup and hair and then is in charge of all the makeup and hair people during shooting.

MUSIC BY: Wrote the original score for the sound track.

CO-PRODUCER: Usually a line producer, in charge of the budget. Also the "bad cop" in charge of hiring and firing people. The co-producer usually has an actual OFFICE, in the production office in Hollywood or Burbank, while the producers are miles way, at their swanky offices in Beverly Hills, and the executive producer is in Cannes or Monte Carlo or jet-setting around with Al Gore. Sometimes the co-producer has done more actual WORK on a movie than all of the producers and executive producers combined.

CASTING BY: The casting agent SUGGESTS what stars should be in the movie, arranges the auditions, brings in the actors who they think are right for the part for the DIRECTORS and producers to see, and then arranges their deals and becomes the schedule liaison with the talent. But the DIRECTOR and producers are the ones who ACTUALLY make the casting decisions. Sometimes the casting director's job is to just DO WHAT THE DIRECTOR SAYS: get who they tell them to get.

CAST: The actors in the movie. Arranged by the size of their role or sometimes— for political reasons—in order of appearance.

At this point in the credits, there's sometimes a card that says something like:

A SUCH-AND-SUCH PRODUCTION

That is the PRODUCER'S PRODUCTION COMPANY.

UNIT PRODUCTION MANAGER: Sort of a line producer, but their job is 100 per-cent to oversee the COSTS of a film: they look at the budgets, make sure every department is staying on budget, and walk around on the set looking tense and staring at their watch. They make sure everyone fills out their cost reports and that those cost reports are accurate and UNDER budget. The GOOD UPMs are real ball busters, and everyone hates them. Except the producer.

FIRST ASSISTANT DIRECTOR: Probably the most important person on set. If the DIRECTOR is Tom Hanks in *Saving Private Ryan*, "The First," or 1st AD, is Tom Sizemore. The DIRECTOR mumbles something about "moving on to the next setup"—the 1st GETS IT DONE. They crack the whip, stay on schedule, and communicate every idea from every department to EVERYONE ELSE. They make sure that everyone knows what's going on. They have heart attacks early, and everyone on set but the DIRECTOR HATES THEM. (If they're any good.)

MUSIC SUPERVISOR: They select and license music (find out who to pay for music and then pay for it) for the movie. Good ones can MAKE a movie. They are walking music libraries—the good ones LOVE EVERY KIND OF MUSIC and know so much about music they are borderline autistic.

FIRST ASSISTANT EDITOR: The editor will spend months, even YEARS in a dark room watching the same footage over and over. He will come to hate the film. He will come to fear the editing room. Everyone will yell at him when things aren't going well and take the credit when the movie looks good. The editor is Frodo Baggins. The movie is the RING OF DOOM. And the FIRST ASSISTANT EDITOR is their Samwise Gamgee. He will be the editor's only friend, their support, their confessor. He will manage the editor's materials, get them coffee, and fill out all of the paperwork. Editing is a lonely job. It takes two.

CAMERA OPERATOR: The guy who PHYSICALLY moves, points, and operates the camera. Some DPs are camera operators. Some are not and hire a CAMERA OPERATOR to shoot the movie for them. The DP tells them where to put the camera, how to move it, what lens to use. The camera op does it. Needless to say, all camera ops strive to become DPs. DPs try to CRUSH that desire out of them so that they will always work for them.

And here's a relatively new credit in the camera department that will be coming up more and more:

STEREOGRAPHER: Now that many films are in 3-D, you need a person on set responsible for JUST THAT ASPECT of the film—the "stereo" of the two lenses creating the depth. This person sits at a 3-D monitor with 3-D glasses on much of the day, fiddling with the beam splitter and making little adjustments to the shot. Love looking at trippy stuff in 3-D? This might be the job for you.

PRODUCTION SOUND MIXER: They sit by the sound equipment mixing board—LISTENING. They makes sure the right mikes are on and that all of them work during the take. Sometimes they MIX the sound as the scene is playing, turning one actor's mike up and another one's down as the scene goes along—DJ-ing. But no one told them to do that, and in the final mix, everyone ignores the "LIVE MIX" the PSM did on set.

SCRIPT SUPERVISOR: Sits at a monitor, script in hand, and makes sure that the words coming out of the actors' mouths are the same ones written down in the

297

script. Sometimes they also help check continuity: "He was holding his cigarette in his left hand, not his right." Or "The writer says they're about to go visit Batman, but Batman died three scenes ago."

SUPERVISING ART DIRECTOR: Makes sure that the set construction team, the set decoration team, and the art department all know what one another are doing. And that the director and producer know what they're doing, and like what they're doing. And that they're ALL keeping under budget.

GAFFER: Head of the electrical department. He's in charge of the electrical generators, the lights, the cables, and all the guys who move all that stuff around. When the DP wants to move a light, the gaffer does it—or, more correctly said: TELLS SOMEONE UNDER HIM TO DO IT. He wires the lights, moves the wires. If it plugs in—DON'T TOUCH IT unless the gaffer told you to.

KEY GRIP: In charge of the grip department. Head grip. The grip bossman. He tells all the other grips what to do.

GRIPS: Work with the lighting and camera department, putting stuff where it's supposed to be and battening it down. If at first you have trouble telling the difference between the surly, tattooed anarchist electricians and the surly, tattooed anarchist grips, just remember: that grips don't get to plug anything in. And they get hammers.

DOLLY GRIP: The train tracks that they put a camera on, to move smoothly across a room (for a dramatic push-in) or to follow a stagecoach and a bunch of Apaches across Monument Valley for a stagecoach chase—that's the dolly. The track has to be perfectly smooth and perfectly level. And who lays the track? Hard-drinking Irishmen, like in the olden days? The dudes in charge of laying down the track, pushing the camera along the track, and then packing the track up again are called dolly grips. And some of them are hard-drinking Irishmen, yes.

CRANE OPERATOR: Operates the big CRANE that the camera is on, for fancy swooping overhead shots.

SET DECORATOR: Puts all of the finishing decorations on the set: the glassware on the tables, the throw rugs, the pillows, the paintings.

IF IT'S BUILT INTO THE SET: It's set design.
IF IT'S PLACED ON SET: It's set dec.
IF AN ACTOR PICKS IT UP DURING THE SCENE: It's a prop.

PROPERTY MASTER: In charge of all the props for a film. ("Prop" is short for "property.") They buy them, rent them, build them, and sometimes design them (under the oversight of the DIRECTOR, PRODUCER, and PRODUCTION DESIGNER). The prop master and their crew is always on set: they hand the actors the props right before they shoot and take them away right after the shot is done, so that the props are safe. If there are GUNS in the movie, they make sure the guns are fake or unloaded, and they show the actors and the 1st AD that the guns are safe or unloaded before they EVER hand an actor a gun. Every time.

COSTUME SUPERVISOR: They make sure that the costume department is under budget and has all of the costumes it needs—including costumes for EXTRAS and DOUBLES of costumes that might get damaged or wet in scenes. They do a breakdown of every scene in the movie—who's in it and what they are wearing.

VFX SUPERVISOR: Supervises the VFX (Visual Effects). The ones that are done LIVE (EXPLOSIONS and stuff) and the CG ones. They make sure that the right people are hired to achieve the special effects, to pull off the VISION of the DIRECTOR (and the STUDIO and the studio's MARKETING DEPART-MENT). They make sure that the right people are on the job and that they are doing it on schedule and under budget.

VFX PRODUCER: Makes sure the VFX department has everything it needs. The VFX producer's and supervisor's jobs overlap a bit, but they usually work together closely.

POSTPRODUCTION SUPERVISOR: Organizes all of the editors. Makes the sched-ule (based on the budget), then makes sure the editors are on schedule and under budget. They also communicate with the STUDIO about their needs and prog-ress. They handle the payrolls of their department (as does every department head) and they makes sure there are enough snacks and cute assistants around to keep the editors alive.

SUPERVISING SOUND EDITOR: Oversees everything that the ADR EDITOR, DIALOGUE EDITOR, SOUND EFFECTS EDITOR, MUSIC EDITOR, FOLEY EDITOR, and all of the mixers are doing. They make sure all the sound work is coordinated, on time, and under budget.

1ST ASSISTANT SOUND EDITOR: Helps. Does the paperwork. Backs up the su-pervising sound editor in arguments.

MUSIC EDITOR: Takes all of the composed and licensed music for the sound track, edits it, and mixes it into the film—so it's all the right length, at the right place, and at the right levels (all under the supervision of the DIRECTOR and PRO-DUCERS).

SOUND MIXERS: Do the same as the music editor, but for ALL of the film's sounds. They put together the tracks that the music, dialogue, foley guys have given them and weave it into one piece of SOUND; that's what you hear when you see the movie.

PRODUCTION COORDINATOR: They make sure that every piece of equipment that needs to be on set is on set. This person needs the fortitude of Patton and the OCD of Monk. Along with the ADs, they make the schedule for the production and make sure that everything is on schedule. And oh my God, the paperwork—they have to document EVERYTHING—all the time cards, all the time sheets, all the receipts—and they make sure all the accountants have copies of everything.

CONSTRUCTION MANAGER: Same as a construction manager in the real world—they coordinate all the construction. All the painters, carpenters, plasterers, designers—they make sure every department that's building shit is on the same page and on schedule and under budget.

SUPERVISING LOCATION MANAGER: Oversees all the location managers.

TRANSPORTATION COORDINATOR: The transpo coordinator is in charge of EVERY VEHICLE it takes to get a movie done: the trucks that haul sets and equipment, the trailers the movie stars rest in, and the big, giant, mobile toilet trucks (called honey wagons). EVERY VEHICLE and EVERY DRIVER answers to, and is hired by, the transpo coordinator.

Why are the mobile toilets called honey wagons? We've heard Teamsters say it was because the goop the sewage truck sucks out of it looks kinda like honey.

TRANSPORTATION CAPTAIN: Second in command of the transpo department, under the transportation coordinator. They put together the schedule.

SENIOR ART DIRECTOR: If you have more than one art director, the senior art director is in charge of all of them.

ART DIRECTOR: Works for the PRODUCTION DESIGNER and tells the set decorator what to do.

ASSISTANT ART DIRECTORS: Work for the art director.

STANDBY ART DIRECTOR: Stands on set to spy on the art department, making sure they are doing everything the production designer told them to do.

PRODUCTION BUYER: Runs out and buys stuff for the SET DEC department. They are supposed to hunt around and find good deals. On GIANT productions, they sometimes don't and instead buy overpriced stuff from their buddies' stores.

GRAPHIC DESIGNER: Creates fake logos for the movie, like the letterhead for Stark Industries and the Ghostbusters sign.

DRAFTSMAN: Draws up plans and blueprints for the production designer's set and props.

CONCEPT ARTIST: Draws artist renderings of what the director or production designer is trying to create—whether that's a Stormtrooper, the Land of Oz, or Scarlett O'Hara's dress.

STORYBOARD ARTIST: When a scene is complicated, a storyboard artist draws out the scene, shot for shot. The drawings look exactly like the shots, from the right camera angles: they show the camera position, what actor is in the shot, what parts of the set the camera will see, whether or not the camera will be moving. If a scene has hundreds of shots, they hang the storyboards up on a wall, so they know what they've shot and what has to be shot. Usually the DIRECTOR explains each shot to the artist meticulously.

ASSISTANT SET DECORATOR: Assists the set decorator. Duh.

ART DEPARTMENT APPRENTICE: Works for the art department to get into the union. They don't get paid much.

ART DEPARTMENT INTERN: Some poor kid earning college credit or trying to brown-nose his way into a job by working eighteen hours a day, FOR FREE, for the art department.

FOCUS PULLER: Believe it or not, it takes more than one guy to work a camera. The focus puller adjusts the camera's lens to focus on the precise point in the scene that the DP wants to be in focus. The DP and camera op are busy pointing the camera and WATCHING the monitor. So the FOCUS PULLER turns the little doo-hickey to adjust the focus. The camera is so precise and delicate it needs the touch of an INCREDIBLY specialized dude. (Or it's just pure union hogwash—we'll never know!)

CLAPPER LOADER: That thing you see on movie sets that looks like a shoe box lid and has a black-and-white-striped thing on top that CLAPS down. Something like "KING KONG, SCENE 1, TAKE 35" is scribbled on it. That's a clapper. That's used so that the editor, when looking at all the footage, knows what scene he's about to see and what take. Why do people still do it now that everything is digitized and filed in a computer system? UNIONS. The person who holds the CLAPPER up in front of the camera and CLAPS it down after the AD says, "Roll 'em!" That's the CLAPPER LOADER. YES, IT'S A REAL JOB. And they make more than schoolteachers.

STEADICAM OPERATOR: A Steadicam is a device that looks EXACTLY like the machine-gun mounts the Space Marines wear in the movie *Aliens*. It attaches to a rig around the steadicam operator's midsection and holds the camera up at eye level. The operator is then able to move the camera around, in all directions, as they walk (and often run) around the set. The shot is as smooth as if it were on a dolly or tripod (if the operator is good).

FILM LOADER: Oh, and all those guys standing around the camera—the DP, camera operator, and focus puller—they NEED ANOTHER GUY WHO PUTS FILM IN THEIR CAMERA. (See Dinosaur.)

DIT (DIGITAL IMAGING TECHNICIAN): The modern version of a FILM LOADER. Makes sure that the DIGITAL cameras (the only type of cameras people use these days, unless you're a film student) are operating smoothly. That all of the data is being stored. They unload the digital information when the camera is full and download it into the storage system.

CAMERA TRAINEE: Low man on the totem pole in the camera department, but it's where you start unless you "know somebody." They fetch coffee and take HORRENDOUS amounts of verbal and psychological abuse from the Mohawked, hard-drinking anarchists who make up the camera and grip department.

B CAMERA OPERATOR: If you're shooting with more than one camera, the second camera is B CAMERA. The operator answers to the DP.

B CAMERA FOCUS PULLER: That focus puller guy we told you about—EVERY CAMERA needs one of those guys.

B CAMERA LOADER: Loads the film into B Camera.

BOOM OPERATOR: Whenever you hear someone say: "BOOM IN THE SHOT!," that's the fault of the boom operator. He works for the sound department. The BOOM mike is a mike on a long pole either over the actors' heads (and in the shot) or under the actor (and in the shot). The boom operator's job is to hold the long pole and point the MIKE at the actors' mouths. And to KEEP THE BOOM OUT OF THE SHOT.

SOUND ASSISTANT: You ask—why does EVERYBODY have an assistant but the writer? You tell us.

SECOND ASSISTANT DIRECTOR: The 2nd AD does more than "assist" the AD. Their primary responsibilities are TALENT WRANGLING and making sure that the 1st AD's orders are being carried out. He makes sure that the CAST is on time, that they're being taken care of, that they're through their makeup and hair process in time to be on set on time. They make call sheets (daily schedules that tell EVERYBODY when they're supposed to be on set) and then get those schedules out to EVERYBODY. All under the supervision of the 1st AD.

BASE CAMP: Where the movie star trailers, production department trailers, hair trailers, makeup trailers, catering, snacks, bathrooms, and equipment trucks are parked all day. Hopefully close to your set, so people don't spend a ton of time going back and forth.

SECOND 2ND ASSISTANT DIRECTOR: Helps the 2nd AD with their workload.

THIRD ASSISTANT DIRECTOR: Usually tells the BACKGROUND EXTRAS what to do.

ASSISTANT COSTUME SUPERVISOR, COSTUME ASSISTANTS, TRAINEE SEAMSTRESS: We bet you can figure out what these guys do yourself at this point.

COSTUME RUNNER: Runs the costumes from the wardrobe trailer or building to the set and makes sure that they are where they need to be—in the actors' dressing rooms, on set, or on the actors.

COSTUMES SUPPLIED BY: Like, when Armani supplies suits for some movie— they get this credit.

MAKEUP AND HAIR ARTISTS: Put makeup on all the actors and do their hair. Everything they do is dictated and designed by the MAKEUP AND HAIR DESIGNER.

CHIEF CROWD MAKEUP AND HAIR ARTIST: In charge of the people who do the makeup and hair for the background extras.

CROWD MAKEUP AND HAIR ARTIST: Does what the CHIEF CROWD MAKEUP AND HAIR ARTIST tells them to do.

MAKEUP TRAINEE AND CROWD MAKEUP AND HAIR TRAINEE: Some poor schlubs, working for free or almost for free, so that one day they can actually make a living doing makeup and hair.

STUNT COORDINATOR: In charge of all the stunts—figuring out the stunts (as envisioned by the director), planning them, hiring the right guys in front of and behind the camera, coordinating with the special effects guys, and making sure things go without a hitch.

STUNT ASSISTANT: Helps the stunt coordinator.

LEAD STUNT DOUBLE: If there are twelve dudes who sometimes double as Robert Downey, Jr.—this is the one who probably looks the most like him.

STUNT DOUBLE: A guy who looks JUST ENOUGH like Robert Downey, Jr., to get slammed into a brick wall dressed as IRONMAN.

STUNTS: Did some stunt in the movie.

STUNT DRIVER: Did some kinda car stunt. Probably has a mustache.

STUNT RIGGER: Tied some sort of equipment in place, so a dude could fall from a bridge safely. Also probably has a mustache. When the stunt is done, the rigger walks up to the stunt guy and says, "That looked awesome."

STUNT PERFORMER: Did a stunt AS A CHARACTER in the movie: a bank robber, played by a stunt guy, who got punched out a window.

FIGHT CONSULTANT: Makes sure the fight looks cool, believable, and authentic. Has probably studied kung fu in Asia and will probably mention that to you at some point.

PRECISION DRIVER: Does car stunts where the car DOES NOT WRECK. Car chases and stuff. They ALL have mustaches and probably Corvettes too.

ASSISTANT STUNT COORDINATOR: Helps the stunt coordinator.

UTILITY STUNTS: Hangs out on set, just in case you need an extra stunt guy or rigger or spotter.

AERIAL GROUND COORDINATOR: If you have one of these, your movie is cooler than our movies.

VISUAL EFFECTS EDITOR: Takes the visual effects elements and, along with the editor, the director, and all the supervisors, integrates them into the cut of the film.

2ND ASSISTANT EDITOR: Does anything the assistant editors tell them to. From "Go find this footage for me" to "Go get us the new issue of *Maxim*."

TRAINEE EDITOR: Some rube the post department has convinced to work for free.

RIGGING GAFFER: Usually goes on the prescout and figures out everything the gaffer is going to need in order to set up his lights and get power to them. The rigging gaffer makes the plan and makes sure the gaffer has everything he needs.

BEST BOY: The assistant to the gaffer or head electrician. (Disappointing, huh?)

CHARGEHAND RIGGING ELECTRICIAN: The guy one below the rigging electrician in rank.

ELECTRICIANS: We bet you can figure this one out.

RIGGING ELECTRICIAN: The electrician in charge of tying and hanging stuff up in the air, above the set.

An easy-to-remember rule: RIGGING guys are in charge of anything up in the air. GAFFERS are in charge of anything on the ground.

GENNY OPERATOR: The Teamster who unloads the generator from the truck, gasses it up, pushes the on or off button, and stands beside it all day, drinking coffee and reporting anybody else who tries to touch it.

PROPS STOREMAN: The guy who knows where all the props are in the giant storage warehouse. He goes and gets them and puts them back where they belong.

STANDBY PROPSMAN: The guy from the props department who stands on set, waiting to see if anything is needed from the props department.

KEY GREENSMAN: In charge of any plants, trees, or plant or tree trimmings on the set.

SENIOR SPECIAL EFFECTS TECHNICIAN: Oversees everyone who's making, rigging, or turning on any of the special effects.

ASSISTANT PRODUCTION COORDINATOR: Assists the person who's making sure that every piece of equipment that needs to be on set is on set.

ASSISTANT TO THE DIRECTOR, ASSISTANT TO MR. STILLER, ASSISTANT TO . . . WHOEVER: If you're important enough, you get your own toady.

PRODUCTION RUNNER: In charge of driving stuff all over town, picking up stuff and dropping stuff off at the production office.

RUSHES RUNNER: "Rushes" are the first prints of the "dailies"—the filming that was done during the day. The rushes runner goes and picks them up and brings them to the screening room or to the set, so that the director can watch them and make adjustments.

PA (PRODUCTION ASSISTANT): If you're the PA and ANYONE on set tells you to do ANYTHING—you have to do it.

HOD CARPENTER, HOD PAINTER, HOD PLASTERER: This is a British credit. Head of Department.

SUPERVISING CARPENTER: In charge of all the carpenters.

SUPERVISING PLASTERER: In charge of all the plasterers.

CHARGEHAND RIGGERS, CHARGEHAND PAINTER: Second in command in the rigging or painting department (below the supervising rigger or painter—but above everybody else). There to make sure the supervisor's orders are carried out or to take command if the supervisor gets blown up.

STANDBY CARPENTER, STANDBY RIGGER, STANDBY PAINTER: Hangs out on set in case someone needs a carpenter, rigger, or painter.

CARPENTERS: They build EVERYTHING that needs building, level the tables and doors—all the carpentry.

TRAINEE CARPENTER: Learning how to be a carpenter/slaving away for free to get into the union.

PAINTERS: They paint.

PAINTERS LABOURER: Hauls the painter's stuff around for them.

APPRENTICE PAINTER: Learning how to paint/slaving away for free to get into the union.

RIGGERS: Again, if it's electric and ON THE FLOOR—gaffers plug it in, tape it down, and haul it in and out. If it's on the CEILING—it gets rigged. By RIG-GERS.

PLASTERERS: Make stuff that's made of plaster and cement.

WOOD MACHINIST: Cuts raw wood material for the carpenters.

LOCATION MANAGERS: They find the locations for the film, usually showing LOTS of locations to the director until they pick one. They find out who to pay to use the location, pay them, fill out all the permits, let the neighbors know there's going to be filming going on, and hang out on set, "troubleshooting." In L.A., folks are pretty savvy to shooting, so the location managers carry around a pocket of twenties to pay off guys who turn on their lawn mowers and crank up their stereos during takes—to get one of the location manager's twenties.

UNIT MANAGER: The production manager for the second unit.

LOCATION ASSISTANT: Assists the location manager. Helps scout, helps with the paperwork.

LOCATION SECURITY BY: Security companies that hang out on the set and in the base camp to protect the equipment, snacks, and movie stars.

PRODUCTION ACCOUNTANT: The head accountant for the production. In charge of budgets, time cards, paychecks—all the bean counting.

FIRST ASSISTANT ACCOUNTANT: Second in command in the accounting department.

ASSISTANT ACCOUNTANTS: The bean counters.

UNIT PUBLICIST: Handles all of the publicity for the film. They handle calls from the press who want to talk to the movie stars—or they call the press to beg them to talk about the movie. They arrange the interviews and organize the red carpet. They usually work for the studio.

STILLS PHOTOGRAPHER: The photographer hired by the studio to take photographs of the action as the movie is being shot.

EPK (ELECTRONIC PRESS KIT) CREW: A small crew that sets up cameras, lights, and directors' chairs in some out-of-the-way corner of the set and interviews the movie stars about the movie to use as publicity. It's usually just a camera guy, a sound guy, and an interviewer—usually a VERY CUTE CHICK, or a guy with a VERY COOL HAIRCUT.

VOICE COACH TO . . . WHOMEVER: The director hired an actor who can't sing and is supposed to sing. Now it's the voice coach's problem.

ACTING COACH TO . . . WHOMEVER: The director hired an actor who can't act. Now it's the acting coach's problem.

MARINE COORDINATOR: If you're shooting a scene in the water or under water, the marine coordinator is in charge of making sure you have the right equipment, manpower, stunt men, safety gear, etc. They're in charge (under the DIREC-TOR) of the water sequence.

ASSISTANT MARINE COORDINATOR: Assistant to the marine coordinator. Usually has to stay later and fill out the insurance paperwork.

MUSICAL ADVISOR: An expert who gives the director his opinion on the music. Very key if you're doing, say, *Amadeus* or a film set in the Haight-Ashbury in 1968. Not so key if you're doing *PORKY'S VII* or *Reno 911!: Miami*.

HISTORICAL ADVISOR: Makes sure historical scenes are accurate. Stands on set and makes sure nobody's wearing Nikes in ancient Rome or says "Right on!" at the Battle of Gettysburg.

SINGING COACH: Makes sure the singing doesn't suck for the WHOLE CAST.

STAND-INS: After the cast and director REHEARSE a scene on set, the actors go away and STAND-INS come in, dressed like the actors. The stand-ins stand where the actors stood so that the DP can light the scene (which takes hours), while the actors work out, hang out by the crafts services table, flirt, or smoke dope in their trailers.

U.K. CASTING ASSISTANT: Wow, you used a U.K. casting agent! Classy! This person was their assistant.

HEAD ANIMAL TRAINER: The animal trainer in charge of all of the animal trainers on your set. Any animal that works in a movie—cobra, cat, or chicken—comes with several animal trainers. They stand to the side as the camera rolls, usually waving a stuffed dog toy, watching helplessly while their "trained" animal stands frozen in panic, flees, or attacks the movie star.

CERTIFIED ANIMAL SAFETY REPRESENTATIVE: Stands on set, making sure that "No Animals Were Harmed"® during the making of your movie.

HEALTH AND SAFETY COORDINATOR: Consultants who make sure that everything on set is SAFE and healthy. The stunts, the water you're flooding the boat with, the food you're pretending to eat . . . they can shut you down in a heartbeat.

UNIT NURSE: Every set has a nurse or medic. They have Band-Aids, aspirin, that cool superglue stuff that makes instant stitches, and LOTS of Emergen-C.

TUTOR/STUDIO TEACHER: If a child is missing school to be in a movie, they must attend class on set and do a certain amount of homework, the amount of which is determined by the state. We would argue—if your kid is already cast in a movie, what does he need an eduction for? They're in showbiz! They're gonna turn out JUST FINE.

CHILD WELFARE WORKER: Hangs around any child on set, making sure they're not working longer than they're supposed to. (Children can work only a limited number of hours a day—it's different for every age group in every state. Canada is much more lenient.) Makes sure that the child has been to their tutor, that the child is safe, not exposed to foul language, that no one is giving the kid blow, etc., etc. Some child welfare workers are a REAL pain in the ass: they decide that a scene isn't appropriate for children or that a child DIDN'T DO WELL ENOUGH on their homework, and they can yank the child from the set—with no due process, no oversight, and there's nothing you can really do about it. They can shut your production down on a whim. We would argue: would Buster Keaton, Mickey Rooney, or Michael Jackson EVER have become the legends if they hadn't been put though the wringer of showbiz at an early age?

UNIT DRIVERS: They drive any CAR on set (not the trucks). They pick up actors, scripts, film, press people—anything that can fit into a car or car trunk.

MINIBUS DRIVERS: The Teamsters who drive the cast and crew between the set and base camp.

TRANSPORT FACILITIES: The company that rents you the vehicles, and hauls THE ENTIRE SET to location: honey wagons, trailers, the whole company. It's like moving Patton's Third Army.

LOCATION FACILITIES: The company that rents you the trailers and tents for base camp.

TRANSPORT FACILITIES MANAGER: The guy in charge of the company move.

TRANSPORT FACILITY DRIVERS: The drivers who drive the company to the next day's base camp at the end of the day. Picture Teamster Trucker Vampires.

CONSTRUCTION TRUCK: The name following this credit is not the name of the truck. It's the name of the guy who drove the truck.

PROPS TRUCK: Same as above.

CAMERA CAR: Any car that you see ON CAMERA is a CAMERA CAR. From the Batmobile to the cop cars that chase the Batmobile to all the background cars the Batmobile passes on the freeway. Anyone driving one of those cars gets the "Camera Car" credit—meaning they DROVE a camera car. Unless they did a stunt—then they get a stunt credit.

CATERING: This is the company that made lunch. Mmmm. Lunch.

SECOND UNIT: When a movie is BIG, they shoot a lot of the scenes that don't have movie stars in them with a second unit: a second crew, with its own camera department, sound department, everything. While the movie stars are shooting one scene on a soundstage, the second unit can be filming a big CHASE SCENE on the other side of town. Big stunt scenes are often second unit. So, then—as movie credits roll by, you'll see the credits REPEAT for the people who do the job on the SECOND UNIT: DIRECTOR OF PHOTOGRAPHY, GRIPS, SCRIPT SUPERVISOR, SOUND RECORDIST, 1ST ASSISTANT DIRECTOR, CLAPPER LOADER, etc., etc.

THEN, AFTER ALL THE SECOND-UNIT CREDITS . . .

POSTPRODUCTION COORDINATOR: Makes sure that the postproduction people have all the equipment they need.

POSTPRODUCTION RUNNER: Kid who goes and gets coffee, lunch, porn, and tapes for the guys who work in postproduction.

POSTPRODUCTION ACCOUNTANT: Keeps track of how much money the post department is spending.

SUPERVISING ADR EDITOR: In charge of ADR—what lines need to be ADR'd, who needs to do them, scheduling the actors to come in and record, recording them, and getting the ADR'd lines into the movie.

ADR means ADDITIONAL DIALOGUE RECORDING: It means RE-RECORDING DIALOGUE that didn't record perfectly when you were shooting the scene—because it was windy, because someone BUMPED their microphone, because someone blew a car horn in the background and it's supposed to be 1776.

It can also mean recording people to sound like BACKGROUND PEOPLE in scenes, to fill out the sound in a crowded restaurant, for example.

ADR/DIALOGUE EDITOR: Edits the ADR'd lines into the movie—makes sure they're synced and mixed and sound good.

DIALOGUE EDITOR: Edits the dialogue into the movie—makes sure it's synced and mixed and sounds good.

SOUND EFFECTS/FOLEY EDITOR: In charge of all of the (nondialogue) sound in the movie.

1ST ASSISTANT SOUND EDITOR: Assistant to the sound editor in charge.

FOLEY ARTISTS: Guys who make the sound effects for the movie in a little room, banging their shoes on tables, breaking bottles, and making noises like the MouthSounds guy or that dude Tom Keith from *Prairie Home Companion*.

FOLEY EDITOR: Puts all the MouthSounds guy sounds into the movie.

ADR VOICE CASTING: Casts new actors to do background dialogue, or makes sure the movie stars show up and do their dialogue.

RERECORDING STAGE: Where they recorded the ADR. Usually somewhere in Burbank.

RECORDIST: The guy who works the mikes that record the ADR.

RERECORDING ENGINEER: The guy who mixes the levels while they recorded the ADR.

DOLBY CONSULTANT: The representative from Dolby Sound whom you HAVE TO PAY because you're using Dolby equipment to mix. It's sort of like if you bought a Toyota and you had to pay a dude from Toyota to sit in the backseat ALL THE TIME to watch you drive. And pay him A LOT.

MUSIC ORCHESTRATED AND CONDUCTED BY: We bet you can guess this one.

MUSIC RECORDED AND MIXED AT: The PLACE where the orchestra laid down the score.

MUSIC RECORDED AND MIXED BY: The guy recording and mixing as the orchestra plays.

1ST ASSISTANT ENGINEER: The guy helping that guy.

2ND ASSISTANT ENGINEER: The guy helping the guy who's helping that guy.

ORCHESTRA CONTRACTOR: The one who HIRED the members of the orchestra.

ORCHESTRA LEADER: The dude with the baton standing in front of the orchestra.

MUSIC PREPARATION: Laid out the orchestra's arrangements.

SPECIAL MUSICIANS: Guys who play instruments that AREN'T so vital that the 20th Century Fox Orchestra keeps them on a full-time payroll, 'cause their instrument doesn't come up too often. We're talking lutes, didgeridoos, bagpipes, washtub basses, ouds, aquaggaswacks, bikelophones, juice harps, and the Samchillian Tip Tip Tip Cheeepeeeee.

CHOIRMASTER: If you have one of these—then, man, you're doing a fancy movie! You're probably hoping for some awards or something! Good luck at the Oscars!

VISUAL EFFECTS BY: The person or company that creates all of the visual special effects.

COMPOSITING SUPERVISOR: The one making sure the effects look good when they get put into the movie. He supervises everyone involved in this process.

CG SUPERVISOR: In charge of all the "computer graphics" (computer-generated special effects).

DIGITAL MATTE AND TEXTURE PAINTING: The people who painted the cool backgrounds that look like Boston in 1776, Dagobah, or Sleeping Beauty's castle. They paint it small, either by hand or animating it with a fancy computer.

CG MODELER: Creates (programs) the first CG models of any CG character, spaceship, prop, or animal based on the director's vision. That model is then used by all the other digital effects guys to create the effects for the movie.

DIGITAL ENVIRONMENTS: Create the digital SETS for the CG or real characters to be composited in front of.

COMPOSITOR: Uses a computer to put the FOREGROUND ELEMENT—Paul Giamatti, Mark Hamill, or Prince Charming—inside the DIGITAL ENVIRON-MENTS and in front of the DIGITAL MATTE.

ROTOSCOPING SUPERVISOR: People who trace over REAL filmed footage to create an animated version of it. Like that awesome A-HA video.

ROTOSCOPING COORDINATOR: Makes sure the rotoscopers have the footage they need and know what they're supposed to be doing.

ROTOSCOPOR: The Korean animator guys who work eighteen hours a day actually DOING the rotoscoping.

CAMERA MATCHMOVING: Oh my God, this is so hard to describe. You know, like in the later, not-as-good *Star Wars* movies, they would walk out of a REAL PLACE and into a BLUE-SCREENED place—like, they'd be in a set that looked real, then they'd step into JAR JAR BINKS's world? Well, the "camera moves" in the two halves of the scene need to MATCH, so that the shot filmed by a real camera in the REAL WORLD and the animated shot in the JAR JAR BINKS world match up and look like the same shot. Matching a "virtual" camera movement in a virtual world with the REAL camera movement in the REAL world is camera matchmoving. If you don't understand, go find some nerd and they'll explain it to you.

TECHNICAL SUPPORT: Could mean they went on a Starbucks run. Could mean they bribed the president of Venezuela to let you leave Venezuela with the film. Could mean they threatened to kill an old lady to let the film shoot in her cornfield.

DIGITAL INTERMEDIATE BY: The DIGITAL print of your movie, transferred from film. You then tweak the colors of your movie in this DIGITAL FORMAT.

SUPERVISING DIGITAL COLORIST: Supervises all of the changes you make to your movie's colors: brightening shots, darkening shots, making the sky bluer, the jungle greener.

DIGITAL INTERMEDIATE PRODUCER: Makes sure all of the people involved in color correction show up on time and have everything they need.

THE PRODUCERS WISH TO THANK: "The producers owe you in a HUGE way . . . but they're not going to pay you anything."

FILMED ON LOCATION AT: Where they filmed the movie. If it wasn't shot on a soundstage.

THANKS TO: "This film wouldn't be possible without you—but we're not going to pay you anything."

ACCOUNTING: An outside accounting firm that oversees and double-checks the bean counting that the production bean counters did.

LEGAL AND BUSINESS AFFAIRS: The most anal people on the planet. They check every name of every character in the movie to see if there's a REAL Indiana Jones or Luke Skywalker who might sue you for using his name. They check the name of every restaurant in the script, every business—to make sure no one can later sue the studio for using their business's name. Every mention of every product—they make sure it's NOT slanderous. Every song, everything that's said in the movie—they make sure there's NOT one in the real world. They make a list of EVERYTHING you might possibly be sued for, write it all up in a 10,000-page memo, and give it to you—to cover the studio's ass.

TITLES DESIGNED BY: The person who thought up the look of the opening titles of the movie.

TITLES BY: The person or company that actually MADE the opening titles.

OPTICALS BY: Dissolves, cross fades . . . stuff like that. Computers do it—but the guy at the computer making sure the cross fade looks how you want it to look gets this credit.

POSTPRODUCTION FACILITIES PROVIDED BY: Sometimes you edit a movie in a post house that's all set up for editing. That is your postproduction facility.

EDITING EQUIPMENT SUPPLIED BY: The company that made the editing equipment. They get paid, and they get a credit.

VIDEO TRANSFERS BY: The company that makes copies of your movie and gets them out to everyone in America.

NEGATIVE CUTTER: See DINOSAUR.

LEGAL SERVICES PROVIDED BY: Let's say you made *Borat*. If you made *Borat*, a lot of people sued you. You needed some legal services. They also do the contracts.

TRAVEL ARRANGED BY: The company that arranges the travel for the crew and cast.

RIGHTS AND CLEARANCES BY: They get the rights to any song, book, TV SHOW, or anything that is legally owned by someone, so you can use it in your movie.

"SO-AND-SO" COURTESY OF, OR "SO-AND-SO" BY ARRANGEMENT WITH: If a singer or artist is under contract to some studio or record company, that studio or record company must be thanked for letting "So-and-So" do your movie.

COLOR BY: After your movie is shot, you correct all of the color with a computer—making your movie prettier, or scarier, or more Oscar-worthy. The company that does this gets this credit.

ACKNOWLEDGMENTS

We'd like to thank David Lincoln. Thank you, Glarn.

INDEX

Page numbers in *italics* refer to illustrations.

Academy Awards, 50, 89, 141, 155, 179
action scenes, 172–73
actors, 188–89, 208
  dialogue and, 156–59
  see also movie stars
"Adaptation by" credit, 127
ADR (additional dialogue recording), 187, 308
agents and managers, 5–9, 15, 29, 37, 50, 186
  acquiring of, 5, 9
  deals negotiated by, 6–7, 30–35
  difference between, 7–9
  functions of, 5–6
  percentages paid to, 32
  rewrites and, 180, 181
  screen rights acquired by, 201, 202
Allen, Woody, 24
Anderson, Laurie, 162
"& or AND" in credits, 127–28
arbitration, 49, 126, 180*n*, 193–97
  arbitration statement in, 196–97
  process of, 194–96
  professional arbiters for, 196, 197
  WGA Arbitration Committee in, 128–29, 194–96
  winning of, 196–97
Avatar, 39

Banks, Elizabeth, 164
"Based on Characters Created by" credit, 127
Bay, Michael, 83
Beer Runners, 22–23
Bernhard, Sandra, 123, 189
Besson, Luc, 116, 118
bidding wars, 31, 127
Blind Side, The, 199
Blue Streak, 77
Bogart, Humphrey, 40, 148
book rights, 201–3
box-office bonus, 34
box-office receipts, xii, 39, 54, 77*n*, 90, 98–99, 100, 103, 115, 161, 167, 193, 199, 211
Brest, Martin, 77
Buddhism, 191–92

Bukowski, Charles, 168
Bündchen, Gisele, 117, 118, 119
Burden of Dreams, 84

Caine, Michael, 27–28
California condors, 188
California State Income Tax, 33
Cameron, James, 39, 55, 148
Campbell, Joseph, 149
Carolla, Adam, 116
carpal tunnel syndrome, 174, 177
Carrey, Jim, 19
cartoon characters, 199
Casablanca, 12, 40, 63, 155, 161
  development of, 65
  drinking and, 205
  structure of, 147, 148–51
Casa La Golondrina restaurant, 132–33
Cat and Fiddler bar, 132
cat videos, funny, 166, *167,* 168
celebrities, 188–89
Chan, Jackie, 120–23, *120*
character development, 12, 125
characters, 154–65, 196
  cartoon, 199
  descriptions of, 171–72
  of *Die Hard,* 162
  entertaining problems faced by, 161–62, 163
  hero, *see* main characters
  initial letter of names of, 153
  maximum ten-page explanation of, 148, 156, 171
  omitting backstory on, 160–61
  real-feeling, 159–60, 163
  specific actors as models for, 156–59
Chaya Brasserie restaurant, 70
Columbia Pictures, 67, 109
  parking at, 58
Comedy Central, 108–9
comic books, 127, 134, 199
Comic-Con video presentations, 112
commencement payments, 31, 50
contracts, 24, 25, 35, 36–37, 59, 169

Cotillard, Marion, 116
coverage, 51–54, 79
creative control, 34
credit bonus, 34
credits, 25, 33–34, 66, 124–29, 180*n*, 185, 187, 199
   "& or AND" in, 127–28
   examples of, 33, 124–27
   glossary of, 295–311
   official, 194
   order of names in, 128–29
   pseudonyms in, 129
   royalties in, 61, 124, 193–94, 196
   studio's suggested, 194
   see also arbitration
critics, 114–15, 192
Cross, David, 22–23
Crystal, Billy, 93*n*, 107

deadlines, 169
Delgo, 77
Del Toro, Guillermo, 85, 87
Diaz, Cameron, 80–81
Die Hard, 12, 99, 167
   characters of, 162
   structure of, 148–50
Diesel, Vin, ix-x, 99, 121–22
directors, 33, 50, 62, 82–88, 89, 91, 92, 186, 208, 295
   of action scenes, 173
   earnings of, 82–83, 86
   first assistant, 297
   helpful attitude toward, 87
   movie star approval of, 190
   patience needed by, 84–86
   production rewrites and, 184, 185
   types of, 86–87
Disney, 22–23, 67, 92–100, 198–99
   parking at, 55
Don Cucos restaurant, 133
DreamWorks, parking at, 57
drinking, 22–23, 61, 174, 176, 204–7

earnings, 6, 31–33, 38, 52, 117, 125
   commencement payments in, 31, 50
   creative spending of, 200, 208*n*–9*n*
   of directors, 82–83, 86
   of movie stars, 189, 190
   from notes, 71
   passive, on sequels, 34, 199
   percentages paid from, 24, 32–33
   residuals, 24, 25, 124, 125, 196
   for rewrites, 183, 185, 186
   royalties, 61, 124, 193–94, 196
economic crisis, current, 30, 36
editors, 5, 88, 296, 297, 299
Eisenberg, Jesse, 159, 277
El Cholo restaurant, 133
Empire, 167

entertainment lawyers, 6, 7, 35, 196, 202
   percentage paid to, 33
Eraserhead, 13, 167
E.T., 109

Fallon, Jimmy, x, 116–19
Faulkner, William, *19*, 206–7
federal income tax, 33
Ferguson, Craig, 191
film festivals, 161
Final Draft computer program, 4–5, 45–46, 48–49, 153, 166, 178–79
firing, 59–61, 73, 89, 92, 95, 180, 183, 191, 293–94
   rehiring after, 34, 60–61, 72, 74
   of studio executives, 4, 67, 90, 106
first-dollar gross, 189
Fitzcarraldo, 84
Focus Features, 67
formatting, 4–5, 38, 40–46
   individual studio requirements of, 43–46
Forrest Gump, 109
Fox, *see* 20th Century Fox
Fox Searchlight, 67
France, 116–18, 169
"fresh eyes," 59–60, 87, 180*n*, 293–94
Frolic Room, 105
Funny or Die videos, 111

Galifianakis, Zach, 156–57, 164
Ganz, Lowell, 60, 99, 126, 128
Garden of Eden, The (Hemingway), 206
Gerard Lounge, 134
Giamatti, Paul, 159
Gigli, 19, 77, 191
Golden Apple Comics, 134
Golden Globe Awards, 141, 188
gracious behavior, 60, 104, 194
   notes and, 71, 72, 73, *73*, 96–97
   pitching and, 20–21
Grant, Hugh, 13
Greenberg, Scott, 33
Grove, 135

Halekulani hotel, 136
Hamburg, John, ix-x, 60
Hangover, The, 53, 54
Helms, Ed, 278
Hemingway, Ernest, 171, 205, 206, 207
Herbie: Fully Loaded, ix, 66, 92–100, 170, 183, 198–99
   incompetent executive's effect on, 92–93, 95–97
Herzog, Werner, 84
"high concept" idea, 127
Hollywood Canteen restaurant, 120–22

I Love You, Man, ix
Incredible Shrinking Man, The, 77–79

Inn on Mount Ada, 136
In-N-Out Burgers, 15, 137–40
  secret menu of, 139–40
Instant Monsters outline, 211, 275–92
internet, 111, 179
  critics on, 114–15, 192
  funny cat videos on, 166, *167*, 168
Island Express Helicopters, 136
Ivy Restaurant, 70, 98

Jackson, Samuel, 278
Jacobson, Nina, 94–95, 198
Jade Mountain resort, 200, *200*
James, Kevin, 80–81, 100
Jobs, Steve, 165
Johnson, Dwayne "The Rock," 157, 158
Jules Verne Restaurant, 169

Knowles, Beyoncé, 142–43

Lady in the Water, 94n
La Serenata de Garibaldi restaurant, 133
Las Fuentes Mexican Restaurant, 133
last-writer bonus, 34
Lawrence, Martin, 77n, 185, 188
lawyers, entertainment, 6, 7, 35, 196, 202
lead role, *see* main characters
Liar, Liar, 19
Lionsgate, 67
Lohan, Lindsay, 70, 92, *92*, 94–95, 98, 170,
  198, 199
Lopez, Jennifer, 191
Lord of the Rings, 98–99
Los Angeles, Calif., 15, 130–43, *130*
  bars in, 22–23, 105, 132, 134–35
  Beverly Park, 105
  "car hobbies" needed in, 130–31, 133
  comic book store in, 134
  getaway destinations from, 135–37
  Grove make-believe neighborhood, 135
  In-N-Out Burger locations in, 137–40
  residing in, 3–4, 24
  restaurants in, 70, 98, 120–22, 132–35
  Robertson Boulevard roller-skater in,
    69–70
  Upright Citizens Brigade in, 5
  writing in public in, 131–32

McBride, Danny, 164–65
McDuck, Scrooge (char.), 199
McKee, Robert, xi–xii, 147
main characters, 53, 54, 72, 94, 154–56, 161
  of *Die Hard,* 162
  heroic quality of, 155
  likability of, 66, 154–55, 162, 163
  maximum ten-page explanation of, 148, 156
  movie star's desire for role of, 18–19,
    154–55
  in structure, 148–52

managers, *see* agents and managers
Mandel, Babaloo, 60, 99, 126, 128
marketing, 30, 53, 54, 105–6, 203
  methods of, 110–13
marketing department, 105–6, 111–13
Market restaurant, 118
Matrix, The, 12, 147
  structure of, 147, 148–51
Mexican restaurants, 132–33
MGM, parking at, 58
Mirren, Helen, 10, 124, 174
Morgan, Tracy, 142–43
movies:
  animated, 25, 77, 155, 187
  art-house, xi–xii, *151*, 152, 167
  box-office receipts of, xii, 39, 54, 77n, 90,
    98–99, 100, 103, 115, 161, 167, 193, 199,
    211
  budgets of, 103–4
  casting of, 54, 62, 112, 117, 185, 188–89,
    296
  cost of, 39, 54, 84, 86, 102, 103–4, 111–12,
    180–81, 211
  critics of, 114–15, 192
  entertainment value of, 11–13, 161–62
  failure of, 32, 37, 85, 116–19
  free ideas for, xii–xiii, 19, 27–28, 72, 80–81,
    127, 142–43, 164–65
  independent, 3, 12, 13, 30, 148
  international appeal of, 103
  "kids'," 94
  long speeches in, 40
  poor quality of, 35, 36, 59, 62–68, 96, 129,
    180
  ratings of, 53, 211–12
  scrapped, 101–7
  structure of, 147–52, 168
  successful kinds of, 13, 18, 169
  target audience of, 53, 106, 111
  test screenings of, 85–86, 117
  3-D, 106, 297
movie stars, 4, 13, 18–19, 50, 54, 59, 62, 171,
  188–92
  actors and celebrities vs., 188–89
  appropriate treatment of, 190, 191–92
  attached contemplative, 105
  bars frequented by, 134
  Buddhist, 191–92
  cold readings by, 102–3
  directors approved by, 190
  earnings of, 189, 190
  in marketing, 111
  notes of, 185, 190–92
  production rewrites and, 184, 185, 189–92
movie theaters, 103, 111
municipal bonds, short-term, 197

Naceri, Samy, 117
"Narration Written by" credit, 126–27

317

INDEX

negotiating deals, 6–7, 30–35, 192
 one-step, 36
Neptune's Net, 134–35
New Line Cinema, 98–99
Newsroom Cafe, 70
New York, N.Y., 5, 23, 69, 116
 Greenwich Village, xi–xii, 3
 Writers Guild of America, East, in, 24, 25
Night at the Museum, 115, 118, 161, 199, 277
notes, 35, 36–37, 39, 49, 71–79, 75, 186
 bad, 65–67, 72, 73–74
 good, 65, 72, 73, 74
 gracious response to, 71, 72, 73, 73, 96–97
 harmless incorporation of, 72, 73–74, 96, 192
 of movie stars, 185, 190–92
 nodding in response to, 72
 payment for, 71
 of producers, 75–76, 75, 97
 producer's draft, 17
 of studio heads, 72, 77–79, 95
 writing down, 72
notes meetings, 71–73, 77–79
 with movie stars, 190–92

One and Only Palmilla, 136–37
one-step deals, 36
Oswalt, Patton, 186
outlines, 166–69, 176
outlines, sample, 168, 211–91
 Instant Monsters, 211, 275–92
 Reno S.O.S.!, 211–12, 213–59
 Scouts' Honor, 211, 261–73
Overture Films, 67

Pacifier, The, ix-x, 12, 99, 121–22
Paramount, 36, 67, 109
 parking at, 56
parking, studio, 55–58
"Patience" (Guns N' Roses), 85
Paul Blart: Mall Cop, 100
percentage of the profits, 33, 83, 91, 193
personal assistants, 9
Pink's Hot Dogs, 51
pitching, 18–23, 98–100, 107, 180–81, 185
 of book rights, 202–3
 dressing for, ix, 19, 19
 drunkenness and, 22–23
 guidelines for, 19–21
 to Jackie Chan, 121–22
 as performance, 20, 23
 of rewrites, 182–83
 to studio heads, 30, 94–95, 96, 97
polish, 49, 190
 optional, 36
postproduction, 88, 89, 299
Principato, Peter, 8

producers, 7, 33, 35, 50, 71, 89–91, 96, 117–18, 202, 295, 296
 notes of, 75–76, 75, 97
 profits percentage of, 91
producer's draft, 71
production companies, 67, 296
production rewrites, 183–87, 190
 ADR jokes in, 187
 movie stars and, 184, 185, 189–92
 payment for, 185, 186
 punch-ups, 4, 161, 185
 reasons for, 184–85
 roundtables, 4, 186
product placement, 111–12
pseudonyms, 129
punch-ups, 4, 161, 185

Queen Latifah, x, 116–19
quotes, 6, 30–32, 94–95
 definition of, 30

ratings, 53, 211–12
readers, script, 51–54
remakes, 34, 77–79, 99, 116–19
Reno 911!, 108–9, 211, 212
Reno 911!: Miami, 211–12
Reno S.O.S.! outline, 211–12, 213–59
representation, *see* agents and managers
reshoots, 186
residuals, 24, 25, 124, 125, 196
rewrites, 4, 9–10, 30, 35, 37, 87, 104, 161, 180–87, 196
 advantages of, 183
 payment for, 183, 185, 186
 pitching of, 182–83
 process of, 181–83
 of unsold script, 14, 16
 see also production rewrites
Robinson, Craig, 164–65, 280
Roosevelt, Teddy, 114–15
roundtables, 4, 186
royalties, 61, 124, 193–94, 196
Rush Hour II, 121

Sandler, Adam, 20, 80–81, 100
Scouts' Honor outline, 211, 261–73
"Screenplay by" credit, 124, 125, 127
screenplays:
 entertainment value of, 11–13
 minimum payments for, 31, 34
 published, 39
 retaining separated rights to, 33–34, 127, 128
 "stories that need to be told" vs., 11–12
 WGA definition of, 125
 see also scripts
screenplay writing:
 action scenes in, 172–73
 assiduous, 9–10, 14–17, 154n, 208

deadlines in, 169
description in, 170–73
dialogue in, 156–59, 160, 171, 182, 189, 196
location in, 170–71
outlines in, 166–69, 176
with a partner, 175–77
in public, 131–32
structure in, 147–53, 156, 168
style development in, 16
see also characters; rewrites
screen rights, 201–3
cost of, 202
"Screen Story by" credit, 125–26, 128, 199
script publication fees, 193
scripts:
Act III problems in, 52, 53, 58, 104
backing up of, 49
coverage of, 51–54, 79
development of, 30, 62, 63–67, 105, 180, 184
fact-checking of, 38, 48
final draft of, 31
first draft of, 31, 35, 36, 39, 52, 94, 176
formatting of, 4–5, 38, 40–46
inciting incident in, 149, 152
initial letter of characters' names in, 153
official draft of, 38, 49
payment for, 38, 50, 52
PDF version of, 38, 48–49, 50
proofreading of, 48
readability of, 53
registering of, with WGA, 38, 46, 49
resale of, to another studio, 108–9
revisions of, 36, 46, 48
right length of, 38–40, 53, 102–3, 156
saved drafts of, 49
shooting draft of, 39
spec, 7, 17, 29, 31, 35, 180–81, 210
spell checking of, 38, 46, 48, 178–79
stalled or scrapped, 77, 101–9
time allowed for writing of, 35–37, 169
title page of, 38, 46–48
turning in of, 50, 53, 65
as unread by studio heads, 52, 53, 78–79
unsold, 11–17
see also screenplays
separated rights to material, 33–34, 127, 128
sequels, 30, 33–34, 116, 117, 118, 127, 151, 198–200, 211–12
jinxing of, 198–99, 211, 212
passive payments on, 34, 199
ShoWest trade show, 111
Shyamalan, M. Night, 94*n*
Simonds, Bob, 117–18
Smith, Will, 30, 58
Solondz, Todd, 54
Sony, 58, 67
source material, 125–26, 127, 128
Speed, 109

Spiderman, 149–50
Spyglass Films, 36
Spy Next Door, The, 99
Starsky & Hutch, 185
Star Wars, 40, 149–51, 161
Stiller, Ben, 155, 156–57
"Story by" credit, 124–25, 128
studio executives, ix, 7, 29, 30, 35, 50, 85, 117
coverage by, 51–54, 79
dumb vs. smart, 65–68, 93, 95
falling asleep by, 99–100
firing of, 67, 90, 106
incompetent, 92–93, 95–97
junior, 52, 65–66
keeping their jobs as goal of, 4, 59, 72, 106, 113
pitching to, *see* pitching
studio heads, 19, 65, 66
notes of, 72, 77–79, 95
pitching to, 30, 94–95, 96, 97
scripts unread by, 52, 53, 78–79
Summit Entertainment, 67
Superman movies, 160

table reads, 4, 102–3
Tallulah Wine Bar, 134
target audience, 53, 106, 111
taxes, 33, 197
write-offs of, 37
Taxi, x, 116–19
French version of, 116, 117
Taxi 2, 117, 118, 199
television, 24, 25, 33, 34, 108–9, 111, 193, 211–12
Terminator, The, 12, 13, 39, 96, 146
test screenings, 85–86, 117
30 Days of Night, 127
3-D movies, 106, 297
Three of Clubs, 22–23
tie-ins, 87*n*, 111–12
Titanic, 39
Towering Inferno, The, 167
Toy Story, 54
Transformers, 54
Transformers 2: Revenge of the Fallen, 22, 84
true stories, 201–3
20th Century Fox, 67, 96, 108–9, 161, 212
parking at, 55–56
standard script formats of, 43–44
Twitter, 125

Universal Pictures, 20, 67, 109
parking at, 57
Upright Citizens Brigade, 5

vamping, 171
Verrone, Patric, 25
Village Idiot bar, 132

319

Warhol, Andy, 167
Warner, Jack, 65
Warner Bros., 63, 67, 109
    parking at, 56
    standard script format of, 45
Weinstein Company, 67
Welles, Orson, 5, *5*
Wilde, Oscar, 170, 204, *205*
Williams, Tennessee, 204, *205*
Willis, Bruce, 148, 149
Witherspoon, Reese, 157
Wong Kar-wai, *151*, 152
word Tetris, 40

work habits, disciplined, 9–10, 14–17, 36
Wrigley, William, Jr., 136
Writers Guild of America (WGA), 24–28, 31,
    33–34, 193–97
    admission requirements of, 25–26
    Arbitration Committee of, 128–29, 194–95
    dues paid to, 24, 33
    protective benefits of, 24, 25
    registering script with, 38, 46, 49
    Screen Credits Manual of, 124–25, 195
    "Written by" credit, 33, 124–25, 128, 199,
    295
Written By magazine, 125

ABOUT THE AUTHORS

ROBYN VON SWANK

ROBERT BEN GARANT was born in Cookeville, Tennessee. He spent the early 1990s appearing in Off-Off Broadway theaters (bars) in New York City with the comedy group The State. The State had a three-year run on MTV, then a forty-four-minute run on CBS. He then created, wrote, produced, and occasionally appeared in three seasons of *Viva Variety* on COMEDY CENTRAL.

Since relocating to Los Angeles, he has written feature film scripts for Disney, New Line, Dimension, Spyglass, Imagine, Fox, Warner Bros., Columbia, and Universal Pictures, as well as working on numerous production rewrites and punch-ups. His writing credits include screenplays for *Taxi, Let's Go to Prison, Herbie: Fully Loaded, The Pacifier, Night at the Museum, Night at the Museum: Battle of the Smithsonian,* and *Reno 911!: Miami* and *Balls of Fury,* both of which he also directed.

He was the cocreator, executive producer, and star of Comedy Central's *RENO 911!* for six seasons. He lives in Hollywood with his three cats, Baby, Heaven, and Pikachu. (He didn't name any of them.)

He is currently adapting a manga by Tokihiko Matsuura for Disney.

THOMAS LENNON is a writer and comedian from Oak Park, Illinois. He attended the Tisch School of the Arts at New York University, where he cofounded the influential sketch comedy group The State. The State's hit television series ran on MTV for three seasons and received an Ace Award nomination for best comedy series. After his work on The State, he and his partner, Robert Ben Garant, created two more hit shows: *Viva Variety,* which ran for three seasons and was also an Ace nominee for best comedy series, and *Reno 911!,* on which he also played Lieutenant Jim Dangle. *Reno 911!* ran for six seasons and was syndicated around the world.

As an actor, he has appeared in numerous films, including *Le Divorce, Heights, Conversations with Other Women, Memento, 17 Again,* and *I Love You, Man.*

As a writer, he has written for the television series *The State*, *Reno 911!*, *Viva Variety*, and *Strangers with Candy*, and he is the author of four of IFC's 50 Greatest Comedy Sketches of All Time.

He and Garant have written nine feature films together, including *Night at the Museum*, *Night at the Museum: Battle of the Smithsonian*, *Taxi*, *Reno 911!*, *Miami*, *Balls of Fury*, and *The Pacifier*.

He lives in Los Angeles with his wife, the actress Jenny Robertson, and their son, Oliver.